KENNETH W. ALLEN

GLENN KRUMEL

JONATHAN D. POLLACK

PROJECT AIR FORCE

Prepared for the
United States Air Force

RAND

Approved for public release; distribution unlimited

PREFACE

In light of the Gulf War, in which airpower played a more dominant, effective, and visible role than in past military conflicts, many nations in the world seem likely to increase their emphasis on airpower. To better understand the potential implications of such a shift in military strategy, Project AIR FORCE at RAND has launched a multiyear effort that addresses the emergent role of airpower.

The analysis is divided into two main efforts. The first portion explores the probable future position of the United States in the global balance of airpower.[1] The second portion of the research analyzes the air forces of various major powers to see how these nations and their air force leaderships think about the past, current, and future role of airpower in support of their national security objectives.[2]

This report, written in support of the second element of this research effort, provides an overview and assessment of China's large and diverse air arm—the People's Liberation Army Air Force (PLAAF). Analysis of the PLAAF has traditionally focused on air order of battle enumerations and projections about equipment procurement. Until the past few years there were very few available primary source materials about the PLAAF. Virtually nothing was written in China to give the air force—or other Chinese military institutions—a detailed

[1]This analysis is discussed in Bowie et al. (1995).

[2]For an analysis of India's air force, see Tanham and Agmon (1995). Other air forces are discussed in as yet unpublished research by George Tanham and Marcy Agmon on the trends and prospects for the Pakistani air force and by Benjamin Lambeth on the fitful emergence of a new Russian air force.

identity. As a result, only two books have been published in the West devoted to the PLAAF (Bueschel, 1968; Allen, 1991). This study, which draws extensively upon newly disseminated Chinese-language sources, should help to fill this gap in our knowledge. Kenneth Allen served as an Assistant Air Force attaché to China between 1987 and 1989 before retiring from the United States Air Force. In response to an invitation from RAND, he compiled and organized the primary source materials and prepared several earlier versions of the study. Glenn Krumel is a U.S. naval aviator (and a former Navy fellow at RAND) who flew combat missions in the Gulf War; he prepared the data on the Chinese order of battle. Jonathan Pollack supplemented and integrated the overall analysis and prepared the concluding chapter.

As part of Project AIR FORCE, this study is primarily designed to provide an overview of the PLAAF to senior Department of Defense and USAF planners. However, the study is also designed to meet the needs of a more specialized audience, including new officers and enlisted linguists and analysts entering the China-watching field, as well as long-time scholars and analysts of the Chinese military. Therefore, the study includes details on the historical roots of the PLA and PLAAF, along with the international setting, that laid the foundation for PLAAF's present organization and that provides additional insight into the PLAAF's future development. The analysis in this report reflects information available as of May 1995.

This research was sponsored by Maj Gen Richard C. Bethurem, the Director of Plans, Headquarters, U.S. Air Force. The research was conducted within Project AIR FORCE's Strategy, Doctrine, and Force Structure Program. Comments and criticisms are welcomed. Please contact the authors or the Program Director, Dr. Zalmay Khalilzad, at 202-296-5000, ext. 5448.

CONTENTS

FIGURES

TABLES

SUMMARY

The People's Liberation Army Air Force (PLAAF) does not constitute a credible offensive threat against the United States or its Asian allies today, and this situation will not change dramatically over the coming decade. If anything, the PLAAF's overall capabilities relative to most of its potential rivals will diminish over the next ten years. These circumstances are a product of constrained strategic thinking in China about the role of airpower, the lack of funds needed for a comprehensive modernization program, logistics and maintenance problems, the limited training available to its pilots, and the absence of a capability to develop and manufacture advanced airpower weapon systems. Although some modern aircraft will be introduced into the PLAAF inventory during the next ten years, the rate and scale of these acquisitions will remain incremental and demonstrably insufficient to redefine the regional airpower balance.

COMBAT HISTORY

During its 45-year history, the PLAAF—using aircraft, antiaircraft artillery, and surface-to-air missiles—claims to have shot down 1,474 aircraft and damaged another 2,344. However, only about 200 of these incidents occurred during air-to-air combat, with most of the remainder purportedly hit by antiaircraft artillery and a small number by surface-to-air missiles. Virtually all of the PLAAF's combat operations took place against U.S. forces during the Korean and Vietnam wars and during small-scale engagements with the Nationalist air force from Taiwan during the 1950s and 1960s. Although the total figure of 3,818 destroyed and damaged aircraft is highly suspect, it is consistently cited in PLAAF literature and has assumed a legitimacy of its own in China. Unfortunately, this may lead decisionmakers in Beijing to miscalculations about the role of airpower during any future conflict with China's neighbors.

Although the PLAAF deployed hundreds of aircraft to southern China during the 1979 border war with Vietnam, none of its aircraft engaged in combat. This was the last time the air force was involved in any large-scale military operations. China's airborne troops, which belong to the air force, are organized primarily for internal control and have only been used twice—during the Cultural Revolution in Wuhan (1967) and during the Tiananmen crackdown in Beijing (1989).

MISSION EMPHASIS

Organizationally, the PLAAF is a multibranch service that is subordinate to the People's Liberation Army (PLA). Only the three most recent commanders of the PLAAF have been aviators; all their predecessors have come from the PLA. Since its establishment in 1949, the air force has been organized to perform its primary role of air defense for China's major cities. The vast bulk of its force structure and resources remains dedicated to this mission.

The PLAAF's primary air defense responsibilities are to protect China's airfields, principal political and economic centers, heavy troop concentrations, and major military facilities and transportation systems. As a result, most fighter airfields and virtually all of the surface-to-air missiles have been concentrated around China's large cities, most of which are located at least 200 km from the nearest potential hostile border. But given the short ranges of most Chinese fighters and the current lack of an appreciable aerial refueling capability, the PLAAF's ability to mount an effective air defense of China remains questionable. In addition, the limited size and poor capabilities of the PLAAF's bomber and attack force mean that the effectiveness of attacks aimed at an adversary's airfields will be highly suspect in an offensive counter-air role.

Surprisingly, the PLAAF still lacks a formal air defense strategy. Moreover, it has yet to create an integrated air defense system that melds fighter aircraft; surface-based defenses; and command, control, communications, and intelligence elements into an efficient defensive network. For example, although the PLAAF merged with the separate surface-based air defense force in 1957, the resulting administrative and operational structure continues to reflect two separate organizations. In an internal air force analysis prepared in 1990, the PLAAF identified the lack of a unified air defense system as among its most serious problems. Each service has its own air defense structure, and it has proven extremely difficult to coordinate the various components, even within a single service, under a single air defense plan. Matters are further complicated by gaps in radar coverage and the lack of airborne early-warning aircraft, although the PLAAF is apparently moving to rectify the last two deficiencies.

The PLAAF describes its secondary mission as support of the army and navy but emphasizes that this must be indirect support only (i.e., airlift and interdiction). Although a subordinate arm of the army, the air force has been—and, by its own admission, will continue to be—largely incapable of providing direct fire support to the ground forces. Moreover, only a small portion of the overall force structure has the capability to deliver air-to-surface ordnance. The PLAAF at present also does not possess any precision-guided weapons, a lack emphasized by the fact that such weapons were highly effective during the Gulf War.

Coordination among the three services and joint training remain extremely limited. This was highlighted by Chinese military performance in the 1979 border conflict with Vietnam and during a large-scale exercise held in 1981. Lack of army and air force coordination is also reflected in the slow pace of organizational change. It was not until 1985 that the air force's military region air force boundaries completely coincided with the army's military region boundaries, and it took another four years for the military region air force commanders to be fully integrated into the military region command staff as the air component commanders. Similar problems affect air force relations with the navy. Although air force and naval aviation were both involved during the 1954–1955 Yijiangshan campaign and the 1958 Taiwan Strait crisis, there are no indications that they train together or have a coordinated command and control system in case of any future conflict.

While the army reorganized along group army lines in the mid-1980s when several small scale joint exercises were conducted, the PLAAF backed away almost completely from the idea of close air support by 1990. The reasons included the lack of an adequate command and control system, the lack of coordination between the army and air force, and an inadequate reconnaissance capability. For example, an internal assessment called for the air force to assign full-time forward air controllers (FACs) to army units at the division level, but the services were still arguing about how to do this in 1990. This air force study also called for an elaborate system of real-time strike requests by the army, but this has yet to be implemented because of the lack of an adequate command and control system.

DEVELOPING STRATEGY FOR THE FUTURE

Despite (or perhaps because of) these constraints, the Chinese air force has slowly begun to identify the requirements for realizing a more credible airpower capability. A recent internal PLAAF study provides some preliminary glimmerings of independent strategic thought emerging in the PLAAF. Indeed, the essence of this assessment is that the PLAAF needs to develop its own strategy and not rely solely on the PLA's strategy. This study pays particular heed to the development of a rapid reaction force—one that can support Chinese political objectives in limited wars around its periphery. But full implementation of an independent airpower force will be hindered by numerous factors, many of which PLAAF analysts have conceded:

- A rapidly aging and obsolescent aircraft inventory
- The aviation industry's inability to design and produce a modern aircraft in meaningful numbers
- A poor logistical support system, with Chinese fighters unable to generate more than one sortie every four to five days
- A rudimentary command and control system
- Lack of airborne reconnaissance, airborne early-warning systems, or assets to suppress enemy air defenses
- Inadequate combat training

- A tightly structured system that stifles initiative and fails to make full use of available resources.

CONTINUING FORCE STRUCTURE LIMITATIONS

With the exception of 26 Russian Su-27s acquired in 1992 (which must be returned to the production facility at Komsomolsk for any major overhaul), the PLAAF relies almost solely on Soviet-designed aircraft from the 1950s that were reengineered, modified and produced in China during the 1960s and 1970s. The Great Leap Forward (1958), the Sino-Soviet split (1960), and, in particular, the Cultural Revolution (1966–1976) had profoundly negative effects on the air force's organizational and operational development. The aviation ministry's acquisition of newly developed Soviet aircraft in the 1950s, which were subsequently to have been coproduced in China, came to a virtual halt after the Sino-Soviet split, and quality control for Chinese-cloned aircraft became nonexistent during the Cultural Revolution.

In addition, the PLAAF's close identification with Minister of Defense Lin Biao and leftist radicals during the Cultural Revolution left the air force politically suspect afterward. China's domestic turmoil shredded the PLAAF officer corps and severely disrupted the country's aviation manufacturing infrastructure. In essence, the Cultural Revolution cost the PLAAF almost two decades of development and sharply diminished its political influence. The air force is still struggling to overcome this legacy. All military forces are products of the "tyranny of the past" to some extent, and the PLAAF is an especially vivid example.

Although the PLAAF has begun purchasing advanced Russian equipment again, such as the Su-27 fighter, the SA-10 SAM system, and a limited number of Il-76 transports, it is unlikely that rapid modernization using Russian-built systems will occur during the latter half of the 1990s. Such purchases would require major infusions of scarce financial resources. China's defense purchasing power declined substantially during the 1980s, and inflation combined with changes in currency-conversion practices have limited the impact of recent increases in defense budgets. But the readiness of the Chinese leadership to allocate appreciable foreign exchange for these recent purchases demonstrates a growing realization of the severity of the PLAAF's modernization problems.

At the same time, the air force and the aviation ministry constantly compete for the limited funds available for aerospace projects. This friction has hindered the development of advanced airpower systems, and no resolution is in sight. Whereas the air force wants to spend the money to build a modernized force today, the aviation ministry needs the same budgetary resources to develop its own technical and industrial capabilities for the future. With occasional exceptions, the aviation ministry's desires have tended to dominate.

One possible solution to China's airpower modernization dilemmas would be a coproduction agreement between China and Russia for a modern aircraft, in an arrangement comparable to transactions undertaken in the 1950s, or a codevelopment arrangement with Israel. Regardless of the specific aircraft in question—e.g., the Su-27, MiG-31, or a Chinese variant of the Israeli Lavi—there are major uncertainties about the long-term prospects for success in any such undertaking. These uncertainties include very long production lead times, the extent of China's budgetary commitment to any such project, the willingness of foreign suppliers to transfer the full spectrum of technologies involved in a modern combat aircraft, the prodigious development costs that would be associated with a full-scale program between China and a foreign supplier, and (perhaps most important) the ability of Chinese research and development personnel to assimilate and integrate newer technologies fully. Even assuming that all these uncertainties can be satisfactorily resolved, there are the equally daunting tasks of maintaining high-technology systems that are well beyond the sophistication of aircraft in the present PLAAF inventory and of the air force being able to utilize such capabilities fully in training and in combat.

At the same time, to garner sufficient political and bureaucratic support within China, any such project must move from the coassembly phase to production with full domestic content. As with numerous joint-venture projects in China, this will be a slow process and might not reach fruition. This would leave the air force unable to modernize its force structure for many years to come while facing a serious block obsolescence problem (in particular, the need to replace the F-6 fighter aircraft, a Chinese-built MiG-19, which constitutes over half of the PLAAF and naval aviation force structure). If Chinese fighter and bomber production continues at its present rate, our estimates indicate the PLAAF will be roughly half its current size in ten years. Moreover, except for a small number of advanced fighters procured from Russia, the preponderance of China's force structure early in the next century will consist of fighters that *today* would be considered obsolescent.

TRAINING DEFICIENCIES

Although the PLA stresses the importance of man in combat, particularly to compensate for acknowledged equipment deficiencies, the PLAAF does not adequately prepare its pilots to fly in combat. Throughout their careers, air force pilots do not fly as many hours as their Western counterparts, taking three months per year off for rest and relaxation. For example, bomber pilots fly an average of 80 hours per year; fighter pilots fly 100 to 110 hours; and A-5 ground attack pilots fly 150 hours. In comparison, for example, the standard minimum training for fighter pilots in NATO is 180 hours per year.

Moreover, there are questions about the value of this training. Most fighter training sorties, for example, last about 45 minutes, and the majority of the flight time is spent on navigation. There is virtually no simulator training, except on very rudimentary systems. According to an internal Chinese assessment in 1990, the poor quality of the training has made the air force deficient in night combat and poor-weather flying, low-altitude attack tactics, mobility and deployment capabilities, and combat flying against dissimilar aircraft.

Attempts to increase training time would be very costly and would also require the PLAAF to address its serious maintenance problems. In addition, there is a lack of combat experience. For example, probably no active-duty pilots are left with any wartime experience in air-to-air combat. Matters are rendered worse by the rigid structure imposed upon the pilots, such as strict ground-controlled intercept and lack of initiative, which will continue to restrict the air force's capabilities.

PROSPECTS FOR THE FUTURE

Changes in the PLAAF's leadership will be important, but the air force's development will still be hampered by its total subordination to the army. When Wang Hai became the air force's fifth commander in 1985, he was the first aviator to hold that position. Although the air force began the transition from older Korean War veterans as Military Region Air Force (MRAF) commanders in the early 1990s, the leadership at headquarters air force still includes some Korean War veterans. The November 1994 appointment of Yu Zhenwu as PLAAF commander (the first post–Korean War aviator to assume command) is very likely to accelerate the leadership transition process. Thus, the shift to leaders without Korean War experience should be complete by the end of this decade. In addition, in the early 1980s under Wang Hai's predecessor Zhang Tingfa, the air force first began sending senior-level delegations, including the MRAF commanders, to other countries and began hosting foreign delegations. This program has continued in the 1990s and has offered the PLAAF a valuable first-hand look at foreign air forces, demonstrating even more how far the Chinese have to go.

There is no doubt that the air force has an uphill battle in its efforts to modernize. Although the PLAAF will continue to replace its older F-6s with F-7s, F-8-2s, and some foreign aircraft, the PLAAF will, in reality, probably not look much different in terms of capability in ten years than it does today. Some important improvements could include the addition of airborne early-warning aircraft, aerial refueling assets, and a limited number of more modern aircraft.

The PLAAF currently has a large number of deficiencies in terms of force structure, training, command and control, surveillance capabilities, and offensive power. Internal assessments, however, indicate that the PLAAF has recognized these problems and seeks to incrementally improve its capabilities. Moreover, while these assessments indicate increased thinking about the role of airpower in support of Chinese national security interests, there is very little probability that the air force will become an independent service.

The challenges facing the leadership of the PLAAF over the coming decade remain formidable. Airpower is a capital-intensive form of military power, and Chinese defense spending remains modest compared to that of the major industrial powers. Moreover, the ground forces are still the dominant service and might resist increased spending on the air force. The navy also appears to enjoy a more politically advantageous position than the air force. In addition, airpower uses high-technology systems, and China's aviation manufacturing sector is in a poor position to help provide the PLAAF with much-needed advanced weapon systems.

The PLAAF's recognition of its problems is an important first step toward the development of a modern airpower force. But improvements in PLAAF capabilities will take many years to achieve. It does not appear that the PLAAF will emerge as an appreciably more formidable player in the global balance of airpower over the next decade. But in twenty years, provided the PLAAF continues to reform, develops its aerospace industrial infrastructure, and enjoys greater access to resources, Chinese airpower could emerge as a much more potent force.

ACKNOWLEDGMENTS

We gratefully acknowledge the contributions of the following RAND staff members: Christopher J. Bowie, who helped guide the research and reshape the manuscript; Michael Swaine, who provided much valuable Chinese language material and advice; and Pamela Thompson, who provided many of the illustrations in this analysis and who prepared the manuscript for publication. We are also greatly indebted to Phyllis Gilmore for her superb and timely editorial assistance. Special thanks go to Paul H. B. Godwin, National War College, for his technical review of an earlier draft and for his contributions to the chapter on PLA doctrine and strategy. Several other people provided information or helped review early drafts: Bill Behymer, Donald Brown, John Caldwell, Jonathan Cohen, Lawrence J. Davies, June Teufel Dreyer, Jeffrey Goldman, Richard Latham, David Laux, Larry Mitchell, Vance Morrison, Mark Roth, Rusty Shughart, Robert Skebo, and Wayne Thompson. There are a few others who will go unnamed, but whose contributions were equally valuable. While these contributors share credit for our analysis, they bear no responsibility for its shortcomings.

This book is dedicated in memory of Mary McGarrahan, who provided inspiration for many young China analysts to learn from the past, search for patterns, and try to predict the future.

ACRONYMS

AAA	Antiaircraft artillery
ADF	Air Defense Force
AEW	Airborne early warning
AEP	Army equivalent position
AWACS	Airborne early warning and control system
CCP	Chinese Communist Party
CMC	The Military Commission of the Central Committee of the Chinese Communist Party (Zhongguo Gongchandang Zhongyang Junshi Weiyuanhui)
COSTIND	Commission for Science, Technology and Industry for National Defense
FA	Field army
FAC	Forward air controller
FEAF	Far East Air Forces
FMS	Foreign military sales
GCI	Ground-controlled intercept
GLD	General Logistics Department
GPD	General Political Department
GSD	General Staff Department
HqAF	Headquarters air force
IDDS	Institute for Defense & Disarmament Studies
IFF	Identification friend or foe
IISS	International Institute for Strategic Studies
IFR	Instrument flight rules
IR	Infrared
KMT	Chinese Nationalist Party
MAS	Ministry of Aero-Space Industry
MND	Ministry of National Defense

MR	Military region
MRAF	Military region air force
NCO	noncommissioned officer
PLA	People's Liberation Army
PLAAF	People's Liberation Army Air Force
PRC	People's Republic of China
R&D	Research and development
SAM	Surface-to-air missile
SAR	Semiactive radar
TOE	Table of organization and equipment
U.K.	United Kingdom
UN	United Nations
U.S.	United States
USAF	United States Air Force
USSR	Soviet Union
VFR	Visual flight rules

Chapter One

INTRODUCTION

Since its founding in 1949, the People's Liberation Army Air Force (PLAAF)—consisting of aviation, airborne, radar, communications, and air defense (surface-to-air missile [SAM] and anti-aircraft artillery [AAA]) units—has become the third largest air force in the world (after the United States and Russia), with over 4,500 combat aircraft in its inventory. According to the PLAAF's official history, the air force has shot down 1,474 and damaged 2,344 aircraft of all types since 1949, including involvement in "liberating Tibet," in the "War to Resist America and Aid Korea," in numerous engagements with Nationalist and U.S. aircraft over the Taiwan Strait, in the "War to Aid Vietnam and Resist U.S. Aggression," and in the 1979 "self-defensive counterattack" against Vietnam. These figures include air-to-air combat and aircraft shot down by the PLAAF's AAA and SAMs (China Today, 1989a; Teng and Jiang, 1990).[1]

While virtually every analysis of the PLAAF since the 1970s has described the PLAAF as an obsolescent force, the acquisition of military equipment from Russia in 1992–1994, including Su-27 fighters, Il-76 transports, and SA-10 SAMs, has brought the issue of PLAAF modernization and its implications for Asian security to the

[1]The PLAAF's most widely circulated publication, *Zhongguo Kongjun* [*Air Force of China*], began publication in April 1986. Although it was not a *neibu* (internal distribution) publication, it was unavailable to the Chinese public until 1988. Ironically, the cover title of the journal's first number was printed in Chinese and English. The probable antecedent was *Renmin Kongjun* [*People's Air Force*], which began publication in April 1950. In 1958, the name was changed to *Kongjun Bao* [*Air Force Daily*]. *Hangkong Zazhi* [*Aviation Magazine*] began publication in April 1955. Publication apparently ceased during the Cultural Revolution.

forefront. The purpose of this report is to analyze strategic and doctrinal thinking in the PLAAF, the air force's performance in combat operations, and trends in its force structure to gain a better appreciation of its present and potential capabilities.

External analysis of the PLAAF has traditionally focused on air order of battle enumerations and projections of future equipment procurement. Until the 1990s, however, there were virtually no primary source materials about the PLAAF, and only two books published in the West have been devoted to the PLAAF (Bueschel, 1968; Allen, 1991). Understandably, the PLAAF was viewed as an organizational clone of the People's Liberation Army (PLA) ground forces. There was no institutional history and no revealed organizational culture. This perception was not so much flawed as it was incomplete. Virtually nothing was written in China to give the air force—or any other Chinese military institution—a detailed identity. In short, China's military was often understood and described in unidimensional terms (Bueschel, 1968; Gregor, 1985).[2]

Beginning in 1978, Deng Xiaoping and other senior leaders began introducing reforms into the Chinese social, economic, and political system, including defense reform. One of the more widely cited doctrinal justifications for Chinese defense reform was the "three *hua*'s": modernization (*xiandaihua*), revolutionization (*geminghua*), and regularization (*zhengguihua*). The exact meaning of revolutionization of the army remains debatable. In many ways, it is a catch-all phrase or process that emphasizes the need for the regeneration of communist ideals and traditional military values. Nearly all substantive military reforms have been introduced under the rubric of regularization. Regularization of the air force has involved people, resources, objectives, processes, and institutions that are internal to the PLAAF. In short, these are factors over which the air force has some degree of control. But modernization of the PLAAF fundamentally applies to equipment, which involves external factors. Until ac-

[2]Bueschel devotes more than half the book to PLAAF aircraft. The first section, which fundamentally is a public account of PLAAF activities, used less than five People's Republic of China (PRC) sources. The point is not that Bueschel failed to use original sources, but that they simply did not exist. Gregor's brief article is not intended to go beyond an order-of-battle comparison of the PRC and Taiwan. Much of the writing about the PLAAF has tended to focus on the "bean counts" in lieu of other sources of information concerning process and policy.

cess to Russian equipment was renewed in 1990, the PLAAF was dependent almost solely on what China's aviation industry (with or without foreign assistance and technology) designed, developed, researched, and produced. For the purposes of this study, however, the term *reform* will be used to refer to all three processes.[3]

During the 1980s, the PLAAF and its officers began to reveal glimpses of the air force's corporate identity, and several unclassified books and periodicals on the PLAAF were published in China, focusing primarily on the 1950s and 1960s (China Today, 1989a, pp. 652, 658, 660, and 675; PLAAF Headquarters Education and Research Office, 1989).[4] In general, the 1980s ushered in an unprecedented proliferation, by Chinese standards, of scholarship and research about defense and national security matters (Latham, 1991). What is typically absent in Chinese literature, however, is research that integrates diverse sources of information into a composite analysis of specific institutions, such as the PLAAF.[5] Even the more detailed studies, for example, do not clearly delineate the air force's present capabilities from those it would like to have if it faced fewer constraints in its future development. As a result, notwithstanding the increased quantity of primary source data, the most comprehensive studies about the PLA are still published outside China (Godwin, 1983, 1988; Joffe, 1987; Lee, 1989; Henley, 1988, pp. 97–118).

REPORT ORGANIZATION

This study seeks to fill some of the major gaps in our understanding of the PLAAF. It is organized into nine chapters. Chapter Two provides an overview of China's dominant military organization, the PLA, from its birth as the Red Army in the 1920s through the various changes in subsequent decades in combat against Japan, the United

---

[3]For a more in-depth analysis of the PLAAF's defense reform in the 1980s, see Latham and Allen (1991).

[4]The trend toward greater openness resulted in the unrestricted publication of some technical PLAAF journals, such as *Hangkong Weixiu* [*Aviation Maintenance*], which is published by the PLAAF Aeronautical Engineering Department.

[5]This is complicated even further because the PLA does not publish order-of-battle information or identify its units publicly using their "true unit designators," such as the 38th air division. Instead, every unit is identified by a five-digit "military unit cover designator."

States, Vietnam, and the Chinese Nationalists. We also discuss the PLA's involvement in China's internal political and social upheavals. This chapter also provides an overview of Chinese military strategy and doctrine during the post–Korean War years to provide a context for the analysis of the present and future challenges faced by the PLAAF.

Chapter Three covers the history of the PLAAF during its crucial formative years, 1924 to 1960. When the PLAAF was formally established in 1949, the main emphasis was on setting up an administrative structure and beginning to train personnel. There were still virtually no aircraft in the inventory, and the existing infrastructure was woefully inadequate to support a large force. However, the ensuing decade was one of major development. The onset of the Korean War and the provision of large-scale assistance from the Soviet Union enabled the PLAAF to organize, equip, and expand at an extremely rapid pace. But the air force's combat record during this period remained very mixed, underscoring the huge challenges faced in effectively protecting China's national-security interests.

Chapter Four discusses the 1960s, during which the PLAAF's evolution was dominated by the effects of the Sino-Soviet split, the Cultural Revolution, and, to a lesser degree, the Vietnam War. This period proved traumatic and highly disruptive. The Sino-Soviet split severely impinged on the aviation ministry's ability to provide the air force with a large inventory of modern aircraft. The Cultural Revolution led to the politicization of the PLAAF leadership and a rapid decline in training and operational capabilities. In essence, the Cultural Revolution set back the PLAAF's development by several decades, and the air force is still struggling to recover from the damage inflicted on it during this period.

Chapter Five reviews the PLAAF's attempts during the 1970s and 1980s to rebuild following this long period of upheaval and decline. The three primary events affecting this situation were the end of the Cultural Revolution in 1976, Deng Xiaoping's ascendancy to top leadership at the Third Plenum of the 11th Party Congress in 1978, and the 1979 border conflict with Vietnam. The PLAAF's activities in the 1980s fit within the broader context of China's opening to the West. During this period, the PLA formalized its relations with the U.S. military, using the concept of the "three pillars" as the basis for the relationship, although these ties were seriously disrupted following the Tiananmen incident.[6] In 1985, China also revised its national military strategy, declaring that it was no longer necessary to prepare for a major (and possibly nuclear) war in the near term. The PLA instead sought to focus its primary attention on preparing for limited war and unanticipated military crises along China's periphery. The PLAAF began the 1990s with a reevaluation of its force structure, the goal of establishing a rapid-reaction force, and the promotion of a new set of leaders.

Chapter Six discusses the PLAAF's missions and strategy. The air force's primary mission is air defense. Although one of the stated secondary missions is support for the ground forces, the air force readily admits that it cannot provide direct support in this context. But as part of its new rapid reaction strategy, the air force has devoted growing attention to the ability to launch attacks against enemy airborne capabilities and against sea-based assaults.

Chapter Seven provides an overview of PLAAF education and training. PLAAF officers attend one of 25 academies and now have the opportunity for further professional military education at the Air Force's Command College and the National Defense University. Despite the higher educational levels of the air force officer corps, the service as a whole remains constrained by the lack of adequate flying time, limited simulator training, and poor training opportunities. Equally telling, China's military as a whole remains seriously disadvantaged by the absence of appreciable joint and combined training.

Chapter Eight describes the PLAAF's weapon procurement process and the air force's order of battle and examines what the PLAAF might look like a decade or so from now. Weapon procurement is a lengthy process, made more complicated because of the contradictions between military and industrial policies. The number of combat air divisions decreased somewhat at the end of the 1980s and will probably decrease even more between 1995 and 2005 as older air-

---

[6]The "three pillars" encompassed high-level visits by senior U.S. officials (Secretary of Defense, service secretaries, service chiefs, and commander in chief of the Pacific), functional exchanges (logistics, training, maintenance, etc.), and technical cooperation (foreign military sales programs). For a more extended discussion, consult Woon (1989).

craft are removed from the inventory. But future access to foreign weapon systems and technology, China's indigenous aircraft design and production capabilities, and overall funding levels will determine the air force's future.

Chapter Nine draws some implications from the analysis. The various appendixes provide details on institutional structure, the defense budget, and related issues.

Chapter Two

THE PEOPLE'S LIBERATION ARMY: INSTITUTIONAL DEVELOPMENT AND DEFENSE STRATEGY

The history of the PLA is closely intertwined with that of the Chinese Communist Party (CCP). As Chairman of the Communist Party, Mao Zedong presented the original concept of "people's war" in the 1930s as an outgrowth of the Communists' battles with the Nationalists and the subsequent strategy for countering Japan's occupation of China. As part of the people's war concept, Mao also formulated the basic military strategy of "active defense," which dominated China's defense thinking through the mid-1980s.

The transition from a peasant guerrilla force to a combined arms army did not begin until the 1950s. This process was hastened by China's involvement in the Korean War, when the PLA encountered modern military power for the first time, and the alliance relationship with the Soviet Union, which provided China a source of advanced weaponry and officer training. During the 1950s, the PLA simultaneously pursued organizational reform and equipment modernization while also undertaking military operations in Tibet, Korea, and along the Chinese coast opposite Taiwan. However, the disastrous effects of successive internal political upheavals, including the Great Leap Forward (1958–1960), the 1959–1961 split with the Soviet Union, and the Great Proletarian Cultural Revolution (1965–1976) greatly impeded the further development of China's conventional military capabilities. Defense reforms virtually came to a halt until after Chinese forces performed unsatisfactorily in the 1979 border conflict with Vietnam.

Under the leadership of Deng Xiaoping, China began to open its doors to the outside world and initiated an economic and military modernization strategy. This also led in 1985 to a dramatic shift away from the concept of preparing for a global war in favor of building rapid-reaction forces to prepare for local wars. The 1991 Gulf War and the sudden breakup of the Soviet Union further hastened this process of change, underscoring the necessity of equipment modernization and organizational changes, as well as providing a renewed source of advanced weapon systems from abroad.

In this chapter, we will review the tumultuous course of China's military development and the legacy of these events as China approaches the 21st century.

BIRTH OF THE RED ARMY

The Chinese Communist armed forces have been called the People's Liberation Army since the last stages of the civil war with the Nationalists (*Kuomintang* [KMT]). These military forces were created from an amalgamation of units of the KMT National Revolutionary Army under the command of officers who belonged either to the Chinese Communist Party, to groups of workers' militia and peasant guerrillas, or to a considerable number of bandit organizations. From the time of the split between the KMT and CCP in 1927, and at least into the early 1950s, the PLA has been a fighting army and inseparably connected with the revolutionary party. Indeed, from 1927 until about 1940, the PLA was the most important part of the Party, and from 1934 until 1937, the Party and army were almost identical. The army was the Party in arms, consisting almost entirely of CCP members and accounting for approximately 90 percent of Party membership.[1]

Following several aborted Communist-inspired uprisings in 1927, Zhu De and Peng Dehuai (two of the PRC's future ten marshals) and their troops joined Mao Zedong's forces in the Jinggang Mountains and established the Central Soviet area, which soon embraced the larger part of three bordering provinces: Jiangxi, Hunan, and Fujian.

---

[1]Party membership in 1986 totaled 44 million in 2.6 million Party branches. This equaled about 8.6 percent of the adult population (Worden, Savada, and Dolan, 1987, p. 116).

In addition, Soviet areas were established in other provinces by units involved in further unsuccessful uprisings.

The Red Army succeeded in defeating three consecutive "extermination campaigns" by the KMT government troops; by the spring of 1933, it numbered approximately 200,000 soldiers. A fourth extermination campaign, however, eliminated a number of guerrilla bases. In March 1934, more than 300,000 KMT soldiers under the leadership of Chiang Kai-shek himself—who was advised by the German General Hans von Seeckt—started the fifth extermination campaign against the Central Soviet Area in southern Jiangxi. By October, the KMT forces, now numbering 550,000, had succeeded in encircling the remaining soldiers of the Red Army, but 90,000 of them finally broke through to begin the 10,000-km Long March, with about 15,000 to 20,000 survivors marching their way into the small Soviet area of Yanan in northern Shaanxi province a year later (see Figure 1).

Japan Invades China: 1937

Until the summer of 1937, the new Soviet area expanded. When the Sino-Japanese War broke out in July 1937, the hostilities between the KMT and CCP ceased.[2] Under the second united front agreement between the two parties, the army, now numbering 80,000 soldiers, was reorganized into the Eighth Route Army of the Chinese Communist armed forces, albeit with full autonomy from the KMT. In addition, the Communist guerrillas who had been operating in scattered areas of southern China were united into the autonomous New Fourth Army. All of these units remained under effective CCP control.

During the Sino-Japanese War, the CCP armed forces mainly fought a guerrilla war against the Japanese, but until the autumn of 1940, they also occasionally engaged in conventional operations. Following a clash between CCP and KMT forces in 1941, the second

---

[2]From China's perspective, World War II began in 1931 when Japan occupied Manchuria. On July 7, 1937, the Japanese initiated an incident at Marco Polo Bridge in Beijing as a pretext to send troops into China and occupy the eastern provinces.

Figure 1—The Long March (October 1934–October 1935)

KMT-CCP united front effectively ceased. From that point on, both sides prepared for the showdown that each expected after World War II. After early 1941, the CCP troops only defended themselves against occasional Japanese attacks. They constantly expanded their base area behind Japanese lines and in the so-called liberated regions in northern China, thereby increasing their military strength. By the spring of 1945, the Communist-led forces had increased the number of regular soldiers in their fold to 910,000, so they were well prepared for the civil war later that year, culminating in an all-out confrontation between the two parties after January 1947.

MILITARY REORGANIZATION AND TERRITORIAL CONSOLIDATION

In July 1947, all armed forces under the leadership of the CCP were unified as the Chinese PLA. Zhu De became the commander of the PLA, and Ye Jianying served as his chief of staff. Their units, already numbering more than 2.5 million men, underwent reorganization into five field armies (FAs) (see Figure 2).

RANDMR580-2

Figure 2—PLA Field Armies

- The Northwestern FA, under the command of Peng Dehuai, operated in Shanxi, Shaanxi, and Ningxia. In February 1949, it was renamed the First FA.
- The Central Plains FA, under the command of Liu Bocheng and with Deng Xiaoping as political commissar, operated in Henan, Hubei, and Anhui. In February 1949, it was renamed the Second FA.
- The East China FA, under the command of Chen Yi, operated in Shandong, Jiangsu, and parts of Anhui. In February 1949, it was renamed the Third FA.
- The Northeast China FA, under the command of Lin Biao, operated in Manchuria. In February 1949, it was renamed the Fourth FA.
- The North China FA, under the command of Nie Rongzhen, operated in Hebei, Inner Mongolia, and parts of Shanxi. In February 1949, it was the only one of the five large PLA units to keep its name.

Having established a more efficient operational structure in 1947, the Communist armed forces prepared for victory in the last stage of the civil war. Between February and November 1948, Lin Biao's forces conquered all of Manchuria and then moved south to assist Nie Rongzhen in capturing Beijing and Tianjin in January 1949. Lin then continued south to the Yangzi River. After very severe fighting all through the spring and summer of 1948, the troops under Liu Bocheng and Chen Yi defeated the main force of the Nationalist army in the Xuzhou-Huaihai battle, which raged from November 1948 to January 1949 and resulted in more than 400,000 deaths for the KMT army and almost 300,000 for the PLA. It was this battle that broke the backbone of the Nationalist troops.

Between April and December 1949, the First FA, in very costly and difficult battles, conquered Shaanxi, Gansu, and Xinjiang in the northwest; the Second FA captured Wuhan and then turned southwest, conquering Sichuan, Guizhou, and Yunnan; the Third FA captured Shanghai and swept south through Hunan and Guangdong, conquering Guangzhou (Canton) in October 1949 and finally Hainan Island in early May 1950. However, the Third FA's attempt to capture the island group of Quemoy (Kinmen/Jinmen) as a stepping stone to the seizure of Taiwan failed with the devastating defeat of its amphibious forces in October 1949.[3]

Although Tibet had lived under the Manchu's Qing Dynasty rule (1644–1911), Lhasa had achieved a certain degree of independence in 1911. As early as 1932, Mao Zedong stated that the Communists would eventually "liberate" Tibet. In October 1949, Beijing announced its intention to "liberate" Tibet, and Liu Bocheng began moving troops into Tibet in October 1950. Although Tibet appealed to the United Nations (UN) for help, it won no support. The Soviet Union supported Beijing's claim to Tibet, which was further strengthened by Nationalist China's unqualified claim to sovereignty over Tibet. Following a series of military engagements and negotiations, Beijing and Lhasa signed an agreement in May 1951 guaranteeing Tibet's right to "regional autonomy," but Beijing was responsible for Tibet's foreign affairs, and Tibet's armed forces were incorporated into the PLA.

THE KOREAN WAR AND REORGANIZATION ALONG SOVIET LINES

After the founding of the People's Republic, the Chinese leadership was concerned above all with ensuring national security, consolidating power, and developing the economy. Toward these ends, the Chinese moved to establish close ties with the Soviet Union and other socialist nations against the United States and Japan. Although, for a time, Chinese leaders may have considered trying to balance Sino-Soviet relations with ties with Washington, Mao Zedong declared by mid-1949 that China had no choice but "to lean to one side"—the Soviet side.

Soon after the establishment of the People's Republic, Mao traveled to Moscow to negotiate the 1950 Sino-Soviet Treaty of Friendship, Alliance, and Mutual Assistance. Under this agreement, China gave the Soviet Union certain rights, such as the continued use of a naval base at Luda (Port Arthur/Dalian) in Liaoning Province in return for military support, weapons, and large amounts of economic and

---

[3]For a detailed review drawing on recently available Chinese sources, consult He (1992).

technological assistance. China acceded, at least initially, to Soviet leadership of the world communist movement and took the Soviet Union as the model for development. China's participation in the Korean War seemed to strengthen Sino-Soviet relations. The Sino-Soviet alliance appeared to unite Moscow and Beijing, and China became very closely associated with and dependent on a foreign power.

Large-scale Soviet aid in modernizing the PLA, which began in the spring of 1951, took the form of weapons and equipment, assistance in building China's defense industry, and the provision of technical advisers. Mostly during the Korean War years, the Soviet Union supplied large quantities of infantry weapons, artillery, armor, trucks, fighter aircraft, bombers, submarines, destroyers, and gunboats. Soviet advisers assisted primarily in developing a defense industry organized along Soviet organizational lines. Aircraft and ordnance factories and shipbuilding facilities were constructed; by the late 1950s, they were producing a wide variety of Soviet-designed military equipment. Because the Soviet Union did not provide China with its most modern equipment, most of the weapons were outdated and lacked offensive capability.

When the PRC decided to attack U.S. and UN forces in Korea in October 1950, all FAs had to send troops to the new combat theater. The combat experience during the Korean War, from 1950 until July 1953, left a complex legacy for the PLA. On the one hand, the armed forces of the PRC could pride themselves on having successfully stopped the offensive of a world power, and their equipment had been thoroughly modernized with Soviet help during the course of the war. On the other hand, the PLA sustained major manpower losses. Although Chinese and American estimates of deaths and casualties are subject to ample uncertainties, these losses demonstrated that China's revolutionary army would have to modernize its structures, its chain of command, and its military strategy and tactics.[4]

---

[4]Western estimates indicate there were between 500,000 and 1,000,000 Chinese casualties (Karnow, 1990, p. 65; Hinton, 1979, p. 334). A recent compilation by a leading Chinese military historian, drawing on extensive access to PLA archives, estimates that Chinese deaths in combat totaled 152,000; casualties totaled 230,000; and hospitalization for illnesses not related to combat totaled 450,000 (Xu, 1993, p. 56).

With the consummation and full development of the Sino-Soviet alliance, China's leaders decided to reorganize the military along Soviet lines. In 1954, they established the National Defense Council, the Ministry of National Defense, and thirteen military regions (MRs): Guangzhou, Chengdu, Fuzhou, Kunming, Lanzhou, Nanjing, Beijing, Shenyang, Jinan, Wuhan, Inner Mongolia Autonomous Region, Xinjiang Autonomous Region, and the Tibet Autonomous Region (Figure 3). The number of MRs was reduced to eleven in 1970 (Figure 4) and to seven in 1985 (Figure 5).

RANDMR580-3

Figure 3—Thirteen PLA Military Regions: 1954–1970

Figure 4—Eleven PLA Military Regions: 1970–1985

The tasks associated with modernization and institutional development were given to Peng Dehuai, who was appointed minister of national defense and thus entrusted with the actual command of the PLA in September 1954. Peng's assumption of office began a period of professionalization for the army, whose personnel in the regional and local administrative machines were either discharged from the military or recalled to the ranks. In 1955, Soviet-style uniforms, military ranks, and insignia were introduced, with ten major leaders receiving the rank of marshal: Zhu De, Peng Dehuai, Liu Bocheng, Chen Yi, Lin Biao, Nie Rongzhen, Xu Xiangqian, Ye Jianying, He

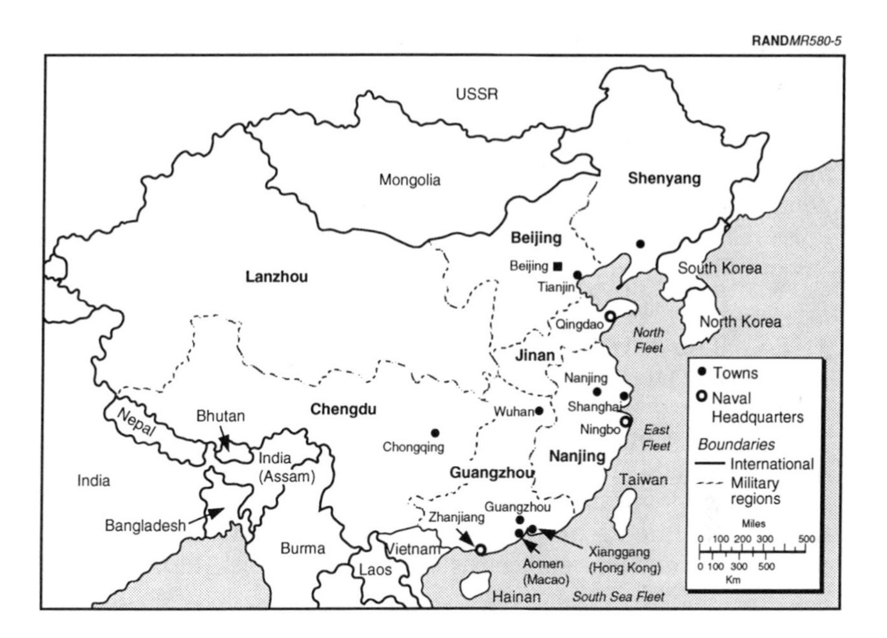

Figure 5—Seven PLA Military Regions: 1985–Present

Long, and Luo Ronghuan. Activities concentrated on professional military training, and the number of soldiers was reduced from 5.5 to 3.6 million. In spite of this drive toward a more professional military, the PLA—in particular, its air force and artillery—suffered a defeat in the Taiwan Strait crisis (August to October 1958). This setback weakened Peng Dehuai's position, and when he attacked Mao's policies of the Great Leap Forward and the people's communes in the summer of 1959, he was purged. Lin Biao succeeded him as minister of national defense.

In Tibet, the socialist revolution that took place after 1950 increasingly became a process of "sinicization" for the Tibetans. Tension culminated in a revolt in 1958–1959 and the flight of the Dalai Lama, the Tibetans' spiritual and de facto temporal leader, to India. Relations with India—where sympathy for the rebels was aroused—deteriorated as thousands of Tibetan refugees crossed the Indian border. There were several border incidents in 1959, as China laid claim to Aksai Chin, nearly 103,600 km^2 of territory that India regarded as its own. In October 1962, the PLA conducted a successful blitzkrieg occupation of disputed territory along the Sino-Indian border, followed by a unilateral Chinese withdrawal from the occupied areas (Figure 6). The Soviet Union provided India moral and political support during the dispute, thus contributing to the growing tension between Beijing and Moscow, which culminated in the Sino-Soviet split.

THE SINO-SOVIET SPLIT AND THE CULTURAL REVOLUTION

During the second half of the 1950s, strains in the Sino-Soviet alliance gradually began to emerge over questions of ideology, security, and economic development. Chinese leaders were disturbed by the Soviet Union's moves under Nikita Khrushchev toward de-Stalinization and peaceful coexistence with the West. Moscow's suc-

RANDMR580-6

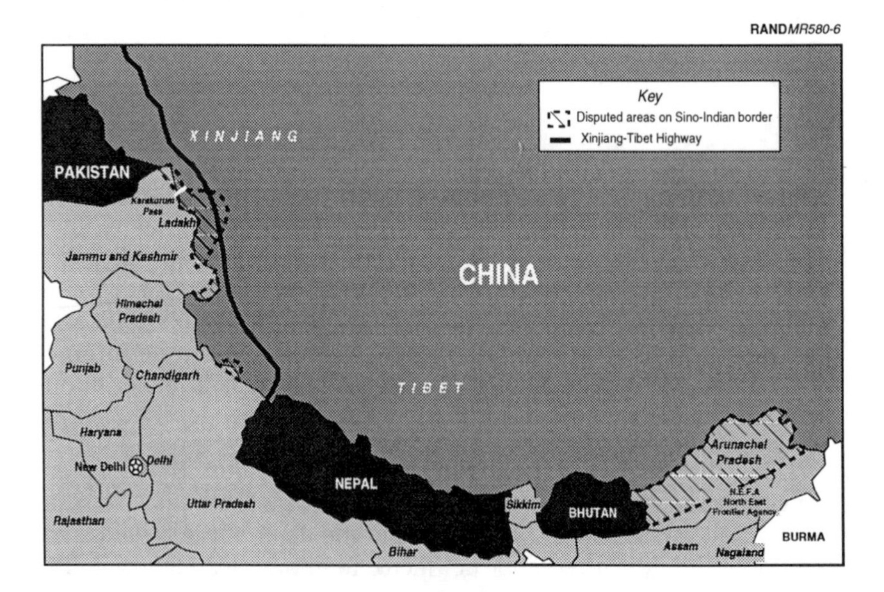

Figure 6—Sino-Indian Border

cessful earth satellite launch in 1957 strengthened Mao's belief that the world balance was in the communists' favor—or, in his words, "the east wind prevails over the west wind"—leading him to call for a more militant policy toward the noncommunist world in contrast to the seemingly more conciliatory policy of the Soviet Union.

In addition to ideological disagreements, there were major strains in the Sino-Soviet security relationship. Mutual antipathies arose in connection with China's attacks on the offshore islands in the summer of 1958, a Soviet proposal in 1958 for a joint naval arrangement that would have put China in a subordinate position, Soviet neutrality during the 1959 tension on the Sino-Indian border, and Moscow's abrogation in 1959 of its 1957 agreement to help China produce its own nuclear weapons and missiles. In addition, in an attempt to break away from the Soviet model of economic development, China launched the radical policies of the Great Leap Forward (1958–1960), which resulted in widespread waste of resources and was partially responsible for a devastating famine in 1960 and 1961. These Sino-Soviet differences led Moscow to withdraw all Soviet advisers from China in 1960.

As a result of the failure of the Great Leap Forward and grievous internal calamities that followed in its wake, Mao Zedong was on the sidelines in the early 1960s. By 1962, however, he began an offensive to purify the Party, having grown increasingly uneasy about what he believed were the creeping "capitalist" and anti-socialist tendencies in the country. More basically, however, Mao used these themes to attack those who had opposed his Great Leap policies, thereby enabling Mao and his political allies to reassert their power.

Toward this end, Mao launched the Socialist Education Movement in 1962 with an emphasis on restoring ideological purity, reinfusing revolutionary fervor into the Party and government bureaucracies, and intensifying class struggle. This movement was tied to Minister of Defense Lin Biao and the movement "to learn from the People's Liberation Army" and to large-scale efforts to send students, intellectuals, and bureaucrats to communes and factories in the countryside. All of these movements were also aimed at dislodging from power Liu Shaoqi and Deng Xiaoping, who opposed Mao's views.

By mid-1965, Mao had gradually but systematically regained control of the Party with the support of Lin Biao, Jiang Qing (Mao's fourth wife), and others. What started as an attack on Liu Shaoqi and Deng Xiaoping in 1965 turned into the Great Proletarian Cultural Revolution. As a result, Mao turned to two separate groups—the PLA and students—to support his movement. Millions of students became Red Guards and, supported by Minister of Defense Lin Biao, virtually shut down the country, shattering the Party organization in its wake. Although the PLA was under Mao's rallying call to "support the left," PLA regional military commanders ordered their forces to restrain the leftist radicals, ultimately restoring order throughout much of China. The PLA was also responsible for the appearance in early 1967 of the revolutionary committees, a new form of local control that replaced local Party committees and administrative bodies. The revolutionary committees were staffed with Cultural Revolution activists, trusted cadres, and military commanders, the latter frequently holding the greatest power.

The radical tide receded somewhat beginning in late 1967, but it was not until after mid-1968 that Mao came to realize the uselessness of further revolutionary violence. Liu Shaoqi, Deng Xiaoping, and their fellow "revisionists" and "capitalist roaders" had been purged from public life by early 1967, and the Maoist group had since been in full command of the political scene.

Viewed in a larger perspective, the need for domestic stability was occasioned perhaps even more by pressures emanating from outside China. The Chinese were alarmed from 1966 through 1968 by the steady Soviet military buildup along their common border and the U.S. involvement in the Vietnam War. The Soviet invasion of Czechoslovakia in 1968 heightened Chinese apprehensions. In March 1969, Chinese and Soviet ground troops clashed on Zhenbao (Damanskiy) island in the disputed Ussuri River border area, although neither air force was involved (Figure 7) (Segal, 1985, pp. 176–193).[5] The tension on the border had a sobering effect on the frac-

---

[5]The 1969 Sino-Soviet border clash and ensuing Soviet threats to eliminate China's nascent nuclear weapon capabilities are special for three major reasons: First, the event involved at least a plausible threat to attack China on a massive scale. Second, this was the first crisis involving the use of Chinese military force against the Soviet rather than the American superpower, thus causing ideological problems. Third, this

RANDMR580-7

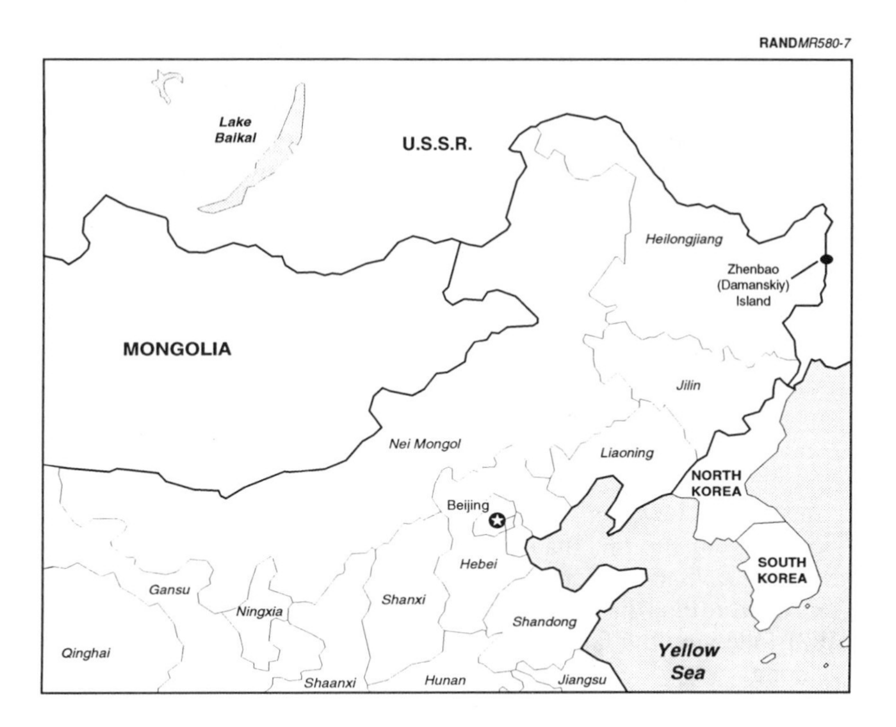

Figure 7—1969 Sino-Soviet Border Conflict

tious Chinese political scene and provided the regime with compelling reasons to end the Cultural Revolution.

The activist phase of the Cultural Revolution ended in April 1969 at the Ninth Party Congress, which confirmed Mao as the supreme leader. Lin Biao was promoted to Party Vice Chairman and was named as Mao's successor. The general emphasis after 1969 was on reconstruction through rebuilding the Party, economic stabilization, and greater attention to foreign affairs.

With Lin Biao as the officially designated successor for Mao, it appeared that the PRC was heading toward military rule. But an active

crisis seemed to have no attainable military objectives for either side. Of particular note, the PLAAF's official histories, including the air force's chronology, do not even mention the crisis.

role of the military in politics also meant that politics entered the military. As the only institution of power left largely unscathed by the Cultural Revolution, the PLA was particularly important in the politics of transition and reconstruction. The PLA was, however, not a homogeneous body. In 1970 and 1971, Premier Zhou Enlai was able to forge a centrist-rightist alliance with a group of PLA regional commanders who had taken exception to many of Lin Biao's policies.

The PLA was divided on policy issues as well as by internal power struggles. On one side was the Lin Biao faction, which continued to exhort the need for "politics in command" and for an unremitting struggle against both the United States and the Soviet Union. On the other side was a majority of the regional military commanders, who had become concerned about the effect Lin Biao's political ambitions would have on military modernization and economic development. In the Lin Biao crisis of 1970 and 1971, the majority of regional military leaders turned against the minister of national defense, who died in an airplane crash over Mongolia in September 1971 following the failure of a purported coup attempt against Mao Zedong.

The Cultural Revolution finally came to a close when Mao died in September 1976, and the infamous "Gang of Four," which included his wife Jiang Qing, were arrested. Mao's death followed that of Zhou Enlai and Marshal Zhu De earlier in the year and opened the way for Deng Xiaoping's second rehabilitation, which was completed in 1978. Deng's rehabilitation, in turn, initiated a process of reform in national defense policy that continues to the present day.

CHINA'S MILITARY STRATEGY

China's overall strategy and doctrine are generally described under the rubric of "people's war."[6] This rubric derives from the PLA's historical experiences and the constraints under which Chinese military power has had to operate. Although necessarily a somewhat amorphous concept, people's war retains a measure of influence in

---

[6]The authors wish to acknowledge the information on the PLA's strategy and doctrine provided by Paul Godwin.

Chinese thinking, at least in broad conceptual terms. It is also sufficiently flexible to encompass a wide array of applications. Thus, people's war has evolved as a blend of defense and offense and has been modified to incorporate active defense, people's war under modern conditions, and rapid-reaction strategy. Within this general structure, the air force has also begun moving to define its own strategy and doctrine.

In its essence, people's war reflects a strategy of weakness. Since the PLA was founded in 1927, it has had to develop strategies for defeating adversaries that have superior weapons and equipment. That this dilemma should continue into the 1990s is no doubt frustrating to members of the current military hierarchy. In some ways, this predicament has become more difficult to resolve than in the army's revolutionary years. In the 1930s and 1940s, the communists could afford to surrender their base areas to maintain fluid battle fronts. Mao could accept the destruction of China's "pots and pans" to maintain the fluid fronts and mobility essential to his concept of strategic defense. With the establishment of a communist state, however, the upholding of China's sovereignty and the protection of its territorial borders became a vital security objective. Even more important, the defense of China's cities and vital industrial centers necessarily became an important component in Chinese defense planning. By the late 1970s, the latter defense objectives were officially enshrined as goals of primary import to China's national security. With the accelerated development of the country's industrial infrastructure since the mid-1980s, China's major urban centers have become even more vital as the nation's focal points of industrial development. Not surprisingly, airpower is seen as a crucial component in guaranteeing the security of China's cities. But the priority accorded these defense goals had to confront the reality of China's military vulnerabilities, to which we will now turn.

People's War

China's communist leaders have long seen themselves as encircled by real or potentially hostile forces threatening the regime's security and have long sought to define a strategy to deal with this situation. Mao presented the original concepts of "people's war" in a series of lectures he delivered between 1936 and 1938. These classic statements of military strategy (*Problems of Strategy in China's Revolutionary War, Problems of Strategy in Guerrilla War Against Japan, On Protracted War,* and *Problems of War and Strategy*) remain the basic reference points for most subsequent innovations in Chinese defense strategy (Godwin 1983, p. 22; Godwin, 1988).

While people's war places special emphasis on defensive strategy and on the factor of manpower over weapons, the PLA has never ignored the need for an offensive strategy. For example, the PLA's involvement in the Korean and Vietnam wars, plus its attacks against India in 1962 and Vietnam in 1979—all of which were followed by a quick unilateral withdrawal—were all described as "defensive" operations. At the same time, Mao long recognized the value of utilizing superior force to overwhelm China's adversaries. As Mao observed in one of his major writings on strategy:

> Make wiping out the enemy's effective strength our main objective; do not make holding or seizing a city or place our main objective. In every battle, concentrate an absolutely superior force (two, three, four or sometimes even five or six times the enemy's strength), encircle the enemy forces completely, strive to wipe them out thoroughly and do not let any escape from the net. Fight no battle unprepared, fight no battle you are not sure of winning.

Thus, Mao was not thinking primarily in terms of guerrilla warfare when he delivered the lectures that were to become the essay *On Protracted War.* In late 1938, he was arguing that the militarily decisive actions would be taken by the main force units and that guerrilla warfare would play a secondary, but important, role in support of the main forces. The basic military strategy Mao formulated, known as "active defense," was one of a protracted, defensive war. The problem was how to develop supporting strategies and tactics to prevent a defensive strategy from turning into a stalemate in which neither side could achieve a military victory.

Active Defense Strategy

The concept of active defense means taking tactically offensive action within a basically defensive strategy. The defending forces undertake offensive operations to wear down the adversary while he is strategically on the offensive and attacking. It is the opposite of passive defense, which means the defending forces simply resist without attempting to weaken the adversary as he prepares to attack or is actually on the offensive.

The active defense strategy consists of three phases: strategic defense, strategic stalemate, and strategic counterattack. In strategic defense the important part of the beginning of the conflict is to smash the enemy's strategic attacks and stabilize the situation. The strategic stalemate phase is designed to stabilize the situation and begin changing from defensive to offensive operations. The strategic counterattack and attack phase is the change to defeating the enemy. China consistently states that its forces are weaker than its potential adversaries and will continue to be so even as the PLA makes efforts to develop and improve its weapons and equipment.

DEFENSE REFORM

The Great Leap Forward and the Cultural Revolution seriously impeded attention to the goals of defense modernization and to China's longer-term military requirements. It was not until Deng Xiaoping reasserted his primacy at the Third Plenum of the 11th Party Congress in 1978 that defense reform was resumed in earnest. No matter how operationally compelling reform was for any of the PLA services, it was virtually impossible to initiate without the explicit (and consistent) support of China's preeminent leader.

Although the current phase of China's defense modernization was initiated in December 1978 as part of Deng Xiaoping's "Four Modernizations" development strategy, the ailing defense establishment had been a major source of debate within Beijing since at least 1975. At a meeting of the Party Central Committee's Military Commission in the summer of 1975, Deng declared that the PLA, with over 4,000,000 troops, was bloated, ill-equipped and too poorly trained to conduct modern warfare.[7] The ensuing debate was not

[7]The Military Commission of the Central Committee of the Chinese Communist Party *(Zhongguo Gongchandang Zhongyang Junshi Weiyuanhui)*, which is sometimes cited as the *"zhongyang junwei"* or *"junwei,"* is commonly translated into English as the Central Military Commission (CMC). In the 1960s and 1970s, it was routinely referred to as the Military Affairs Commission (MAC). The name of the commission in Chinese

over whether the PLA should be rebuilt and rearmed, but over what priority this goal had relative to the needs of China's economy. This fact was driven home when the PLA conducted an ineffectual and very costly campaign during the Sino-Vietnamese border war of February through March 1979. This experience strengthened those forces in the army advocating a thorough modernization of the army's organizational structures, as well as its equipment. The debate concluded with Deng's assessment that, although the USSR did present a major threat to China's security, it was not an immediate military threat, thereby enabling China to turn to long-deferred defense modernization goals.

This decision reflected two important factors. First, the late 1970s rapprochement between the United States and China provided Beijing with a tacit security partner against the Soviet Union. Second, Deng's goal was not simply to modernize the arms and equipment of the PLA but to rebuild China's entire defense establishment—i.e., the armed forces, the defense science and technology community, and the defense industrial base. Consequently, modernizing national defense was viewed as a long-term strategic program that would reconstruct the defense establishment in coordination with the modernization of China's economy and science and technology capabilities. Defense modernization was therefore placed fourth in China's development priorities—known as the "Four Modernizations"—following agriculture, industry, and science and technology.

In the years following the 1975 decision and the Third Plenum, defense reform assumed specific patterns that reflected Deng's overall strategy. The long-term objective was to provide China with the capability to design and build its own weapons and equipment with only limited dependence on external sources of technology. With this goal achieved in the 21st century, China would be able to take its place among the world's leading military powers in both nuclear and conventional forces. The near-term objective was to take the current force structure and rebuild and train it to increase its immediate

---

has not changed—only the English translations. Properly speaking, "*zhongyang*" refers to the Central Committee. It is understood in Chinese as an abbreviated noun rather than an adjective.

combat effectiveness. Weapons and equipment would be improved primarily through upgrading existing weapon systems.[8]

The primary focus of military reform for the first decade, however, was not on weapons and equipment but on redesigning the armed forces, modifying the concepts of operations with which they fought, and improving the technical, managerial, and leadership abilities of the officer corps. The first stage was designed to reform the armed forces so that they would be capable of absorbing and effectively using more advanced weapons and equipment as they became available in the future.

This period saw China reduce, at least on paper, the size of its armed forces by some 1,000,000 personnel and reform the officer recruitment process by requiring that most candidates earn their college degrees from military academies (only a handful of officers came from civilian colleges).[9] In addition, the professional military education system was revamped; the structure of the armed forces was adjusted to make them more compatible with combined arms warfare; and China's national military strategy was reconceptualized to take account of the rapidly changing security environment. Furthermore, on August 1, 1983, the PLA received new uniforms, modeled (as they had been in the 1950s) after Soviet uniforms. Having been abolished in 1965, ranks and insignia were also reintroduced in 1988.

Even without the introduction of modern weapons, the first decade of military reform represented a significant change. Similar reforms were being made across the rest of the defense establishment as de-

---

[8]Thus, the standard T-59 main battle tank derived from the Soviet T-54 was upgraded with Israeli and British technology. Similarly, the MiG-21–derived F-7 fighter benefited from imported technologies. Other major weapon systems in all of the services received similar upgrades.

[9]The first step in reducing the 4.5 million–member PLA was to relieve the PLA of some of its nonmilitary duties. The Railway Engineering Corps was civilianized, and in 1983 the PLA internal security and border patrol units were transferred to the People's Armed Police Force. The headquarters staffs of the three general departments, the MRs, and the military districts were streamlined, and the sizes of the air force and navy were reduced by retiring older, undereducated, or incompetent officers. County- and city-level people's armed forces departments, which controlled the militia, were also transferred to local civil authorities. In addition, many PLA factories were "civilianized" but still funded by the PLA.

fense research and development (R&D) institutes effectively ended their isolation and were integrated into China's science and technology community, and the bloated defense industrial base went through a conversion process designed to reduce the number of enterprises producing military equipment and to permit simultaneous manufacture of civilian and defense products.

REVISING CHINA'S STRATEGY

The PLA's poor performance against Vietnam accelerated the process of debate over reforming China's national military strategy. The initial focus of the debate was on how to defend against a Soviet blitzkrieg attack on northern China. The Red Army's 1945 "August Storm" assault on Japanese forces in Manchuria was the model. The debate, which was resolved in the summer of 1982, is important for two reasons. First, it became clear following the 1979 border conflict with Vietnam and a large military exercise in North China in 1981 that the ground and air forces of the PLA had not trained together in combined arms warfare. As training very slowly began the transition to a combined arms strategy, the PLA started focusing on integrating infantry, artillery, and tank operations. However, close air support and battlefield interdiction did not receive much attention.

Second, Chinese planners recognized that the strategy and concepts of operations chosen to defend against a Soviet attack were less than optimal. In the view of Chinese strategists, the PLA's arms and equipment did not permit them to conduct the maneuver warfare operations they would have preferred. The complaint that the limited capabilities inherent in the armed forces' obsolescent weapons and equipment severely limited the PLA's combat effectiveness became more insistent with a major change in China's national military strategy in the late spring of 1985. As part of this change, the number of MRs was reduced from 11 to 7, streamlining command and control to facilitate the rapid-reaction strategy (Figure 5).

Near the end of this debate, two events occurred almost simultaneously. First, the PLA quietly began reorganizing its ground fighting forces from an infantry-heavy field army structure to corps size units called "group armies." Generally, group armies combine several infantry divisions with armor divisions or brigades—as well as artillery, engineering, anti-aircraft, communications, and other specialized forces—into an integrated, combined-arms fighting force. Second, the PLA published a series of documents defining support by each of the services and their branches for "The Campaign to Defend Group Army Field Positions" during future wars. The premise of defending field positions was based on the "people's war" strategy of "active defense."

Revised Strategy: Local and Limited War

Following the debate on China's national military strategy, the Military Commission declared in June 1985 that it was no longer necessary to prepare for a major and possibly nuclear war, but, instead, the PLA should focus its attention on preparing for limited war and unanticipated military crises on China's periphery.[10] As analyses of these types of wars appeared in Chinese military journals, it soon became evident that the Chinese armed forces were entering yet another stage of military reform. Wars limited in geographical and political scope required quick, lethal responses if China was to prevail. The first engagement could be critical in determining the outcome of the conflict. Thus, the earlier concepts of defensive operations conducted while the society was mobilized for war, followed by offensive operations when the entire country was prepared, were no longer applicable.

Given this change in thinking, Chinese military journals designated five types of limited war on which the PLA should focus: (1) small-scale conflicts restricted to contested border territory, (2) conflicts over territorial seas and islands, (3) surprise air attacks, (4) defense against deliberately limited attacks into Chinese territory, and (5) "punitive counterattacks" launched by China into enemy territory to "oppose invasion, protect sovereignty, or to uphold justice and dispel threats."

Preparation for local wars required the PLA to review its defense posture around the periphery of China and to make an assessment of the most likely conflicts to be fought in each sector. Given the diversity

---

[10]The material in the subsection draws heavily on Godwin (1992), pp. 191–201. Unless otherwise noted, quotations in this subsection are taken from that source. See also Sheng (1992).

of terrain, weather, and potential adversaries, different border areas were faced with different operational requirements. This led to the conclusion that each of China's seven MRs should conduct independent training and field exercises for local war. The concept of a "war zone" was introduced, with the observation that "war zone independent campaign operations will probably be the most frequently seen mode of action in the Army's campaign operations for some time to come."

In 1988, four major MR exercises were conducted under the direction of the MR commanders. These were designed to test the extent to which the previous three years of preparation had developed new capabilities within the armed forces to respond to the changing threat environment. Three of the exercises focused on the USSR and one on Vietnam as the potential adversaries.[11]

The exercises primarily tested rapid deployment and combined arms operations responding to "border clashes, accidents, and local warfare." Equally important, however, was the testing of theater operations desired and executed by MR commanders as independent campaigns. In each of these maneuvers, the MR commander was clearly defined as being responsible for the campaign and, presumably, the concept of operations behind the campaign.

The maneuvers all referred to the use of special forces identified as "fist" (*quantou*) units and have been the focus of considerable discussion in Chinese military journals since the late 1980s. Air mobile units, using helicopters assigned to the new Army Aviation Troops organized in 1987, are one focus of Chinese interest. In addition, the PLA's airborne forces, which belong to the air force, have been selected for training as "fist" units and rapid-response units capable of being deployed anywhere in China within 12 hours.

Even if military force is not applied, a credible capacity to respond quickly to a crisis must be available if China is to maintain an effective deterrent posture at this level of warfare. Current levels of

---

[11]The three exercises oriented against the USSR were West-88 in the Lanzhou MR, Yanhang-88 in the Beijing MR, and Qianjin-88 in the Shenyang MR. The Vietnam-related exercise was Guangzi-15 in the Guangzhou MR. No exercises aimed at Taiwan or India were conducted.

Chinese military technology severely limit both the mobility and lethality of the PLA and, by implication, its credibility. The approach taken by Beijing since the mid-1980s has been to modernize selectively. The military leadership has chosen to upgrade key units. It appears that fist units have received the most modern equipment and have tested it in field exercises. While undoubtedly the most sensible way to introduce new weapons and equipment into the armed forces, this practice will not result in a fully modernized PLA except over a very long period of time.

THE IMPACT OF THE GULF WAR

As the PLA developed its tactics and concepts of operations for limited war, there was a steadily increasing expression of unease from the armed forces that their weapons and equipment were not up to the demanding tasks assigned the PLA under the new national military strategy.[12] A chorus of complaints was reinforced by the success of the American-led coalition in the 1991 Gulf War, which demonstrated the significance of high-technology weapons and equipment when applied by skilled and extremely well-trained forces. In particular, the pivotal consequence of complete domination of the air by coalition air forces required Chinese military strategists to rethink the role of airpower in modern warfare.

In the defense reform debate initiated in the late 1970s, airpower had played a role in the PLA's revised concepts of operations, but the ground forces remained the primary focus of attention. This focus reflected the traditional dominance of the army within the Chinese military. If it were not for China's interest in enforcing its claims to sovereignty over the Paracel and Spratly islands in the South China Sea, it is unlikely that the navy would have received as much attention as it has over the past decade, running second in importance to the army. This priority also appears reflected in the higher stature of the navy leadership in the political process.

The Gulf War air campaign demonstrated the critical role of airpower in modern wars. While airpower was viewed as important in China's military modernization effort, it was not until the Gulf War that the

---

[12]The introduction to the Gulf War was provided by Paul H.B. Godwin.

senior leadership of the PLA demonstrated any real appreciation of the implications of complete domination of the air. Commentaries on the Gulf War by senior Chinese military leaders since 1991 have used the Gulf War to highlight their own need for advanced military technologies, especially combat aircraft and airborne command and control capabilities.

In March 1991, the Military Commission issued instructions for the PLA's General Staff, Political, and Logistics Departments and all military academies to study the Gulf War from different angles so that the Chinese military could learn from the experience. The Chinese National Defense University also made a study of the impact of the Gulf crisis on world strategy, drawing seven major conclusions:[13]

- The "Big Peace" (U.S.-Soviet relaxation and the end of the Cold War) cannot help prevent the outbreak of "small wars" (or regional conflicts); at a time when global nuclear war and European conventional war have become less likely, regional conflicts are escalating.
- Power politics and gunboat diplomacy still remain an important factor in the 1990s and even in the next century; the intensification of competition based on comprehensive national strength does not mean the reduction of the role of military power.
- The Gulf crisis would not change the general trend of disarmament carried out by the United States, the Soviet Union (later Russia), and other countries, but it will stimulate arms races in some regions, which may lead to new "prosperity" for weapon manufacturers.
- To diminish their military vulnerabilities, small and medium-sized countries will form regional alliances and set up regional security structures and crisis control mechanisms through bilateral or multilateral cooperation.
- The Gulf crisis will have a major impact on future nuclear strategy. A possible future development is that nuclear powers will

---

[13]"CPC Views Various Aspects of Gulf War," March 14, 1991, in FBIS-CHI-91-050, pp. 30–32.

maintain a "low-level deterrent," with more attention on dealing with nuclear and missile threats from Third World countries.

- The results of the Gulf War will produce far-reaching changes in global conventional strategy. A possible future trend is that the United States and the Soviet Union (subsequently Russia) would place particular stress on mutual deterrence while focusing their attention on actual combat in dealing with regional Third World conflicts. The U.S. theory of "low-intensity conflict" will therefore face a new set of challenges.
- The Gulf War has set higher demands on future national defense capabilities, with particular attention on higher-intensity conventional combat, the formation of elite units, the application of high technology, and quick-response operations.

Summing up this experience, the Chinese National Defense University study pointed out that the PLA should (1) reduce the number of soldiers and improve the armed forces' equipment, training quality, and actual combat capability; (2) give priority to conventional arms over nuclear weapons; (3) introduce high technology, including advanced guidance systems, pinpoint accuracy bombing, weapons of mass destruction, and stealth aircraft; and (4) build a rapid-response force.[14]

During 1993, the PLA leadership reaffirmed that "Mao Zedong's military thought will always be the guideline for our army building and for our military operations," and that Deng Xiaoping's military

---

[14]One military academy under the General Staff Department paid particular attention to four aspects in studying the Gulf War: (1) ways to restrict air attacks by using camouflage and by using mobile missiles like the Iraqi Scuds, (2) the widening gap between the forces equipped for night combat and those that are not, (3) the continuing importance of mechanized troops as the main attack force, and (4) the importance of electronic warfare as a force multiplier.

The General Logistics Department's Logistics Academy focused its study on logistics supply during the Gulf War, including troop mobility; material, fresh water, and oil supplies during desert operations; and the influence of geographical environment and meteorological conditions on high-technology weapons. Finally, the Gulf War enabled officials in the military academies to pay more attention to personnel training. While there are some improvements in China's military equipment, it is conspicuously backward if compared with developed countries. In a future war, the studies all indicated that the PLA should improve the quality of its soldiers if it wants to use less-advanced equipment to defeat the enemy. Therefore, the decisive factor is still man.

thought essentially "inherits and develops" the Maoist military heritage. However, the PLA must "strengthen and improve military exercises in view of the nature of modern warfare" in an international situation that is still turbulent, and "since the PLA possesses inferior weaponry, we must display confidence and bravery in order to defeat well-armed enemies." Furthermore, the leaders asserted that the "long-term military build-up and modernization program for 1991–1993 aims at acquiring military capabilities, including sophisticated modern weapons, to meet the challenges of local and regional wars." Despite the PLA's reiteration of this grand strategy during and since the 14th Party Congress in October 1992, the PLA leadership concedes that it must meet the challenges of future local wars and regional conflicts through the modernization of tactics and force structures, relying primarily on existing if obsolete weapon systems (Bodansky, 1993, pp. 1–8).

Such developments demonstrate the inescapable dilemmas confronted by the PLA as it faces the future. On the one hand, the challenge faced by the application of advanced technology to warfare finds only limited precedent in the PLA's previous combat experience. Institutional restructuring and the recruitment and development of a more highly educated officer corps represent part of the answer, but these measures cannot by themselves address the acute military vulnerabilities that China would face in most local war scenarios. Even after more than a decade of defense reform, the cumulative consequences of political and institutional upheaval within China have yet to be overcome, lending a problematic forecast to the PLA's ability to address some of the security challenges it could well confront in the coming decade.

Many of these political problems are manifest even more acutely when we turn attention to the Chinese air force. The enhanced role of modern airpower in potential conflicts for which the Chinese armed forces must prepare leaves the air force highly disadvantaged. To understand the challenges that the air force leadership must address over the coming decade, we need to turn our attention to the combat experiences and development changes faced by the PLAAF in earlier periods, since these seem likely to shape Chinese policies and programs for many years to come.

Chapter Three

THE PLAAF'S FORMATIVE YEARS: 1924–1960

The PLAAF traces its origins to 1924. Two individuals—Chang Qiankun and Wang Bi—are regarded as its founding fathers. In 1924, during the first KMT and CCP united front, Sun Yat-sen's Guangzhou Revolutionary Government established an aviation bureau and a military flying school at the Huangpu (Whampoa) Military Academy, where two classes (50 people) received 12 months of training. Eighteen of the students (9 KMT and 9 CCP), including Chang and Wang, were sent to the Soviet Union from 1925 to 1927 for advanced flight training.[1] Chang remained in the Soviet Union until the CCP sent him to Communist headquarters in Yanan in 1940. Over the next several years, he served in several positions, including director of the aviation bureau (the PLAAF's predecessor) and PLAAF deputy commander. In 1927, Wang moved from Moscow's Sun Yat-sen University to the Soviet air force's ground support school, where he graduated in September 1929. He then served in the Soviet air force before being sent to Yanan in 1940. After 1949, he served primarily in political commissar and aircraft maintenance positions, but retired as a PLAAF deputy commander.

---

[1]Of particular note, the Soviet Union helped Sun Yat-sen's and Chiang Kai-shek's KMT and the CCP establish the same organizational structure during the 1920s. In response to Japanese actions in China, beginning with Japan's invasion of Manchuria in 1931, the Soviets supported the Nationalists by providing arms and advisors. From late 1937 until Germany attacked the Soviet Union in June 1941, Stalin provided about $300 million in credits to Chiang Kai-shek's regime to finance Soviet aid, including hundreds of planes, pilots to fly them, and instructors to train Chinese pilots. Soviet advisors were also attached to Nationalist army units. (See Schwartz, 1973, pp. 133–134.)

From 1941 to 1945, the CCP Central Committee's Military Commission laid the groundwork for the eventual establishment of the PLAAF. In 1941, the Military Commission established an air force engineering school to teach basic aviation theory and aviation armament, even though the Communists had no aircraft or airfields. In addition, the Military Commission established a subordinate aviation section in 1944, which was responsible for all aviation work. Chang and Wang shared leadership positions in each organization.

But the idea of a Communist air force was only a concept throughout the Party's struggle for power. There were no aircraft, no airfields, and no pilots. When the Japanese surrendered in 1945, the Communists quickly occupied the northeast provinces, commonly known as Manchuria, and began training a core of pilots on captured aircraft, using Japanese personnel as instructors and for ground support.

In September 1945, the aviation section sent a 30-member team from Yanan to northeast China and eventually established the Northeast Old Aviation School. The first class began in July 1946 with four basic trainers and a few ex-Japanese Tachikawa Ki.55 type 99 advanced trainers. Many of the initial instructors and ground-support personnel were Japanese Air Force personnel who remained in China after the surrender in 1945. By July 1949, the school had trained 560 people, including 126 pilots. The rest received various ground-support training.

BIRTH OF THE PLAAF

The PLAAF underwent some of its most significant and far-reaching changes during the PRC's first decade. These included establishing an administrative structure in Beijing, building several schools to train pilots and support personnel, acquiring thousands of the Soviet Union's most sophisticated combat aircraft, and engaging in combat against the world's strongest airpower—the United States—and against Chinese Nationalist forces.

When the Nationalists retreated to Taiwan in 1949, the strength of the Communist forces was concentrated within the five FAs in the north and northeast. The PLAAF formally established its headquarters in Beijing on November 11, 1949, and established six military region air force (MRAF) headquarters organizations within the five FA operations areas by the end of 1950.

By the end of 1949, the PLA had established 16 antiaircraft artillery (AAA) regiments stretching from Shenyang to Changsha to protect the major cities they had liberated from the Nationalists. However, they still did not control Fujian Province or the eastern portion of Guangdong Province.

To control all of the air defense forces, the Military Commission formally established the PLA Air Defense headquarters in October 1950, with Zhou Shidi as the commander and Zhong Chibing as the political commissar. At that time, there were two AAA divisions, 16 AAA regiments, one searchlight regiment, two radar battalions, and one aircraft observation battalion. Shortly thereafter, four air defense headquarters were established in the MRs.[2]

However, from the air force's earliest years, no consideration was ever given to making the air force a service independent of the army. The PLA leadership did not want an autonomous aviation force and chose the first commander, Liu Yalou, and political commissar, Xiao Hua, directly from the army. Neither had any aviation experience.[3] In addition, 2,515 members of Liu Yalou's army unit transferred from Wuhan to Beijing to form the core of the PLAAF headquarters. The

---

[2]In addition, other subordinate air defense command organizations were formed. The Air Defense Force also established five schools (advanced air defense, AAA, air defense, radar, and maintenance) plus five preparatory schools.

[3]Wu Faxian (1965–1971) succeeded Liu Yalou (1949–1965) as PLAAF commander. During Liu's tenure, Wu was a political commissar. In September 1971, Wu Faxian was implicated in the Lin Biao affair and was sentenced in 1981 to 17 years of imprisonment. For almost two years, the air force did not have a commander; the official PLAAF histories list no events for 1972 at all. The next PLAAF commander was Ma Ning (1973–1977), who had an illustrious army career before transferring to the PLAAF in 1949. He served in the 21st Air Division (Shanghai) until 1967 when, as the division commander, he transferred to Changchun in the Shenyang MR. He was apparently politically adroit during the Cultural Revolution. In 1968, he was on the Jilin Provincial Revolutionary Committee standing committee. Ma Ning later served as the Lanzhou MRAF deputy commander prior to becoming the PLAAF commander. Ma's political savvy allowed him to become PLAAF commander before Zhang Tingfa, who had been a deputy commander before the Cultural Revolution. Zhang, who subsequently followed Ma Ning as commander, had the most diversified headquarters experience of any PLAAF commander. Zhang served as the PLAAF commander (1977–1985), political commissar, deputy commander, chief of staff and CCP Politburo member. Wang Hai, the commander from 1985–1992, was the first pilot to command the air force.

administrative structure at PLAAF headquarters reflected the air force's needs at the time and consisted of six major departments: headquarters, political, training, engineering, logistics, and personnel. This structure was mirrored in each of the MRAF headquarters.

For the first few years, most of the PLAAF's regional headquarters were merely administrative organizations without any significant operational forces, and the Nationalists still controlled the skies over southeast China as far north as Shanghai. For example, Nationalist B-24 bombers attacked Beijing on May 4, 1949. The most serious attack was in February 1950, when 1,400 people were killed (China Today, 1989a, p. 109). Therefore, the air force's immediate task was to provide air defense for the major cities, such as Shanghai, Beijing, and Tianjin.

China's vulnerability to air attack underscored the imperative need to build an air force. In early August 1949 (i.e., several months prior to the establishment of the People's Republic), Liu Yalou led a Chinese delegation to Moscow seeking rapid Soviet support in this area. The delegation remained in Moscow for a full two months, with the USSR agreeing to furnish 434 aircraft and to assist the PLA in establishing schools for training Chinese pilots (He, 1992, pp. 4–5).

The PRC's first flying squadron was established in July 1949 in Beijing with four flights (two fighter, one bomber, and one transport), including six P-51s, two Mosquito bombers, and two PT-19 trainers. However, the first actual PLAAF aviation unit, designated the 4th Division (two fighter, one bomber, and one attack regiment), was established in Nanjing in 1950 but moved shortly thereafter to Shanghai. When the Korean War broke out, the four regiments were split and became the backbone of the first four aviation divisions.

At the time of the Communist victory, the PLAAF had fewer than 3,000 trained aviation personnel, including 202 pilots; 30 navigators; 2,373 mechanics; three engineers; and miscellaneous personnel. There were only 159 foreign-made aircraft (the 21 different types constituted a logistical nightmare) but 542 airfields. Airmen from the communist movement constituted 88 percent of the pilots but only 15 percent of the mechanics. Personnel "accepted" from the Nationalist forces represented 85 percent of the mechanics and an even higher percentage of technical personnel (China Today, 1989a, pp. 37, 89).[4] More than 100 Japanese pilots and technically trained ground personnel remained in Manchuria after 1945. They were part of the initial contingent of instructors at the Northeast Old Aviation School (China Today, 1989a, pp. 18–19).[5]

The PLAAF established its first development plan for the years 1950 to 1953. The plan called for training 25,400 technical troops, establishing about 100 aviation regiments, repairing over 100 airfields, setting up eleven aircraft repair factories, and increasing the size of the PLAAF to 290,000. For the most part, these goals were reached by the end of 1953.

Notwithstanding the many difficulties the PLAAF faced, it had reason to be heartened by its early growth (Table 1). By 1954, the Soviet Union had supplied the PLAAF with 3,000 aircraft, which were organized into 28 air divisions and 70 regiments, and had trained the pilots and technicians that manned and maintained them. At least 12 academies or schools had been founded. These institutions trained 5,945 pilots; 24,000 technicians; 396 cadres; 690 political cadres; and 310 logistics cadres. PLAAF histories, however, are unclear as to whether or not their goal of 290,000 airmen was realized by 1954 (China Today, 1989a, pp. 49–50, 53, 69, 88).

THE TIBET CAMPAIGN: 1950

In January 1950, the Military Commission ordered the PLA to send troops into Lhasa to "liberate" Tibet and unify the nation. Once the

Table 1

PLAAF Expansion, 1949–1954

	Aircraft	Pilots	Mechanics/ Technicians
1949	159	202	2,373
1954	3,000+	5,945	24,000

[4]The PLAAF repaired or expanded only 94 of the 543 airfields between 1949 and 1953. Most of the dirt runways were simply reclaimed for agricultural use.

[5]In April 1988, China sent an aviation delegation to Japan to commemorate the contributions of the Japanese airmen. (See *Hangkong Shibao*, November 24, 1988, p. 1.)

operations began in February, the troops advancing from the northwest and east faced extreme difficulties receiving supplies and traversing the difficult terrain. Mao Zedong ordered the PLAAF to begin air-dropping supplies to them.

As a result, the PLAAF established its transportation aviation troops, but only had one unit with 12 C-46 and C-47 transports located in Beijing with the capability of air-dropping supplies. Eventually, the air force deployed six of these aircraft plus four others from southern China to Chengdu to carry out the air-drop operations. This unit soon acquired several Il-12 transports from the Soviet Union and changed its name to the 13th Air Division. From April 1950 to the conclusion of air operations in November 1952, the air force opened up 25 navigation routes across the Tibetan Plateau; flew 1,282 sorties; and dropped 51 tons of supplies.

As the Communists gradually consolidated their gains, the PLA began conducting operations against armed "bandit" groups in Sichuan and Gansu provinces. The air force took part in these operations from December 1952 to July 1953, using six Tu-2 bombers and five La-9 fighters, plus Il-12 transports from the 13th Air Division. For example, during one month of intense fighting in 1953, the combat aircraft dropped 72 bombs; fired 1,300 rounds of ammunition; and flew 237 transport sorties.

THE KOREAN WAR: 1950–1953

Historical Setting

Several significant events that began in the late 1800s placed Korea at the center of an intense geopolitical struggle among China, Russia (later the Soviet Union), and Japan.[6] These events, along with the growing role of the United States in Asia, helped lay the basis for the Korean War. Japan's actions stemmed from increasing Sino-Japanese tensions on the Korean peninsula, where China had traditionally exercised suzerainty. But Japanese ambitions also clashed directly with Russia's desire for expansion into the Far East in search

---

[6]The material in this subsection draws from Fairbank, Reischauer, and Craig (1973), pp. 553–556 and 882–884. Unless otherwise indicated, quotations in this subsection are from that source.

of a warm-water port. Tokyo described Russia's expansion into Korea as a "dagger pointed at the heart of Japan." At the center of Moscow's plans were several concessions made by a rapidly decaying government in China that allowed Russia to build the Trans-Siberian Railway across Manchuria to Vladivostok and south to the warm-water port of Dalian (Port Arthur) on the Liaodong Peninsula. Construction began in 1891 and was completed in 1903.

Following several years of increasing tension with China, Japan's army seized all of Korea, and its navy defeated Chinese forces in the Sino-Japanese War of 1895. Meanwhile, tensions with Russia increased as Moscow expanded its influence in Manchuria. The resulting Russo-Japanese war of 1905 ended when the Japanese fleet destroyed the Russian Baltic fleet as it entered the Tsushima Strait. The ensuing Treaty of Portsmouth recognized Japan's "paramount interest" in Korea. As a result of these two events, Japan ruled Korea until the end of World War II. During this period, the Soviet Union began training a Korean communist army, which formed the basis for the subsequent establishment of the North Korean army and government.

The next significant event took place during the Cairo Conference of December 1943, where Britain, China, the United States, and the Soviet Union agreed to an international trusteeship of Korea following Japan's defeat. Soviet troops entered northern Korea on August 9, 1945, just before Japan's surrender on August 15, and American troops arrived in southern Korea on September 8. By arranging to take Japan's surrender north and south of the 38th parallel, the two powers created two separate zones and, ultimately, two separate countries. Within a year after separate elections were held in the north and south in 1948, Soviet and American forces had been largely withdrawn from the divided peninsula. By June 1950, the North was a stronger state, both industrially because of its mineral and hydropower resources and militarily because the Soviets had armed it for offensive warfare.

The North Korean surprise attack on June 25, 1950 was at once condemned by the UN Security Council. (The Soviet Union had boycotted the Security Council for six months in protest against the presence of Nationalist China and was not present to cast a veto.) None of the official PLAAF histories on the "War to Resist America and Aid Korea" comment in any detail on the war's origins. The sections dealing with the war merely state that "the Korean civil war erupted on June 25, 1950." However, a burgeoning array of archival materials and interview data have enabled preparation of pioneering studies of the interactions among Moscow, Beijing, and Pyongyang that led to the outbreak of the war.[7]

Immediately following the North Korean attack, President Truman sent forces to defend South Korea and secured the support of the UN in the name of collective security. Forces were sent from Britain, Turkey, and 13 other member countries, although South Korea supplied two-fifths of the ground forces and the United States one-half of the ground forces, as well as most of the naval and airpower. All were put under the command of General Douglas MacArthur.

The war had four phases. First, under the well-prepared Soviet-armed North Korean assault, the outnumbered Korean-American forces initially were forced back southeast of the Naktong River to protect a fifty-by-fifty mile perimeter around Pusan in the extreme southeast. They fought off North Korean attacks while garnering reinforcements from abroad. In the second phase, MacArthur demonstrated the offensive power of modern military technology with a massive amphibious landing on September 15 at Inchon, a gamble that succeeded brilliantly and was soon followed by recovery of Seoul and destruction of the North Korean invasion force.

The war entered the third phase when UN forces crossed the 38th parallel in early October and, shifting their war aim from repulsing of the Northern invasion to reuniting Korea by force, pushed north toward the Yalu River. The two main American thrusts were under separate commands, divided by 50 miles of seemingly impassable mountains. In mid-October, a massive force of Chinese "volunteers" began to cross the Yalu into North Korea to defend China's interests on the frontier of its northeast industrial base and to solidify its new alliance with the Soviet Union.[8] Marching long distances through

---

[7]For two exemplary treatments, consult Goncharov, Lewis, and Xue (1993) and Chen (1994).

[8]For the official Chinese military history of the war published initially for internal reference (*nei bu*), consult Military History Department (1988). Although this study pro-

the mountains by night, lying hidden from air reconnaissance by day, Chinese forces waited until they totaled 300,000 or more by late November. Unexpected flank attacks then forced the American columns into a costly retreat of 275 miles in the winter cold, to well south of Seoul. However, massive UN firepower eventually enabled a stalemate at the 38th parallel. General MacArthur's disagreement with the policy to limit the war led to his dismissal in April 1951. In the fourth phase of the war, truce talks began in July 1951 and dragged on at Panmunjom for two years. An armistice was finally signed July 27, 1953, shortly after the inauguration of President Eisenhower and the death of Joseph Stalin.

The FEAF and PLAAF

The PLAAF was the primary air force involved in the Korean War on the communist side, although the small North Korean Air Force and pilots from the Soviet Air Force also took part.[9] On the UN side, the largest force was the Far East Air Forces (FEAF), which was the air component of the Far East Command. FEAF was composed of the U.S. 5th Air Force (the largest subordinate command), the 20th Air Force, the 13th Air Force, the Far East Air Materiel Command, plus a few other small units. In addition, U.S. Navy and Marine Corps aircraft, plus other friendly foreign air units, including the Royal Australian Air Force's No. 77 Squadron and the small South Korean air force, participated (Futrell, 1983, pp. 689–693).[10]

---

vides a wealth of detail on Chinese combat operations during the war, it offers only limited (if suggestive) insight into Chinese decisionmaking during the conflict.

[9]As part of the "People's Volunteer Army," China's air force was organized and known as the "People's Volunteer Air Force," but the term PLAAF will be used in this chapter.

[10]During the war, FEAF's personnel strength more than tripled as it grew from 33,625 in June 1950 to 112,188 in July 1953. Counting an average of two groups and seven squadrons of Marines and three squadrons of friendly foreign air forces, FEAF possessed or controlled an average of 19 groups and 62 squadrons from June 1950 to July 1953. These squadrons possessed an average of 1,248 aircraft, of which an average of 839 were kept combat ready. A total of 1,040,708 UN aircraft sorties were flown during the war. FEAF units flew a total of 720,980 sorties, including 66,997 counterair; 192,581 interdiction; 57,665 close-support; 181,659 cargo; and 222,078 miscellaneous sorties. Marine units flew an additional total of 107,303 sorties; land-based friendly foreign air units flew another total of 44,873 sorties; and the U.S. Navy flew an additional 167,552 sorties.

From the PLAAF's perspective, the Korean War accomplished several goals. The most important of these were to establish a command organization, to repair and build suitable airfields, to acquire substantial numbers of modern combat aircraft organized into over 25 air divisions, and to gain combat experience for its pilots, staff, and support personnel. The basic organizational structure still exists today, and the Korean War veterans who led the PLAAF in the 1980s are only now being replaced by postwar aviators.

The official PLAAF and USAF histories of the Korean War describe the conflict chronologically, but focus on different considerations. Whereas both describe the organizational changes in air force commands during the war, the acquisition of new equipment, and the constant challenge to achieve air superiority, PLAAF accounts necessarily differ from the USAF histories, given that the PLAAF could not provide direct support for the ground troops.

PLAAF Order of Battle

The PLAAF force structure expanded very rapidly following the PRC's intervention in Korea. Within several months of China's entry into the war, the PLAAF had a total of 650 combat aircraft. By mid-1951, the number had expanded to 1,050 aircraft in 17 divisions (each with two regiments), including 12 pursuit divisions (MiG-9, La-9, and 445 MiG-15s), two attack divisions (Il-10), two bomber divisions (Tu-2 and La-2), and one transport division (Il-12). By late 1952, FEAF estimated the PLAAF had attained a strength of 1,485 aircraft opposite Korea, including 950 jet fighters, 165 conventional fighters, 100 Il-28 jet bombers, 65 conventional light bombers, 115 ground attack planes, and 90 transports. By the time the armistice was signed in 1953, the PLAAF had a total of 28 air divisions (56 regiments). At the same time, each division also began changing from two to three regiments, so that, by early 1954, there were 28 air divisions (70 regiments) with 3,000 aircraft.[11] This was a most impressive achieve-

[11]Information on the PLAAF's order of battle was compiled from data throughout China Today (1988a), PLAAF Headquarters Education and Research Office (1989), and Futrell (1983). The standard table of organization and equipment for an air division has historically consisted of 75 aircraft divided into three regiments of 25 aircraft each. Each regiment has three groups of eight to nine aircraft. Each group has three squadrons of two to three aircraft each.

ment considering the state of the PLAAF in 1949 and the losses sustained in the war.

PLAAF Combat Operations

During the first few weeks of the Korean war, FEAF airmen easily destroyed the small North Korean Air Force, largely by destroying the aircraft while they were still on the ground. This early attainment of air superiority paid large dividends. Without the hazard of hostile air attacks, UN ground forces could maneuver freely by day to resist the more powerful Communist ground forces, who were able to move and fight primarily at night. Following the defeat of the North Korean Air Force, FEAF "owned" the air to the Yalu River, but here air superiority ended, because UN airmen were forbidden to violate the sanctity of the Chinese borders (Figure 8).

Since the UN command's politico-military restrictions confined FEAF air operations to North Korea, the Chinese were free to build and refurbish airfields on Chinese soil to house the expanding inventory of combat aircraft provided in large part by the Soviet Union. The main PLAAF airfield was just across the Yalu at Andong, but MiG-15s were eventually stationed at four other bases, each capable of supporting continuous operations of up to 300 aircraft. By American standards, these airfields were poor, lacking facilities for maintenance and service of aircraft, but the PLAAF showed that they could accept lower standards of flying safety and personal comfort and still operate at a fairly high sustained rate of operations.

The first missions flown from China against the allies occurred on November 1, 1950, prior to the large-scale entry of Chinese ground forces later in the month. During the first months of the war, the Chinese recognized that their ground campaigns could not succeed without air support. Therefore, in late 1950, the PLAAF commander, Liu Yalou, was ordered to begin devising a plan to support a PLA ground offensive that would begin in the spring. Like the FEAF commanders, he also had political and operational restrictions placed on him. He was told not to strike UN forces in the south for fear of retaliatory strikes on bases inside China, and he was limited by the range of the MiG-15, which could not be used to attack tactical targets lying more than 100 miles away from its home base. As a result, he decided to begin renovating and building more bases

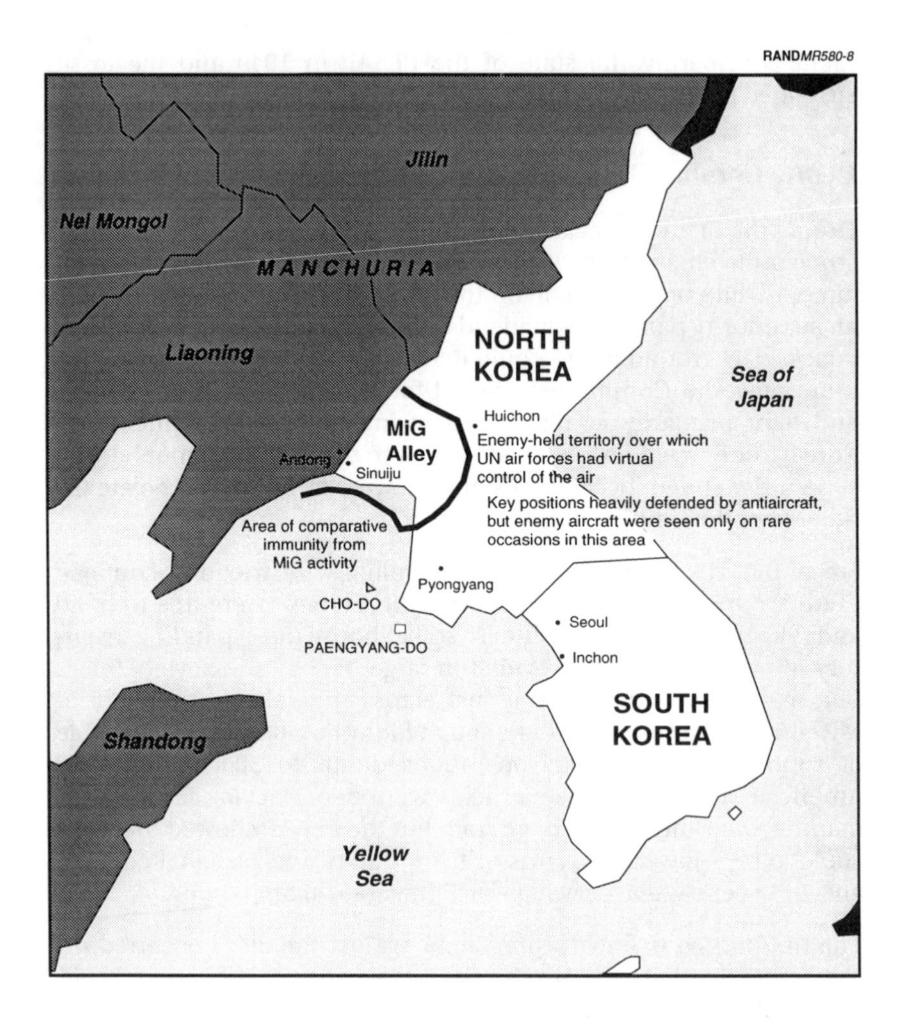

Figure 8—Korean War: MiG Alley

inside North Korea, including "secret" bases near the 38th parallel, and to begin establishing a zone of air superiority over northwestern Korea.

As part of the war plan, the PLAAF and North Koreans were able to build up an extensive network of early warning and ground-control intercept (GCI) radar sites that fed information to a joint PLAAF-North Korean Air Force operations center at Andong. The early-warning coverage extended well south of the 38th parallel, and the GCI coverage was most effective along the west coast of Korea and particularly within a 90 mile radius of Andong. Employing MiG-15s by day and a miscellany of jet and piston day-fighters by night, the PLAAF began to integrate GCI techniques into their air defenses. The GCI radar at Andong could position the PLAAF pilots within 2 to 5 miles of UN aircraft to a distance of 70 miles. This was the technical limit of available GCI radars, because the "blips" of friendly and enemy planes merged on the ground radar scope when they were closer.

In addition, the AAA order of battle around North Korean airfields consisted of about 786 AAA guns and 1,672 automatic weapons by late 1952. The Communists also made extensive utilization of searchlights, eventually deploying about 500 mobile systems, which could illuminate a target up to 30,000 feet on a clear night.

Throughout 1951 and 1952, the PLAAF tried to carry out its airfield construction plan inside North Korea. Initially, FEAF employed its B-29s in an "airfield neutralization program" to attack the airfields during daylight, but the Chinese-North Korean coordinated air defense system throughout northwestern Korea seriously hampered these attacks. Therefore, FEAF equipped its B-29s with the Shoran beacon system to conduct effective night attacks. The Chinese worked feverishly to repair the bomb damage and even tried piling dirt on the runways to make it appear that the runways had been damaged. But these efforts did not prove successful. As a result, the PLAAF was never able to directly support its ground troops during the war.

Pilot Training

One of the most important PLAAF priorities was to train its pilots. To create a cadre of experienced pilots, the PLAAF devised a training cycle consisting of five phases: The first involved three steps: (1) route familiarization into the battle area when no UN forces were in the area, (2) flying into the battle area when UN forces were there but were not a very big threat, and (3) flying missions as the threat gradually increased.

The second consisted of three steps: (1) attacking small flights of bombers, (2) attacking small flights of F-86s, and (3) attacking large formations of aircraft.

The third consisted of flying with experienced leaders, then flying independently.

The fourth consisted of alternating between flying with experienced and new pilots.

The fifth was a period of rest and relaxation, so that no one was in continuous combat for too long. During this period, the pilots summarized their combat experience.

Although FEAF commanders did not have access to the specifics of this training cycle, they did determine most of the details. For example, FEAF intelligence reports indicated that the PLAAF appeared to fly in a predictable three-month training and operational cycle. A new "class of trainees" would fly their MiGs across to meet the Sabres for several weeks but would maintain a high altitude and would not engage in combat. When the "trainee" pilots could be brought under attack they were apt to display utter confusion. Some forgot to drop their external tanks; others fired their guns wildly; and many ejected from their aircraft without particular provocation. As the "class" gained flying proficiency, the PLAAF pilots would become more aggressive and more effectively engage the Sabre pilots. It was during this phase that the Sabre pilots attained their peak aircraft kills. This period would be followed by a near stand-down, then a new "class" would begin all over again.

From the FEAF perspective, the pilots ranged in skill from the very few "honcho" pilots down to the predominant mass of "recruit" pilots. FEAF intelligence officers always insisted that the Sabre pilots did not need to know the nationality of the men they fought. However, Sabre pilots believed that most of the "honcho" pilots were Russians and the "recruits" were Chinese and North Koreans. In the last months of the war—when the "honchos" had apparently gone home—many MiG pilots refused to engage the Sabre force. Although the PLAAF history makes no mention of the role of Soviet pilots, the Russians have recently acknowledged that Soviet pilots flew missions in North Korea from Chinese bases (Gordon and Rigmant, 1993, p. 114). Detailed histories of the Korean War based on Soviet and

Chinese archival holdings also provide ample evidence of the role played by Soviet pilots during the war (Goncharov, Lewis, and Xue, 1993).

Air-to-Air Tactics

From the very beginning of the war, the inexperienced PLAAF pilots tried different tactics and adjusted them as necessary. Until the first F-86 Sabres arrived, the MiG-15 pilots aggressively attacked and "boxed" the slower F-80s and F-84s as they escorted the B-29s and B-26s on their bombing runs into the northwest. However, FEAF pilots gained kills when they caught the planes in turns, something they were able to do at the less-than-20,000-ft altitudes where the fights were waged.

During early 1951, only about one-fourth of the PLAAF pilots sighted by the FEAF sought to engage UN airpower. As FEAF bombers approached the northwest, as many as 50 MiG-15s would scramble and fly to meet the bombers and their escorts, but not all of the MiGs would move in for the attack. By mid-1951, the PLAAF was trying a "yo-yo" tactic: 20 or more MiGs established orbits over UN air formations; then, preferably from up-sun and usually in elements of two, the MiGs dived downward and attacked from high astern; and, finally, the elements zoomed back up into the pool of orbiting MiGs overhead.

By the end of 1952, when the two primary air-to-air combat aircraft were the F-86 Sabre and the MiG-15 Fagot, the PLAAF (sacrificing quality for quantity) was attempting to devise air superiority tactics and to develop fighter interceptor cadres. It experimented again with line-abreast passes against Sabres, using the Sabres to simulate bombers. In an effort to probe UN radar defenses and test the scramble time for the Sabres, it also penetrated south only to withdraw immediately when the Sabres were scrambled. During this period, it was trying to work out the mechanics—command, staff, maintenance, supply, and related problems—of sizable counter-air efforts against the most advanced airpower force in the world.

The decisive factor in U.S. air victories was the experience of the FEAF pilots. The Chinese never adequately or consistently exploited the advantageous characteristics of the MiG-15s, probably because their pilots and their commanders lacked experience in air warfare. The PLAAF consistently misused its available assets by failing to exploit its numerical advantages and the superior high-altitude capabilities of its equipment. The Chinese paid a serious price for the limited experience of their pilots.

During combat, the light MiG-15 consistently outclimbed the heavier F-86 at all altitudes, especially at the higher altitudes. As a general rule, the MiG-15 had a greater rate of initial acceleration than an F-86 in a dive, but the F-86 had a higher terminal velocity at all altitudes and consequently the advantage in a sustained steep dive. The ability of the MiG to convert speed into a high-angle "zoom" was outstanding. The F-86 appeared to enjoy a very slight speed advantage at all altitudes, and it had a slight advantage in very high speed turning duels.[12]

Recognizing the tactical advantages granted to the MiG pilots by their sanctuary inside China, the combat situation over MiG Alley, and the relative performance characteristics of the MiG and Sabre, FEAF Sabre wings developed innovative tactics to maintain air superiority. Perceiving their inability to provide maximum protection to friendly aircraft from flying escort, the Sabres emphasized fighter interceptor "screens" or "sweeps" in conjunction with small escort forces which accompanied the friendly aircraft. Since the MiG airfields were concentrated in a small geographical area just over the Yalu inside China, the Sabre sweeps and screens represented an optimum employment of interceptor aircraft.

But the Chinese pilots were almost totally incapable of providing direct support for their ground forces. The PLAAF attempted to directly support the ground troops on only a few occasions. In June 1951, Il-10 ground attack aircraft were used for the first time to dis-

---

[12]Interestingly, neither aircraft had an armament system well suited for air-to-air combat between jet fighters. The standard MiG armament consisted of 23-mm and 37-mm cannons, combined with a gyroscopic gunsight, which had mechanical range controls. This system performed well against bombers but was not well suited to attacks against maneuvering targets. The Sabre had six 0.50-caliber machine guns. Early models used lead computing gunsights, which performed poorly against the MiGs. Later in the war, radar ranging sights were deployed. These were not totally successful, but proved the concept in combat and led the way to truly effective systems.

lodge South Korean forces off Sinmi-do island. Two Il-10s and six Yak-9 fighters were destroyed en route, while three more Il-10s and four MiG-15s that were flying cover for them were damaged during the attack. Another occasion occurred in November 1951, when F-86s destroyed eight Tu-2 bombers, three La-9 fighters, and one MiG-15 en route to attack South Korean troops on the offshore island of Taehwa-do (Futrell, 1983, p. 415).

The PLAAF's Lessons Learned from Korea

As part of its official history, the PLAAF provided an analysis of the war and drew six principal conclusions (China Today, 1989a, pp. 203–211). The first focused on the policy of trying to repair North Korean airfields as stepping stones toward the south and for providing direct support to the ground forces. It was not until the end of 1951 that the Chinese military leadership conceded that this policy would not work because the UN forces controlled the skies over North Korea and could bomb the airfields at will. The Military Commission also determined that the PLAAF could not directly support the ground troops. As a result, the mission changed to maintaining air superiority in northwestern Korea, to providing point protection of key transportation lines and military and industrial targets, and to providing indirect support for the ground forces. The second lesson was the primacy still placed on the human factor. Even though the UN forces had higher-quality equipment and technology, the PLAAF insisted that its forces were superior because they had come from the ground forces accustomed to difficult situations and were willing to sacrifice themselves for China. This seemed an implicit admission that the Chinese sustained serious losses in the air.

The third lesson was that high technical skills among pilots and maintenance personnel are the keys to victory. For example, the PLAAF compared the kill ratio and aircraft malfunction ratio during the war. From September 1951 to May 1952, according to PLAAF data, the USAF kill ratio was purportedly 1.46:1 and the PLAAF had an average of one maintenance malfunction for every 558.8 sorties. After October 1952, when the F-86 became the primary fighter, the USAF kill ratio was 1.42:1, but the PLAAF had an average of only one malfunction for every 1,003 sorties. However, the kill ratios calculated by the PLAAF do not appear credible. U.S. figures indicate that the Sabres enjoyed an exchange ratio of closer to 10:1 (see Table 2). The fourth lesson was the imperative need to improve the command level to ensure victory. Several instances were cited of missions being conducted mechanically, resulting in the needless loss of aircraft, including the Il-10 mission discussed earlier.

The fifth lesson was the pivotal importance of equipment. Specific examples included PLAAF's claims of a kill ratio of 1:7.8 against the F-80 and F-84. The situation changed when the UN forces acquired the F-86, but the PLAAF's acquisition of MiG-15Bis evened up the odds. For example, of the 125 air battles engaged in during 1952, 85 were with F-86s. Of these, the PLAAF purportedly won nine of them (i.e., shot down at least one F-86 with no PLAAF losses), came out ahead in 15 (it had fewer losses than the UN forces), tied 34, and had more losses in 27. In the remaining 40 battles against other aircraft, the PLAAF won 20, came out ahead in 10, tied 8, and lost 2. The final lesson was the continued importance of the political commissar system's emphasis on political work among the troops to ensuring victory.

But these "lessons learned" were neither comprehensive nor fully candid. Indeed, China's authorized version of these events—even in the 1980s—reveals an unwillingness to fully and accurately portray the record of the conflict. The wide discrepancy in air-to-air combat figures cited by both sides of the Korean War is a good illustration of the PLA's difficulties in analyzing the effectiveness of airpower (see Table 2). These claims suggest that the Chinese continue to delude themselves about the capabilities and performance of their aircraft during the war.

According to the PLAAF's published history, the PLAAF shot down 330 aircraft and damaged another 95 in air-to-air combat, compared

Table 2

Korean War Aircraft Losses/Claims

	Communist			Allies	
	Destroyed	Probable	Damaged	Destroyed	Damaged
PLAAF data	330		95	231	151
Allies' data	976	193	1,009	1,041	
F-86 vs. MiG-15	792			78	

to having only 231 aircraft shot down and 151 damaged—a ratio of 1.1:1 in favor of the PLAAF (China Today, 1989a, pp. 200–201). According to USAF data, UN forces (FEAF, Marines, and friendly foreign aircrews) destroyed 976 enemy aircraft in air-to-air combat. In the course of its operations, UN forces lost a total of 1,986 aircraft, of which 1,041 were destroyed by hostile action and only 147 were lost in air-to-air combat. The number of UN aircraft damaged in air-to-air combat was not given.[13] It should be noted that the USAF had gun camera film to support most of its claims, and it is doubtful if the Chinese had any similar accountability system. Some of the differences may be explained by Russian and North Korean participation. For example, in 1993 a pair of Russian authors challenged the authority of gun camera film by stating "some of these MiG-15s, seemingly shot down on Sabre gun camera film, actually landed at their airfields with damage." More interesting is their revelation that Soviet losses totaled 345 MiGs (Gordon and Rigmant, 1993, p. 114).

The real key to analyzing the war and the effectiveness of the PLAAF's air-to-air capabilities, however, comes from examining combat between the F-86 and MiG-15. By the conclusion of the war, Sabre pilots had destroyed 810 enemy planes, including 792 MiG-15s, some of which were piloted by Soviet airmen. Meanwhile, FEAF lost a total of 139 aircraft in air-to-air combat, including 78 Sabres. The Sabre pilots thus maintained a 10:1 margin of victory over the MiG-15.

Despite its problematic record in certain areas, the PLAAF nevertheless scored some significant accomplishments. In only a few years, the PLAAF had grown from a force of only a few obsolescent combat aircraft to over 20 divisions and 3,000 aircraft, many of which were highly advanced systems for their time. Chinese forces virtually stopped the FEAF B-29s from flying daytime missions and shot down over 100 aircraft in air-to-air combat. (The number actually shot down by Chinese pilots is certainly much less than this figure, because of the participation of Russian pilots alongside the Chinese and North Koreans, but the PLAAF had gained a training edge that put it ahead of most of the world's air forces.) The PLAAF had also gained valuable combat experience, established a command organi-

[13]Of the total of 1,986 allied aircraft lost, 945 were lost to nonenemy causes and 1,041 to enemy action, including 147 in air-to-air combat, 816 to hostile ground fire, and 78 to unknown enemy action.

zation and administrative structure, built and refurbished countless airfields, and trained a cadre of maintenance and logistics personnel under combat conditions. The Korean War experience also helped the PLAAF lay the foundations for future growth, and provided the operational experience for the PLAAF's leaders in the 1980s and 1990s.

POST–KOREAN WAR REORGANIZATION

Coincident with the fuller development of defense ties with Moscow, China made an effort to reorganize along Soviet lines. In 1954, China's leaders established the National Defense Council and the Ministry of National Defense and, as noted in Chapter Two, reorganized the PLA's five FA areas into 13 MRs.

In 1955, the Air Defense Troops became the PLA Air Defense Force (ADF), with Yang Chengwu as the Commander. At this point, the ADF became a service equivalent to the air force and navy. In May 1957, however, the ADF was merged with the PLAAF. At that time, the ADF had four MR air defense headquarters (Shenyang, Beijing, Nanjing, and Guangzhou), one ADF corps (Fuzhou), and eight schools, plus AAA troops, searchlight troops, and aircraft reporting troops, totaling 149,000 personnel. The PLAAF gained substantially in end-strength through the merger, and the logic of a more integrated organizational structure was thus more fully in place.

When the PLAAF and ADF merged, the new PLAAF leadership consisted of the commander (Liu Yalou), political commissar (Wu Faxian), and seven deputy commanders—five from the PLAAF and two from the ADF. Although several elements with similar responsibilities were merged and some redundant elements were eliminated, the administrative and operational structure continued to reflect two separate organizations. To some degree, this situation has persisted in subsequent decades, and has hampered a true integration of the aviation (combat aircraft) and air defense (AAA, SAM, radar, and communications) assets.

In conjunction with this reorganization, the air force renamed its six MRAF headquarters in May 1955 as the Shenyang, Beijing, Nanjing,

Guangzhou, Lanzhou, and Wuhan MRAFs. Although four of the MRAFs remained in the same location, two of them moved.[14] Because of the lack of an adequate command and control system, the MRAF headquarters were responsible primarily for those units surrounding the six major cities.[15]

In addition to realigning the MRAFs, the headquarters air force (HqAF) organization in Beijing was restructured in May 1955, and the six major departments were expanded to 11, plus a military law division, to handle the increasing responsibilities and missions. The 11 departments were the headquarters, political, personnel, military training, schools, engineering, procurement, airfield construction, logistics, finance, and directly subordinate political departments (Allen, 1991a, p. 2-6). This administrative structure was mirrored at each subordinate level, beginning with the MRAF headquarters.

The significance of these changes was that the air force was beginning to expand its operational and administrative command and control structure to perform its primary air defense mission. However, the changes also reveal that the air force was not organized to perform a support role for the ground forces. For example, the structure of the six MRAFs covering all of the 13 MRs was designed for air defense, not ground support. Furthermore, the air force and army headquarters were not (and are still not) colocated. This helped cause further organizational separation between the two services.

THE CONFRONTATION WITH THE NATIONALISTS

After the Nationalists retreated to Taiwan in 1949, Beijing repeatedly emphasized its intention to "liberate" Taiwan.[16] The PLA began stationing some of its ground forces opposite Taiwan in Fujian

---

[14]The South Central MRAF in Wuhan moved to Guangzhou as the Guangzhou MRAF, and the Southwest MRAF in Chengdu moved to Wuhan to become the Wuhan MRAF.

[15]In addition, two other types of operational organizations subordinate to headquarters air force or the MRAF headquarters—air corps and command posts—were established to control aircraft defending the other major cities within China.

[16]Information from this discussion is drawn from Young (1968), p. 137–162; Pollack (1976); Oksenberg and Oxnam, (1978), pp. 179–182; Segal (1985), pp. 7–139; and Worden, Savada, and Dolan (1987).

Province in 1949 and began repairing various airfields in Fujian and Guangdong Provinces in advance of deploying additional troops there in 1950. However, these preparations were put on hold during the Korean War in order to concentrate forces in the Northeast.[17] Meanwhile, the Nationalist air force controlled the airspace over Fujian, eastern Guangdong, and southern Zhejiang Provinces, to facilitate raids against other targets. In addition, it controlled a series of islands just off the coast of Zhejiang and Fujian Provinces, using Dachen Island, Quemoy (Kinmen/Jinmen), and Matsu (Mazu) as the key centers (Figure 9). In 1954, the PLA successfully occupied the Dachen island group in what is known as the Yijiangshan Campaign. It also tried unsuccessfully to dislodge Nationalist forces from Quemoy and Mazu islands in 1954 and 1958.

Other than individual engagements with U.S. aircraft over Chinese airspace during the Vietnam War, the 1958 Taiwan Strait crisis was the last time the PLAAF aircraft engaged in any type of large-scale direct combat. The preparation phases for this operation are quite similar to other PLAAF operations and provide insights into how the PLAAF might prepare for a future conflict.

Political and Military Setting

Shortly after the May–July 1954 Geneva Conference on Indochina, the PLA began shelling Quemoy, a Nationalist outpost consisting of two islands covering 130 km^2 and located just 2 miles from the mainland port of Amoy (Xiamen).[18] This opened up eight months of artillery, air, and naval exchanges, centering on these and other offshore islands held by the Nationalists. As a counterpoise to Beijing's massing of troops on the mainland, President Eisenhower concentrated sea and air forces in the Taiwan area, withholding American forces from the offshore fighting while sustaining Quemoy and Matsu logistically. At the culmination of the crisis in March

[17]For a detailed, highly revealing account of the events leading to the deferral of plans to attack Taiwan that draws extensively on newly available Chinese source materials, consult He (1992).

[18]For an insightful account by a Chinese military analyst, see Li (1992).

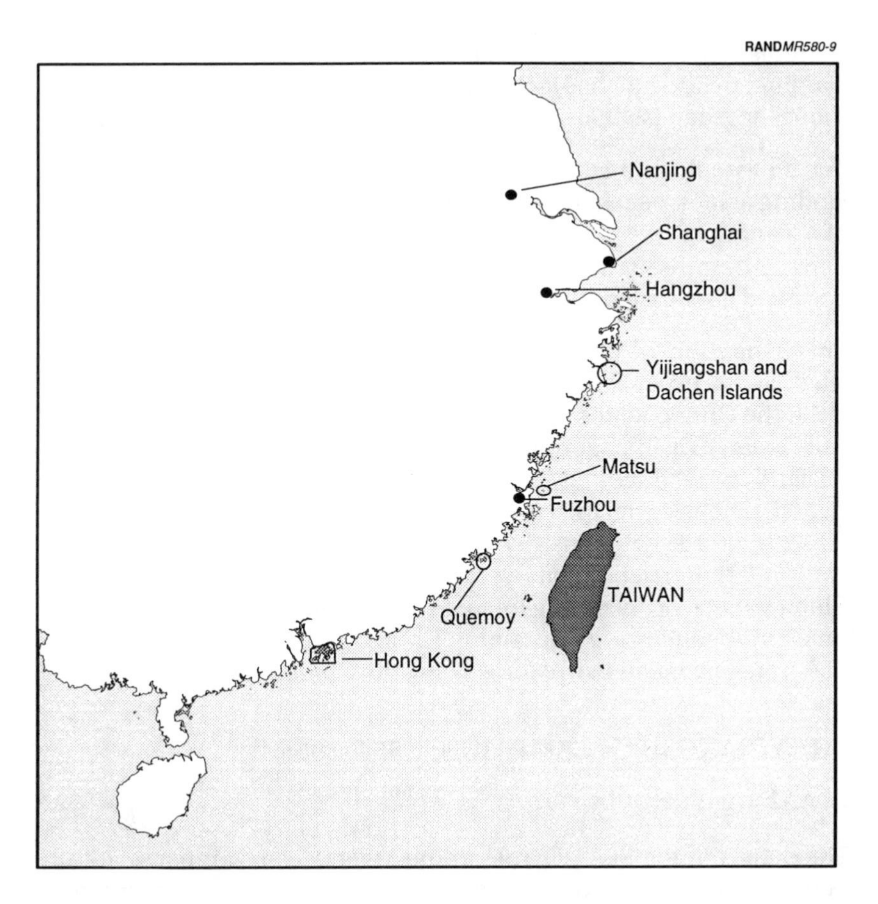

Figure 9—Taiwan Strait Crisis and the Yijiangshan Campaign

1955, Beijing backed off and called for talks with Washington, which began in Geneva in August.

By 1954, the Nationalists had one division and six assault groups on Dachen Island itself and 8 to 12 vessels in the surrounding waters, for a total of about 20,000 troops. They also had about 1,000 troops deployed on the Yijiangshan Islands, which are part of the Dachen Island group and consist of two small islands covering 1.7 km^2, strategically located about 10 n mi from the mainland coast. At the same time the PLA began shelling Quemoy and Matsu, the Military

Commission ordered the PLA's East China MR (headquartered in Nanjing) to liberate the Dachen Islands, beginning with an assault on the Yijiangshan Islands.

The air assault on the Dachen Islands began on November 1, and the landing assault began on January 18, 1955. Following the occupation of Yijiangshan, the U.S. Navy helped evacuate Nationalist forces to Taiwan from the remaining islands in the Dachen group. The PLA occupied all the islands by February 25th.

This expansion of Beijing's military activities, however, was paralleled by an expansion of American commitments. In September 1954, the United States created a joint defense system, the Southeast Asia Treaty Organization, to include Britain, France, Australia, New Zealand, the Philippines, Thailand, and Pakistan. Washington also signed defensive alliances with Seoul (October 1953) and Taipei (December 1954). Thus, by the time the Communist-Nationalist confrontation over Quemoy and Yijiangshan occurred in 1954, China's activity concerning four contiguous areas was matched by an American-led effort at containing Chinese power and deterring the PLA from any major use of force along the Chinese coast.

THE YIJIANGSHAN CAMPAIGN: 1954–1955

PLAAF Involvement

The details of the PLAAF's role in the Yijiangshan Campaign are instructive, because the campaign was the PLA's first true combined arms operation.[19] The campaign also provided the framework for the 1958 attempt to dislodge Chinese Nationalist forces from Quemoy and Matsu, as well as the border conflict with Vietnam two decades later.

As part of the PLAAF's command post in Zhejiang Province, the PLAAF established a forward command post under Nie Fengzhi, who was the Commander of the East China MRAF. PLAAF and naval aviation units used for the operation included elements of one bomber division, one ground attack division, three fighter divisions,

---

[19]The material in this subsection draws from China Today (1989a), pp. 319–328. Unless otherwise indicated, quotations herein are from that publication.

two independent reconnaissance regiments, and three naval aviation fighter divisions, for a total of 200 aircraft deployed to five airfields. The PLAAF pilots were flying the MiG-15Bis, Tu-2, and Il-10 aircraft. At that time, the Nationalists, flying F-84s and F-47s, were just beginning to be equipped with F-86s.

Phase I: Planning

A decision was made in September 1954 to conduct the operation in two phases. The first phase would consist of the navy and air force gaining air and maritime superiority. Army troops would deploy secretly to Toumenshan and wait for high tide to begin the assault. The PLAAF's missions were as follows:

- Use fighters to support ground air defense troops and to gain air superiority.
- Use bomber and ground attack units to mass force to attack resupply ships sent from Taiwan.
- Use small formations to attack military fortifications continuously.
- Support the army and navy amphibious landing.
- Conduct airborne reconnaissance flights.

However, during preparations for the campaign, the air force encountered numerous problems, even though many of the units had taken part in the Korean War:

- There were no reliable data on Nationalist fortifications.
- There was no previous experience in coordinating among the three services.
- There was virtually no capability to hit hardened ground targets.
- The bombers and ground attack aircraft had no experience flying in bad weather or over water.

As a result, the PLAAF undertook various steps to overcome these obstacles while preparing for the air assault:

- It studied amphibious assault theory.
- It established a command structure. Besides setting up a command post at each airfield, it also set up alternate command posts at four sites, set up a forward air controller (FAC) site on a mountain, sent aviation representatives to work with the fleet to coordinate air and naval operations, and sent FACs to work with the first echelon at the army's regiment and battalion levels to coordinate all air and ground operations.
- It practiced flying over Hangzhou Bay and dropping bombs on an island.
- It conducted 60 aerial reconnaissance sorties.
- It conducted battlefield preparations, such as increasing the amount of fuel and bombs available.
- It strengthened troop indoctrination about the PLAAF's combat policy. For example, the U.S. 7th Fleet, which was conducting operations in the area, flew 294 sorties in June and August. The PLA was ordered not to respond, to keep the United States from becoming involved.
- It carried out a coordinated operations plan.

Phase II: The Attack

The PLAAF initiated the first bombing of Yijiangshan on November 1, 1954. At exactly 11:00 a.m. on a clear day, fighters, ground attack aircraft, and bombers departed their airfields and formed up using radio silence. Four Il-10s struck AAA positions and then supported nine Tu-2s as they attempted to strike ships in the harbor—but failed to hit anything because they found the targets too late. Overall, the air force flew a total of 288 sorties, including 168 sorties for air cover and 72 bomber (Tu-2s) and 48 ground attack (Il-10s) sorties on the first day of the campaign. They dropped 851 bombs (127 tons) and fired 3,741 rounds of ammunition.

From November 2 through December 20, five bomber and ground attack aircraft groups attacked various targets. They were effective against land targets, but not against any vessels. On January 10, under high-wind conditions, the air force sent a total of 130 sorties in four separate time periods and sank or damaged five Nationalist vessels. In addition, the air force sent out 297 sorties to blockade the Dachen Islands.

On January 18, the landing assault began according to the plan. The first group of fighters took off at 4:00 a.m. and formed up to cover the loading of troops at Toumenshan and Gaodao. From 8:00 to 8:15 a.m., Tu-2s and Il-10s conducted concentrated bombing on military fortifications on Yijiangshan. The successful landing assault took place that day, which essentially ended the campaign. During the entire Yijiangshan Campaign, the air force lost 19 aircraft to AAA. According to the PLAAF, 35.9 percent of the bombs dropped hit their targets (the accuracy of this statistic is suspect).

As with the Korean War, the PLAAF and naval aviation massed aircraft from several different units to conduct the campaign. Unlike the Korean War, however, there was no real air threat to the aircraft because the Nationalist aircraft were flying out of Taiwan. Besides the few unsuccessful ground attack missions described in the Korean War section, this was the only other time in its history that the PLAAF has conducted a direct support role for ground or naval forces. Indeed, quite remarkably, the lack of coordination among the three services during the planning phase has continued to the present day.

THE 1958 TAIWAN STRAIT CRISIS

Beginning in 1956, the PLA began building a new group of airfields in Fujian, Zhejiang, and eastern Guangdong Provinces and had begun making preparations to move the air force into Fujian. By 1958, Beijing estimated that the Nationalists had six infantry divisions with 85,000 troops and over 400 artillery pieces stationed on Quemoy and Matsu. In the aftermath of a two-month-long meeting of the Military Commission between May and July of 1958, Beijing began a sharp upsurge in propaganda calling for the "liberation" of Taiwan. The plans called for the air force to enter Fujian first, and for Chinese artillery to begin shelling Quemoy. In response, Washington announced that its forces in the Far East were going on alert and would conduct naval and air force patrols north to Okinawa and south to the Philippines. In addition, Taiwan put its forces on alert on July 17 and began conducting reconnaissance flights along the coast of

Fujian and Guangdong, publicly calling this "preparations to quickly counterattack the mainland."

Several factors helped explain Beijing's decision to initiate hostilities against Quemoy. First, the West appeared preoccupied with the Middle East crisis under way since the late spring, a fact that was probably central in the timing of the attacks.[20] Second, the Chinese believed they had an unbeatable hand. The evidence strongly suggests that Beijing never intended to launch a frontal assault on any of the offshore islands but believed that, by interdiction, Chinese forces could compel the Quemoy garrison to surrender, which would lead to the automatic collapse of the other offshore islands. The Chinese seemed to base their calculations on a judgment widely held in the West—that once air and sea interdiction became effective, the offshore islands could not be supplied, unless Nationalist and American forces were prepared to bomb the coastal provinces on the Chinese mainland. A third calculation was that Mao sought to stimulate greater popular effort for the "Great Leap Forward" and the commune program that he launched in July 1958. Fourth, the offshore island venture must also be looked upon as a calculated probe of U.S. intentions, to see just how far Washington would go in defending the islands. Finally, and perhaps most important, Mao seemed determined to demonstrate his independence from Soviet control and initiated military actions without fully informing his allies in Moscow.

PLAAF Preparations

Overall, the PLAAF's battle for air superiority took three months and can be divided into two phases.[21] Phase 1 took place from July 27 to August 22 and consisted of the PLAAF moving into Fujian and Guangdong. Phase 2 took place from August 23 to mid-October and consisted of air cover for the naval and army artillery shelling and the blockade of Quemoy. The air force's plan for these two phases consisted of the following four parts:

---

[20]For suggestive evidence in this regard, see Li (1992), p. 36.

[21]The material in this subsection draws from China Today (1989a), pp. 333–351. Unless otherwise indicated, quotations herein are from that publication.

- Before the aircraft moved in, the air force had to quickly establish a command structure in Fujian and first had to deploy small numbers of AAA, radar, and searchlight troops into the area. The air force's 1st Air Corps in Fuzhou, which was acquired during the 1957 PLAAF–Air Defense Force merger, was responsible for the air defense of Fujian but was not equipped to handle a large influx of troops. Therefore, the decision was made to use the 1st Air Corps as the core but to transfer experienced operations personnel from the 5th Air Corps in Hangzhou to Fujian to establish the Fuzhou MRAF command staff. The personnel from the 5th Air Corps were already combat veterans, having been involved in the Korean War and the Yijiangshan Campaign.

- The air force began moving key staff and ground personnel into various airfields in Fujian on July 24 to prepare for the arrival of elements of five PLAAF fighter divisions, two bomber regiments, AAA and radar units, and part of the naval aviation's 4th Division. The actual aircraft deployments began on July 27th. During the first two weeks of August, elements of four more air divisions deployed to Zhangzhou, Liancheng, Longtian and Fuzhou. By this time, there were six fighter regiments deployed along the first line and 17 regiments on the second line for a total of 520 aircraft. In addition, maintenance field stations, trucks, and supplies were brought in from throughout China to support the aircraft.

- The air force clarified its "operational command philosophy," which consisted of five parts: (a) use small forces to achieve large victories; (b) protect yourself and destroy the enemy; (c) military battles must be subservient to political battles; (d) the air force must strictly adhere to the Military Commission's operational policy; and (e) personnel must study lessons of the Korean War.[22] The reaction of the rank and file to these lofty sentiments is unknown.

- As in the Korean War and, subsequently, in the 1979 Sino-Vietnamese border conflict, the PLA's and PLAAF's political

[22]This paragraph is presented to show what type of guidance the air force leadership has given, and will probably give in the future, to its troops prior to engaging in combat.

commissar system expended considerable propaganda efforts to increase political mobilization by explaining to the troops and local Chinese populace that the reason for entering Fujian was to support the struggle of the Middle East people against imperialism, protect socialism, smash the Nationalists' military abilities, and to train the people's air force under real conditions.

During preparations for the assault, the Military Commission also established the following three rules of engagement for the air force:

- The air force could not enter the high seas to conduct operations.
- If the Nationalist air force did not bomb the mainland, the PLAAF could not bomb Quemoy and Matsu.
- The air force was not allowed to attack the U.S. military but could defend against any U.S. aircraft entering Chinese territory.

PLAAF Operations

Once the general plan and rules of engagement were established, the air force gave the order on July 19 to begin implementing the plan.[23] In spite of Fujian being hit by a typhoon that same day, which caused massive flooding, 5th Air Corps personnel deployed and established the Fuzhou MRAF command post at Jinjiang. They also set up 21 radar sites and set up AAA sites along the coast. Once these were in place, the first aircraft (MiG-17s) deployed to Liancheng and Shantou on July 27th. Prior to these deployments, the United States and Taiwan were not fully cognizant that the Soviets had provided the PLAAF with the MiG-17—a significant upgrade to the MiG-15. During this period, the Nationalists responded by preparing to bomb naval targets and conducting reconnaissance flights along the coast. According to PLAAF statistics, each day during this period, the Nationalists flew about 100 sorties, using F-86s to fly cover for RF-84s.

During Phase 1 of the air operations (July 29 to August 22), PLAAF statistics showed that the air force units that had deployed to Fujian

---

[23]The material in this subsection draws upon China Today (1989a), pp. 333–351. Unless otherwise indicated, quotations herein are from that publication.

and Guangdong flew 1,077 sorties in 255 groups and engaged in four battles, shooting down four aircraft, damaging five, and losing one. Assuming that only the six regiments (about 200 aircraft) deployed along the front line conducted these sorties, each fighter flew an average of five sorties over the 23 day period—one sortie every four days. If the number of aircraft was greater, the number of sorties declines accordingly. This indicates that the PLAAF logistical support capabilities were still far from adequate.

The first air battle took place on July 29th over Shantou, where four MiG-17s had a three-minute air battle against four Nationalist F-84Gs. According to the PLAAF, the battle ended with the PLAAF having shot down two and damaged one with no losses. The Military Commission had originally planned to begin shelling Quemoy on July 24 but delayed this until the beginning of Phase 2 on August 23. On the first day of shelling, the PLA fired over 30,000 rounds at the islands. Since the PLAAF had not been able to gain air superiority, the Military Commission used the policy of "shelling but not assaulting, blockading but not killing."

Phase 2 was also highlighted by further deployment of aircraft on both sides of the Taiwan Strait and larger air battles. The PLAAF redeployed some of its aircraft to airfields in Fujian and eastern Guangdong. The United States also deployed more troops and 140 F-100s and F-104s to Taiwan. In addition, the Nationalists, who began using U.S.-supplied Sidewinder air-to-air missiles for the first time, flew 100 to 200 sorties a day, including 30 to 80 aircraft at a time along the coast. During this period, there were seven air battles, with the largest ones on August 25, September 24, and October 10.

To prepare for the possibility of the Nationalist air force conducting retaliatory bombing raids on the mainland, the PLAAF and Naval Aviation began preparations for conducting bombing attacks on Taiwan. On August 21, two Il-28 and one Tu-4 bomber regiments entered Zhangshu airfield in Jiangxi Province. In addition, two MiG-15 and one Il-10 ground attack regiments prepared to deploy if necessary. Two AAA battalions were also deployed to the area. In the end, the Nationalists did not conduct bombing raids on the mainland, so the PLAAF did not retaliate with its bombers.

On August 25, the Nationalists sent 48 F-86s to fly over Quemoy and eight more aircraft to fly in the area of Zhangzhou. In response, the Fuzhou MRAF scrambled 68 Soviet-supplied MiG-17Fs and equivalent indigenously produced F-5s. According to PLAAF statistics, some F-5s engaged four F-86s and shot down two aircraft, but one aircraft was shot down by friendly AAA en route home. As a result of the AAA shootdown, the air force and artillery commanders met and came up with the following principles, which guided all future air and ground combat coordination:

- If there is an air battle in progress, the ground artillery will not fire.
- If PLAAF aircraft cannot take off or if there are no friendly aircraft in the air, the ground artillery will engage the enemy.
- If the enemy is conducting bombing, the ground forces will engage the aircraft even if there is an air battle going on between enemy and friendly forces.
- Coastal forces should not open fire, except when enemy forces are attacking their specific positions.

During the two weeks following the opening of Phase 2, KMT forces used two methods involving the U.S. military to resupply the troops on Quemoy. The first method matched Beijing's tactical innovation with technological innovation. The U.S. Navy used a convoy of landing ships to carry preloaded, tracked amphibious craft manned by Nationalists to a point 3 mi from Quemoy, where they disembarked from the landing ships, darted through the shellfire, and scurried ashore to inland unloading areas. The scheme worked, and by September 21, the siege was lifted. The Nationalists also continued to use a second method to resupply the troops after September 21, whereby F-86s flew cover for C-46 transports as they air-dropped supplies. In addition, the United States flew air cover 20 to 40 km south of Quemoy. To hinder the resupply effort, the Military Commission decided on October 2 to attack the air transports and deployed a squadron of MiG-17s to Jinjiang to conduct the mission.

At 3:00 p.m. on October 3, the Nationalists dispatched 24 C-46s to Quemoy with 48 F-86s flying cap at 12,000 to 13,000 m. The attack began when the Fuzhou MRAF command post scrambled 24

MiG-17Fs each from Liancheng and Shantou airfields and ordered them to fly to a position near Quemoy to distract the F-86s. At the same time, the command post scrambled four MiG-17Fs from Jinjiang and vectored them at low altitude to a point where they shot down two of the C-46s once the F-86s went after the MiG-17s.[24] This was the last time the Nationalists flew daytime air-drops.

The final air battle took place on October 10, when a PLAAF pilot shot down two F-86s. By the end of October, Beijing deescalated the crisis with a temporary cease-fire followed by intermittent shelling. The strait's air defense situation had reached a stalemate, with the Nationalists controlling the airspace over the strait and the PLAAF gradually controlling the airspace over Fujian, Zhejiang, and Guangdong provinces. Over the next few years, the Nationalists continued to probe the mainland's defenses with reconnaissance flights (including high-altitude U-2 flights of which the PLAAF shot down five between 1962 and 1967).

As in many cases, the data on combat victories and losses reported by the opposing sides vary widely (Table 3). For example, according to PLAAF data, the air force and naval aviation flew 3,778 sorties in 691 groups from July 18 until the end of October. Their aircraft were engaged in 13 air battles, shooting down 14 and damaging nine

Table 3

1958 Taiwan Strait Crisis Aircraft Losses

Source	Battles	PLAAF	ROC	AAA
PLAAF	13			
Lost		5	14	—
Probable		—	0	—
Kills		—	—	2
Damaged		5	9	2
U.S./ROC	25			
Lost		32	3	—
Probable		3	—	—
Kills		—	—	—
Damaged		10	—	—

[24]According to his biography, Cao Shuangming, the PLAAF commander between 1992 and 1994, was one of the MiG-17 pilots (Xinhua, 1992).

Nationalist aircraft. The PLAAF lost only five aircraft and had five damaged. In addition, PLAAF AAA units were involved in seven battles, shooting down two and damaging two aircraft (China Today, 1989a, pp. 350–351).

On the other hand, according to USAF data, there were 25 air-to-air engagements from August 23 to October 6. Nationalist pilots destroyed 32 aircraft, downed probably three more, and damaged ten. Nationalist forces lost four of their own aircraft (USAF Historical Division, 1962, p. 39).

The only positive outcome for the PLAAF of the crisis was that it now had a permanent presence opposite Taiwan, and the Nationalists no longer owned the airspace over Fujian and eastern Guangdong provinces. On the negative side, the PLA was not able to take Quemoy or Matsu, and the Nationalists had an 8:1 kill ratio over the PLAAF. Coordination between fighter forces and ground-based defenses had been found wanting as well. Although the PLAAF deployed over 500 aircraft to the area, they did not capitalize on their numerical superiority, nor did they show any type of surge capability. The incident also helped hasten the split between Beijing and Moscow.

Despite mounting frictions with Moscow, China continued to receive military assistance from the Soviet Union. In October 1958, China received its first SA-2 missiles (five launchers and 62 missiles) from the Soviet Union. Following the merger and the addition of the SAM troops in 1958, the PLAAF consisted of five branches (aviation, AAA, SAM, radar, and communications) plus airborne and logistics troops. This basic structure has continued to the present day.

By the close of the 1950s, therefore, the PLAAF had gained ample combat experience and had (with very substantial Soviet assistance) emerged as a major force in military aviation. The units and pilots who trained and fought together during this period became the backbone of the air force in subsequent decades. Indeed, the air force's organizational relationships have remained largely unchanged ever since.

By decade's end, the air force leadership had thus built up a sizeable air defense force, first in the northeast and later opposite Taiwan. It had also acquired some sobering experience in combat against forces that were superior in technology and in tactics. But the air force continued to labor under severe constraints in developing concepts of operations appropriate to the challenges that it faced. Even more ominously, Mao Zedong's growing defiance of the Soviet Union meant that the sole source of advanced equipment for the PLAAF was increasingly jeopardized. The decade of the 1950s was a momentous period of development, but subsequent years involved setbacks from which the air force even today still struggles to recover.

Chapter Four

"LIVING IN INTERESTING TIMES": THE PLAAF IN THE 1960s

THE BREAK WITH THE SOVIET UNION

The split with the Soviet Union and the excesses of the Cultural Revolution in the 1960s all but stopped the PLAAF's drive toward modernization. The cumulative effects of the 1960s devastated the air force organizationally and operationally, leaving it merely a shell of what it had been at the outset of the decade.

When China tried to manufacture several new aircraft on its own, the aviation factories ended up producing aircraft during the Cultural Revolution that were dangerous to fly. Meanwhile, the air force all but ceased training its pilots and maintenance personnel, leading to serious aircraft malfunctions and crashes. Thus, the breakup of the Sino-Soviet alliance was especially traumatic for the PLAAF. With nowhere else to turn for advanced technology, self-reliance became an imperative. At the same time, the PLAAF found itself increasingly embroiled in China's internal political convulsions—even as the security challenges to China mounted to the south and to the north.

PLAAF and aviation industry leaders quickly recognized the need to address airpower in terms of China's independent defense needs. This effort proved to be a tortuous and lengthy process (China Today, 1989a, pp. 266–271). PLAAF staffs began a multiyear effort to compile rational regulations, rules, manuals, and guidance that reflected the air force's needs. The education and training system was reformed, and there was an emphasis on indigenous skills and education for PLAAF officers and technicians.

But the consequences of Mao's break with the Soviets and the effort to recover from the debacle of the Great Leap Forward were very severe. With the withdrawal of Soviet advisors in 1960, there was an immediate need to consolidate incomplete Soviet scientific and technological projects. The problems were especially pressing for the PLAAF. Because of a lack of engines and engine parts, flying hours fell by 41 percent in 1960. They continued to be low through at least 1963.

In 1961, quality control in the manufacture of aircraft also became a serious problem. The scarcity of aviation equipment and parts also compelled the PLAAF to adopt new flight training measures. These were summarized as "train harder on the ground; fly with precision through the air" (China Today, 1989a, pp. 251–256).[1] Perhaps only briefly between 1963 and 1966—before the chaos of the Cultural Revolution began—did the PLAAF feel it was finally on the threshold of recovering from the setbacks caused by the break with Moscow. These were years during which there were efforts to imbue all services with a sense of professionalism, refine the education curricula, improve the training schools, take advantage of the more modern aircraft in China's inventory, and create an underpinning of doctrine and regulations that could give direction to the air force.

THE CULTURAL REVOLUTION AND THE PLAAF

The Cultural Revolution proved a disaster for the PLAAF. Without question, the turning point was Minister of Defense Lin Biao's abortive coup attempt and his subsequent death in a plane crash as he fled China in September 1971. The immediate consequence was a steady erosion of the influence of the left-wing radicals. Lin Biao's closest supporters, including PLAAF commander Wu Faxian, were purged systematically. Wu Faxian was arrested immediately after Lin's death and was finally sentenced a decade later to 17 years of imprisonment. Because of deep suspicions among other senior military and civilian leaders about the PLAAF's loyalties, the air force was

---

[1]Even during the 1980s, photographic stories in *China Pictorial* and PLAAF pictorial books often showed PLAAF pilots watching an instructor demonstrate an aircraft maneuver with a hand-held model airplane. This technique was indicative of the emphasis on ground training.

immediately put in a stand-down for three months after Lin's death (PLAAF Second Aviation School, 1982, p. 282). These suspicions continued long after the stand-down ceased and are illustrated by the fact that the air force did not have a commander for almost two years and that none of the official PLAAF histories list any events for 1972 at all.

Biographies of PLA and PLAAF leaders are often glaringly silent about these years. Although a number of books have been published in the West about the difficulties of the Cultural Revolution years, there have been no similar books that specifically focus on the consequences for the Chinese military. Recent military histories are guarded in their assessments. While not understating the problems that arose, they have not "hung out the wash," as has been the case in some of the personal accounts.[2]

Because of the political and economic turmoil during the Cultural Revolution, the PLAAF stagnated. In matters involving flight safety, education, training, strategy, and tactics, PLAAF historians claim there was actual atrophy (China Today, 1989a, pp. 480–491; PLAAF Headquarters Education and Research Office, 1989, pp. 195–202). Civilian units, under the guise of making revolution, often occupied military bases. In many cases the military property was never returned to its units. In other instances, military school compounds were destroyed as well as teaching materials, books and equipment. Instructors, researchers and staff were often scattered throughout China. In the worst cases, they were killed or died.

Ironically, the war in Vietnam, plus Lin Biao's paranoia about China facing an imminent large war, led to an increase in flying hours. However, the training was haphazard, maintenance was poor, and the "serious accident rate" for aircraft soared to 0.6 per 10,000 sorties from 0.249 in 1964 (China Today, 1989a, pp. 271, 299, 510–514).[3]

---

[2]For example, in China Today (1989a), the PLAAF historical chronology has no entries for 1972. The period from September 1971 to May 1973 is the only time the PLAAF did not have a commander. For first-hand accounts of the Cultural Revolution, see Milton and Milton, 1976; Liang and Shapiro, 1983; and Cheng, 1986.

[3]In 1984 the serious aircraft accident rate was 0.204. Between 1950 and 1953 the rate was 4.716, but dropped to an average of 1.5 until 1959, when it finally fell below 1.0. The PLAAF's three categories of aircraft accidents are (1) aircraft and pilot lost; (2) aircraft lost, pilot safe; and (3) aircraft damaged, pilot safe.

Almost all PLAAF schools were closed for nearly six years, halting almost all nonflying and ground training. This was the "lost generation" for China's youth, and it was no less true for the PLAAF.

For the air force, the cessation of education was more complicated than it was for society as a whole. The problems resulting from the "stop classes, make revolution" activities were disruptive but did not pose the most harmful consequences. The major problem was Lin Biao's advocacy of an imminent war doctrine. An emphasis on war preparations and political activism led to far-reaching changes. In November 1969, this view led to the elimination of 13 of approximately 16 technical schools and academies in the PLAAF. The expected training goal for the Cultural Revolution years was 21,900 students, but only 5,650 graduated. In 1967 and 1968, the achievement levels of graduates were so low they could not be used in the units to which they were assigned. At the PLAAF's Second Aviation School, authorities claimed that the elimination of aviation theory courses between 1967 and June 1970 "resulted in an increase of aircraft accidents at the school and operational bases." (PLAAF Second Aviation School, 1982, p. 7.) There were similar results in 1970 when some technical courses resumed for periods of only three to eight months (China Today, 1989a, pp. 298–300, 524).

The reason for this devastating cutback in nonflying education was a major expansion of flight training in preparation for imminent war. Four flying schools were added in 1967 and 1968. Annual flying hours for flight schools increased dramatically: 1966 (180,000), 1968 (260,000), 1970 (310,000), and 1972 (400,000) (China Today, 1989a, pp. 299–300).

Impact on the Aviation Ministry

The relationship with the Soviet Union in the 1950s also had a lasting impact on the development of China's aviation industry. During the 1950s, China acquired vast numbers of Soviet aircraft, including transports (An-2), helicopters (Mi-4), trainers (Yak-18), fighters (MiG-15, MiG-17, MiG-19, and MiG-21), ground attack aircraft (Il-10), and bombers (Il-28, Tu-2, Tu-4, and Tu-16). Of these, China received production rights to the MiG-15, MiG-17, MiG-19, MiG-21, Il-28, and

Tu-16 but did not receive the technical material or machinery for these aircraft and bombers before the Soviets withdrew in 1960.[4] China also received its first surface-to-air and air-to-air missiles from the Soviet Union in the 1950s. Although the Chinese did not receive the production rights, they had reverse engineered most of these systems by the mid-1960s. These included the SA-2 SAM and the K-5 ALKALI and AA-2 ATOLL air-to-air missiles.

Once the Soviet advisors withdrew, China took several years to either modify or reverse engineer some of the aircraft and missiles furnished by the Soviet Union. Chinese efforts reached a peak around 1965 only to be severely disrupted by the Cultural Revolution (1966–1976). Between 1969 and 1971, continued disruptions led to profound quality control problems. As one history of the aviation industry notes, it was a time of industrial "anarchy or semi-anarchy . . . the whole industry was in the difficult position of trying to preserve order." (China Today, 1988, p. 83.)

The aviation industry places the blame on the direct interference of PLAAF commander Wu Faxian and the "military." Official accounts claim, for example, that, in 1971 alone, 27 types of aircraft were authorized to be developed. Even though there were no blueprints for any of them, the industry was expected to bring them to the production stage in two to three years. Development time for aircraft stretched out for 10 to 15 years or more because production decisions were constantly delayed by protracted development problems or by leadership indecision. According to the official history of the aviation industry, 46 projects went into operation without the necessary materials or designs between 1969 and 1971; 36 of the projects had not even been approved (China Today, 1988, pp. 83–84). Three specific aircraft production programs—F-6, F-8, and A-5—graphically illustrate the effects of the Cultural Revolution on China's combat aviation infra-structure:

- In 1957, the Soviets agreed to transfer production rights for the MiG-19 to China, but the first aircraft, designated the F-6, was not produced until December 1963. Following several modifica-

---

[4]China did not actually produce any MiG-15s, choosing to produce the MiG-17 when it became available.

tions, the F-6-3 conducted its first flight in August 1969. Because of the turmoil caused by the Cultural Revolution, this aircraft was produced with defective design modifications, without any quality control, and suffered numerous accidents over a four-year period. This led to a recall of several hundred aircraft for complete overhauls in 1975.

- In 1964, the Shenyang Aircraft Corporation began a development program to design, manufacture, and test-fly the F-8, whose baseline was the MiG-21. Because of serious design and economic problems related to the Cultural Revolution, F-8 validation was not completed until December 1979—15 years after development began.[5]
- The only successful design program during the 1960s was the A-5 ground attack aircraft, derived from the MiG-19. Initial design work on the A-5 began in 1958, and following many setbacks, the first flight was conducted at Nanchang in 1965. In November 1975, the Military Commission ordered all of the A-5s in the inventory to be returned to the factory for overhaul because of failures in manufacturing quality control.

THE VIETNAM WAR: 1966–1969

Although the PLAAF ground-based air defense units were operationally engaged in Vietnam from 1965 to 1969 and in Laos from 1970 to 1973, official PLAAF histories dedicate only a few pages to this period (compared with over 100 pages for the Korean War).[6] By comparison, the Yijiangshan Campaign and the 1958 Taiwan Strait crisis have more detailed coverage. The most likely reason is that the PLAAF's aviation units were not involved in hostilities, and the

---

[5]According to the senior author's discussions with PLAAF officers and officials at the Shenyang Aircraft Corporation, the program continued despite these problems because the government's investment in the program was high and China wanted to encourage the construction of the aeronautics industry, including the infrastructure for R&D, manufacturing, and flight testing. Although the F-8 entered service in 1979, the PLAAF still considered it "an operational test aircraft" as late as 1989.

[6]The material in this subsection relies on China Today (1989a), pp. 396–397 and 651–677, and China Today (1989b), pp. 681–719. Unless otherwise indicated, quotations herein are from these publications.

ground-based air defense systems are not as highly regarded as the aviation units.

According to the PLAAF's account, the air force began deploying units to Guangxi and Yunnan for war preparations to help the North Vietnamese in August 1964 following the Gulf of Tonkin incident. When U.S. forces began crossing the 20th parallel in May 1965, Vietnam asked China for assistance. As a result, the PLAAF began sending troops to Vietnam on August 20, 1965. These units included eight groups of AAA units from seven AAA divisions, 26 AAA regiments, eight AAA battalions, nine searchlight battalions, and 14 radar companies.

Altogether, the PLAAF states that its AAA units were involved in 558 battles, shooting down 597 U.S. aircraft and damaging 479, losing 15 AAA pieces and four AAA radars, and with 280 troops killed and 1,166 troops wounded. Like the PLAAF's figures cited during the Korean War and the Taiwan Strait crisis, they appear highly inflated, but they are the ones the Chinese leadership is likely to use for future planning purposes.[7]

In addition to aircraft shot down over Vietnam, the PLAAF histories describe in detail how its pilots purportedly shot down three U.S. Air Force aircraft (one F-4B and two A-4Bs, even though the USAF did not fly A-4s) and two Navy (one A-3B and one A-6) and 17 unmanned reconnaissance drones over or near Chinese territory. The official naval aviation history also identifies two U.S. drones and four aircraft (F-4B, F-104C, F-4C, and A-1) that naval aviation pilots purportedly shot down over Hainan Island.[8]

The PLAAF withdrew the last of its troops from Vietnam on March 14, 1969. The official histories do not give any specific reasons why they departed at that particular time. From December 29, 1970 to November 14, 1973, the PLAAF also sent AAA units to Laos to support Chinese road construction. During this period, the units allegedly shot down 17 aircraft and damaged three.

---

[7]A search of USAF histories was unable to find any specific references to casualties inflicted solely on Chinese troops.

[8]Taken from throughout China Today (1989b) and PLAAF Headquarters Education and Research Office (1989).

The PLAAF's histories do provide detailed data on each of the aircraft shot down in air-to-air battles and sum up the AAA units' experience in three areas:

- AAA must be concentrated along key flight routes and at important targets. In general, a reinforced regiment or two regiments were used to protect a single target. The guns were deployed by companies so that their coverage overlapped.
- Concentrate as many AAA guns on a single aircraft as possible, but do not open fire until the aircraft is quite close.
- Employ camouflage and mobility to move the AAA around to areas where enemy aircraft would pass over.[9]

It is significant that, unlike the historical accounts of the Korean War, Yijiangshan Campaign, and Taiwan Strait crisis, the PLAAF histories do not draw any conclusions or lessons learned about the impact of political decisions, leadership, command and control, and equipment from the Vietnam War. There was not even any mention of U.S. tactics and new weapons, such as large-scale helicopter assaults, laser-guided bombs, TV-guided bombs, semiactive radar homing (SAR) missiles, drone reconnaissance vehicles, large-scale active jamming, and numerous sensors. Although China acquired some of these weapon systems from downed aircraft and from the Vietnamese after the war, the country's preoccupation with the Cultural Revolution and the virtual noninvolvement of aviation troops apparently led the PLAAF and aviation ministry to miss these changes in air warfare and fall even farther behind. The consequences of these developments continue to be felt even today. To understand these consequences in their fuller context, we need to turn our attention to the reform efforts of the Deng Xiaoping era.

---

[9]PLAAF Headquarters Education and Research Office (1989), pp. 207–215.

Chapter Five

THE REFORM PROCESS BEGINS

The PLAAF entered the 1970s still under the influence of Lin Biao and the leftists. This phase came to an abrupt halt when Lin Biao was killed in a plane crash over Mongolia in September 1971 and the PLAAF commander, Wu Faxian, was arrested. The air force languished without a commander, and then under an ineffective transitional commander, until 1977. Even then, the air force did not begin to recover until Deng Xiaoping's rehabilitation in 1978 following Mao Zedong's death and the arrest of the "Gang of Four" in 1976.

Of the four PLAAF commanders since 1977, three (Zhang Tingfa, Wang Hai, and Cao Shuangming), were Korean War veterans. The PLAAF's newest commander, Yu Zhenwu, is the first of the post–Korean War aviators to assume command. All have brought a more personal style of leadership to the air force, emphasizing direct contact with foreign air forces. These contacts have helped the senior air force leaders in Beijing and in the MRs to move away from theoretical study to a first-hand understanding of modern airpower.

In addition, the air force's lackluster performance during the 1979 border conflict with Vietnam and the 1981 exercise in north China forced the PLAAF to reassess its relevance in light of new security challenges faced by the PRC. Although the air force did not engage in any direct combat during the 1979 conflict, major logistics, maintenance, reconnaissance, and command and control deficiencies would have severely inhibited its performance. As in the Korean War and the 1958 Taiwan Strait crisis, the air force was not capable of conducting surge operations during the 1979 conflict, and it did not attempt to practice any such operations during the 1981 exercise. All of these developments prompted the air force to begin a process of administrative, operational, and equipment reform in the 1980s. Although these efforts have proved only partially successful, they have highlighted the challenges that the PLAAF has continued to face in making the transition to a more credible, modernized fighting force.

REGENERATION: 1972–1985

The PLAAF emerged from the Cultural Revolution—including the residual years of leftist influence in the early 1970s—as an organizational shell. The air forces were intact, but their effectiveness had been severely degraded. Given growing concern about the Soviet buildup along the northern border and the need to streamline its own forces, the PLA reduced the number of MRs from 13 to 11 in 1970 and further reduced them to 7 in 1985 (Figures 3, 4, and 5). Although the basic administrative infrastructure was still in place, the routine functions, operating procedures, training, education, tactical and strategic planning, and corporate identity of the air force were nearly moribund. Discipline had seriously eroded, and standards of competency (e.g., leadership, flying, technical support, and administration) were also low.[1]

The PLAAF clearly needed to pursue a new course, but no military service in China had ever unilaterally undertaken reform. In 1973, Ma Ning, a former deputy commander of the Lanzhou MRAF and a politically active figure in Jilin during the Cultural Revolution, became PLAAF commander. However, he was a transitional figure. Although Ma Ning had been a commander, his rise to prominence in the PLAAF seemed linked more to his compliance with the political needs of the leadership in the post–Lin Biao period than to his aviation skills. As a consequence, neither the PLA as a whole nor the

[1]The PLAAF Second Aviation School, for example, sent 1,669 of its staff to 11 provinces and 68 work units to carry out "three-supports and two-militaries" activities. The school slowly brought back staff members, even though there had been considerable atrophy of skills and knowledge. In 1964, the total authorized strength of the school was 1,745, while in 1971 it had risen to 4,778. It appears that almost the entire school staff was dispersed early in the Cultural Revolution (PLAAF Second Aviation School, 1982, pp. 15, 42).

PLAAF seriously addressed its pressing problems during the early 1970s.

The mid-1970s, however, proved a critical turning point. The death of Mao Zedong, Zhou Enlai, and Marshal Zhu De in 1976 and the subsequent arrest and purge of the Gang of Four were singular events in redirecting China's political orientation. In the aftermath of these events, Deng Xiaoping moved steadily to consolidate his political and military power.[2] Amid these profound leadership changes, the PLAAF took its initial steps toward reform. Zhang Tingfa, who began his career in the army and had previously served as the PLAAF political commissar, deputy commander, chief of staff, and member of the Party's Politburo, became the new PLAAF commander in 1977 and served in this capacity until 1985.

A broad array of institutional reforms was also associated with the transition to new service leadership, as well as to the broader array of military reforms that Deng subsequently sought to launch. In 1966, the PLAAF had reorganized its administrative structure into 11 major departments under the commander and political commissar. However, this structure was too unwieldy and was reduced in 1969 to three major departments—headquarters, political, and logistics. Finally, because of the need to deal directly with major aircraft maintenance problems, the PLAAF established aeronautical engineering as the fourth major department in 1976. This four-department structure still exists in the mid-1990s (Figure 10). In addition, in 1977, all military services embarked on a five-year program to

---

[2]Deng was born in 1904 and went to France to study after World War I, where he became good friends with China's future premier, Zhou Enlai. Deng went from France to Moscow to attend Sun Yat-sen University, then returned to China in 1929, where he served as a political commissar at various levels in the PLA from 1937 to 1949. He became the secretary-general of the Communist Party and a deputy premier in 1954. The following year, he was named to the Politburo. After Mao removed him from all of his posts at the beginning of the Cultural Revolution in 1966, he quietly reappeared as the deputy premier and Party vice chairman in 1973 with the help of his mentor Zhou Enlai. He became the PLA's Chief of the General Staff in 1975. However, he was purged again in April 1976 shortly after Zhou died. When he was rehabilitated for the second time at the Third Plenum of the Ninth Party Congress in July 1977, he retained his three previous positions, but also became a vice chairman of the Military Commission. Yang Dezhi replaced Deng as chief of the general staff in 1980, and Deng became chairman of Military Commission in 1981. Although Deng stepped down from the last of his official positions in November 1989 and is in increasingly problematic health, he still remains the most important political figure in China.

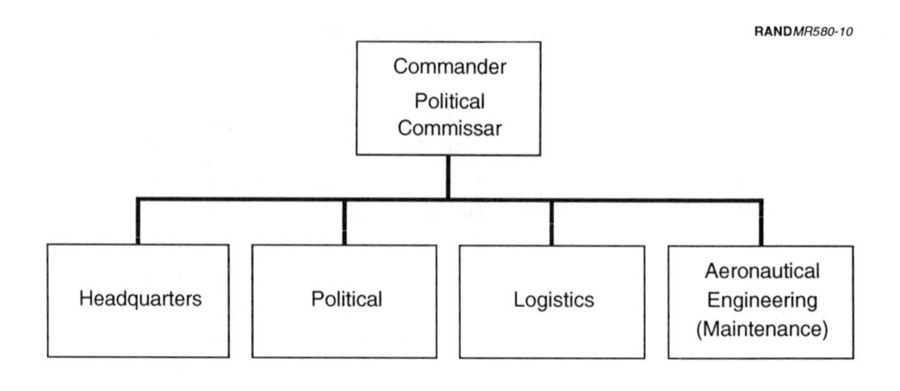

Figure 10—PLAAF Administrative Structure

reestablish military training and education (China Today, 1989a, pp. 237, 492).

The first impulses toward defense industrial reform (including in the aviation sector) were also manifest during this period. China's aviation industry entered the late 1970s much further behind world standards than it had been in the late 1950s. The deficiencies were complicated by Mao's determined efforts during the 1960s to build key aviation factories and research institutes in distant, inland areas. The results of relocating industries to the "third line" (i.e., to remote areas of the interior) have continued to inhibit Chinese defense industrial reform ever since: It has simply proven far too expensive to relocate the factories and research institutes and all their personnel to major population centers.

The aviation industry cites December 1971—three months after the death of Lin Biao and arrest of Wu Faxian—as its turning point. Zhou Enlai and Marshal Ye Jianying called for a conference on the continuing problem of quality control in the aviation industry. The Military Commission subsequently addressed deeper, underlying problems; within three months, it "adjusted" the leadership of the industry. According to official historical accounts of the aviation industry, the Military Commission abolished the "air force relationship with the aviation industry and restored direct subordination [of the aviation industry] to the State Council" in March 1972 (China Today, 1989a, p. 85).[3]

DEFENSE REFORM TAKES HOLD

Following Deng Xiaoping's full return to power at the Third Plenum of the 11th Party Congress in 1978, the PLAAF embarked on numerous reforms and changes in its operating style. The first step was an overall rectification of organizations, practices, and procedures. Air force leaders held numerous conferences during which they addressed the need to improve organizational standards and practices. PLAAF leaders began to focus more intently on specific missions for aircraft in the inventory, strategic research, safety guidance, and logistics work. A renewed emphasis was placed on drafting operating regulations. Air force units also participated in several small joint-service exercises. Budget planning was undertaken in three-year plans. The Military Commission authorized the restoration of flying grades and flight pay.

PLAAF personnel also began to attend international conferences. As PLAAF officers traveled abroad, the air force became more visible as a military service and organization, and exposure to the outside world brought new information to bear in reshaping the orientation of the PLA as a whole. This knowledge proved of undoubted importance as China's air force undertook extensive reforms of its institutions, forces, and personnel.

Changes In Leadership

As discussed in Chapter Two, the PLA initiated four significant PLA-wide structural changes during the mid- to late 1980s that had major effects on the personnel structure of the air force.[4] Changes also took

---

[3]Even prior to the leadership of Wu Faxian, the PLAAF frequently had senior officers who served as deputy ministers of the aviation industry. The aviation industry clearly wanted full autonomy from the PLAAF.

[4]These were the Military Commission's mandated reduction of personnel by 1,000,000 persons beginning in 1985, which was achieved by the end of 1989; the reduction in MRs from 11 to 7 in October 1985; the introduction of a military civil service system in August 1988; and the reinstitution of military ranks in October 1988.

place in the PLAAF's leadership. The PLAAF has had eight commanders and nine political commissars since 1949. Lieutenant General Yu Zhenwu became the newest commander in November 1994, replacing General Cao Shuangming, who had been promoted to commander in November 1992 along with political commissar Lieutenant General Ding Wenchang. (Ding was retained as political commissar following Yu's appointment as air force commander.) All three leaders have further promoted the reform process begun in 1977 with the commander–political commissar combination of Zhang Tingfa and Gao Houliang and continued in 1985 with Wang Hai and Zhu Guang. External observers of the PLAAF gave high marks to the cooperative spirit of the Wang Hai–Zhu Guang and Cao Shuangming–Ding Wenchang teams. Although there was considerable political soul-searching within China's military after June 1989, the PLAAF's senior leadership seems to have weathered it well. One reason is that the air force leadership concentrated on the tasks assigned by the Military Commission and avoided significant embroilment in the political upheavals surrounding the Tiananmen crisis and its aftermath.

The PLAAF leadership changes have become more stable and predictable. Cao Shuangming and Ding Wenchang were successful in continuing the long-term plan that Wang Hai and Zhu Guang mapped out for a leadership transition to the next generation of senior but younger air force leaders. The Military Commission and three PLA general departments have combined to approve all senior-level PLAAF personnel changes. The accession of Yu Zhenwu to top leadership position in the fall of 1994 also seems congruent with this pattern. In a word, the PLAAF promotion process has been regularized.

Leadership stability has been easier to predict, because a number of career and experience indicators are now more evident. First, future PLAAF commanders are henceforth likely to be aviators; nonaviators will be the exception. Second, antecedent assignments for the air force commander and deputy commanders will be jobs as an MRAF deputy commander and commander or a senior position in the Air Force Command College in Beijing. While Wang Hai had been the Guangzhou MRAF deputy commander and commander and PLAAF deputy commander, Cao Shuangming had been the Shenyang MRAF deputy commander and commander.[5] Career progression to the political commissar position may involve some variations in this pattern. Zhu Guang, whose previous air force command experience was as the Shenyang MRAF deputy political commissar, came directly to HqAF from jobs in the General Political Department (GPD) and the Military Commission. Ding Wenchang was previously the Director of the Political Department at HqAF.

Third, Yu Zhenwu is the first post–Korean War veteran to be named commander.[6] Although Cao Shuangming was a Korean War veteran, almost all of the senior leaders at HqAF and in the MRAFs with Korean War experience had been replaced by younger leaders by early 1994. Prior to Cao Shuangming becoming the commander in November 1992, three of the HqAF deputy commanders; four of the seven MRAF commanders, including Cao; and at least two MRAF deputy commanders in 1989 flew with Wang Hai during the Korean War. By early 1994, HqAF had reduced the number of deputy commanders under Wang Hai from four to three, and only two of Wang's deputy commanders remained. Yu Zhenwu had joined the PLAAF after the Korean War but followed Wang Hai as the deputy

---

[5]Cao Shuangming was born in 1929 and joined the PLA in 1946. Having served in the Second Field Army, he was later sent to pilot training, which he completed in 1952. In 1953, he joined the "People's Volunteer Air Force" and participated in the Korean War as a deputy squadron commander (each squadron only has two to three aircraft). During the 1958 Taiwan Strait crisis, Cao was deputy commander of the 16th Air Division's MiG-17–equipped 48th Regiment. While Wang Hai was commander, the HqAF deputy commanders who are Korean War veterans were Lin Hu, Li Yongtai, and Liu Zhitian. The other three MRAF commanders were Liu Yudi (Beijing), Sun Jinghua (Lanzhou), and Hou Shujun (Chengdu). The MRAF deputy commanders were Yao Xian (Beijing) and Han Decai (Nanjing). Cao Shuangming had replaced almost all of these leaders by mid-1994.

[6]Lieutenant General Yu Zhenwu (born in 1931) became the PLA commander in November 1994, following General Cao Shuangming, who had held the post for only two years. Yu joined the PLAAF in its earliest years, and was briefly assigned to Korea in the waning months of the war. As one of the PLA's first test pilots, he conducted the first flight of China's indigenously developed, but never produced, FT-1 trainer in July 1958. From his position as director of the Training Department at HqAF, he replaced Wang Hai as the Guangzhou MRAF commander in 1982 and became a PLAAF deputy commander when Wang Hai was promoted to commander in July 1985. As the deputy commander, he was responsibile for schools, training, and engineering (maintenance) and was selected as an alternate member of the 13th Party Congress Central Committee. Under Wang Hai and Cao Shuangming, Yu was the youngest deputy commander, but he was the senior ranking deputy on the protocol list.

commander and commander of the Guangzhou MRAF, and Lin Hu was Wang Hai's commander in the Korean War. The third deputy commander, Yang Zhenyu, a Korean War veteran without any MRAF command experience, came from being the commandant, and before that the deputy commandant, of the PLAAF Command College. Like Yu Zhenwu, who had previously been the director of the Training Department at HqAF, and Lin Hu, who had been a deputy commandant at the PLAAF Command College, Yang Zhenyu's appointment confirms the heightened importance that the PLAAF now places on training.

Fourth, Yu Zhenwu, Cao Shuangming, and Ding Wenchang have continued the process begun by Wang Hai and Zhu Guang of moving younger officers into key HqAF and MRAF command positions. The reinstitution of ranks in October 1988 made this task easier, since retirement ages were linked to the "Army Equivalent Position" (AEP). It became possible, for example, to put talented younger officers in command positions with lower ranks than an older deputy, because the AEP was the real reflection of responsibility.[7] Cao and Ding began replacing some of the older MRAF leaders in mid-1993, and Yu Zhenwu should finish the process by the end of 1995. Overall, the new officers are better educated than their predecessors. Many of them have been given the opportunity to travel abroad with Wang Hai or other PLAAF and PLA delegations.

Fifth, the PLAAF has begun to emphasize direct contact with foreign air forces at all levels. It has sent close to a hundred delegations to over 20 countries and regions for goodwill visits over the past decade. Hundreds of groups and close to 2,000 personnel have been sent abroad for importing foreign advanced technology and equipment, placing orders, and training. Over a hundred groups and hundreds of personnel have been sent abroad for academic exchanges. The PLAAF has received over 100 visiting foreign air force delegations from over 40 countries and regions, which include 38 foreign air force commanders (BBC, 1993a). Furthermore, Cao Shuangming continued Zhang Tingfa's and Wang Hai's practice of traveling

[7]There are still several cases in which deputy unit commanders outrank their commanders because they have more time in service. It will therefore take several years before the oldest officers reach retirement age and the rank structure becomes more predictable.

abroad and taking their key headquarters department directors and regional commanders with them to gain first-hand knowledge. For example, Zhang Tingfa made approximately ten trips abroad (China Today, 1989a, pp. 670–675), and Wang Hai visited, among others, his counterparts in the United States, Pakistan, Bangladesh, Chile, Peru, Colombia, and the United Kingdom, and hosted, among others, his American, Egyptian, Pakistani, Zimbabwean and Tanzanian counterparts. The PLAAF Chief of Staff, Lieutenant General Yu Zemin, accompanied President Yang Shangkun to Pakistan in October 1991. Cao Shuangming hosted his Zimbabwean counterpart in November 1993. In addition, Cao led a six-member delegation on a visit with his counterparts in Pakistan, Thailand, and Bangladesh in May 1993.[8] In May 1995, Yu Zhenwu became the second PLAAF commander to visit the United States. Former Political Commissar Zhu Guang visited the United States in 1988, and the Political Commissar during the early 1990s, Ding Wenchang, has also traveled abroad, accompanying the former Director of the General Political Department, Yang Baibing, on visits to several Eastern European countries.

Although the personal style of the air force's leaders has had a major impact on air force operations, the PLAAF remains clearly subordinate to the army and to overall shifts in PLA strategy. In the next chapter, we will examine the PLAAF's involvement in changes to the PLA's overall strategy in the 1980s and 1990s.

THE SINO-VIETNAMESE BORDER WAR

Two specific events stand out in the process of institutional change in the 1980s: the PLA's unsatisfactory performance during the 1979 border conflict with Vietnam and the results of major military exercises in North China undertaken in 1981.[9]

The Sino-Vietnamese conflict resulted from a host of historical and contemporary factors. Deng Xiaoping deeply resented what he construed as Vietnamese ingratitude for Chinese support of Vietnam that began even prior to the establishment of the People's Republic.

---

[8]Multiple Chinese publications.

[9]The material in this subsection draws from Chen (1987), pp. 10–69, 96–118. Unless otherwise indicated, quotations herein are from that publication.

As Vietnam's cultivation of the Soviet Union mounted during the latter half of the 1970s, Deng's convictions hardened on the need to demonstrate China's displeasure in more overt form.

According to various Chinese accounts, Beijing provided more than $20 billion in economic and military assistance for Vietnam between the early 1950s and late 1970s, including the deployment of more than 300,000 Chinese military personnel to Vietnam during the second Indochina war. Beijing also rendered ample political support to the Viet-Minh during the 1954 Geneva Conference. However, by the time that Hanoi took full control over Vietnam in the mid-1970s, tensions had already begun to build. The Vietnamese leadership had accused Beijing of blocking the early liberation of all Vietnam during the 1950s and 1960s, and the Vietnamese were deeply suspicious that the growing U.S.-China accommodation of the 1970s was coming principally at the expense of Vietnamese interests. The Vietnamese and Chinese also traded accusations as both began occupying potentially oil-rich islands, known as the Spratlys (Nansha) and Paracels (Xisha), in the South China Sea in 1974 (Figure 11).

RANDMR580-11

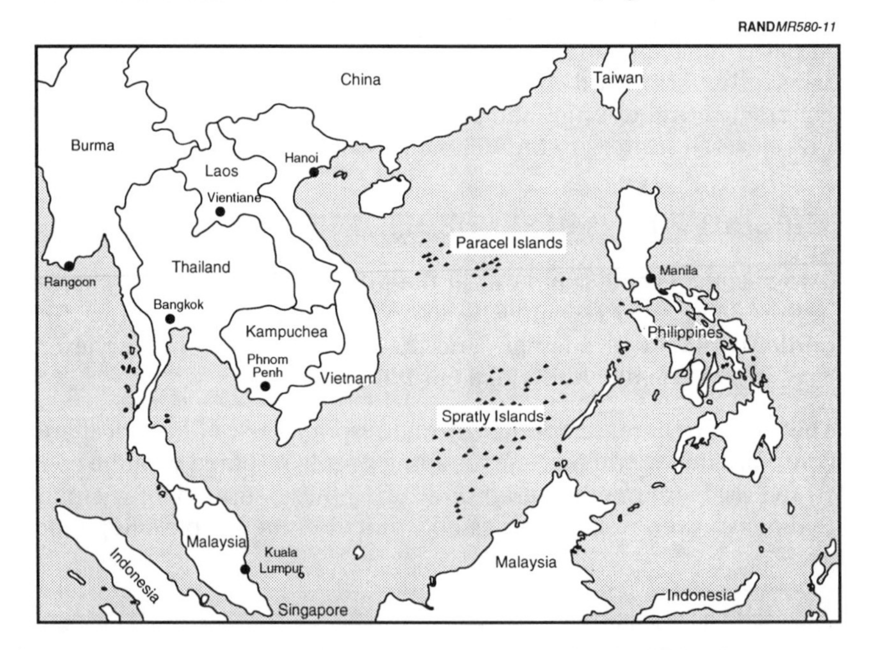

Figure 11—Paracel (Xisha) and Spratly (Nansha) Islands

The final issue concerned Vietnamese treatment of ethnic Chinese who lived in Vietnam and constituted a very important business community. From 1975 to 1978, the Vietnamese government carried out a series of measures for socioeconomic transformation that hit the Chinese community especially hard. The 1978 through 1980 confiscation of Chinese businesses and the expulsion of hundreds of thousands of overseas Chinese deeply rankled Chinese sensibilities, prompting Beijing to consider more coercive actions against Vietnam.

Several other significant events took place in 1977 and 1978 that set the stage for the 1979 border conflict. In September 1977, Pol Pot, the top leader of Cambodia's xenophobic regime, visited Beijing seeking more aid and military support to strengthen his hand against Vietnam. Large-scale skirmishes along the Vietnam-Kampuchea border took place in December 1977, and Hanoi broke diplomatic relations with Phnom Penh immediately thereafter.

In February 1978, the Vietnamese leadership began making preparations to oust the Pol Pot regime and to strengthen ties with the Soviet Union. Shortly before Hanoi and Moscow signed the Soviet-Vietnamese Treaty of Friendship and Cooperation in November 1978, the Soviets began special air shipments of MiG-23s and other weapons to Vietnam via India. The year culminated with a two-week Vietnamese blitzkrieg, using 100,000 troops, that took Phnom Penh on January 7, 1979.

The Chinese immediately put in motion their plans for a punitive retaliatory attack on Vietnam. Although Beijing sought to justify its actions on the basis of purported border violations by Hanoi, these accusations were largely a fig leaf for military moves that the Chinese (especially Deng) were determined to undertake.

Overview of the Conflict

China's so-called "punitive war" or "self-defensive counterattack" can be divided into three periods: (1) February 17–26, (2) February 27–March 5, and (3) March 5–17. Deng Xiaoping was named the overall commander of Chinese forces, Marshal Xu Xiangqian and Marshal Nie Rongzhen were appointed deputy commanders, and Geng Biao was named the chief of staff. Under the central command, two fronts were established—northern and southern. The Northern Front, which included the Shenyang, Beijing, Jinan, Lanzhou, and Xinjiang MRs, was placed under the command of Li Desheng, who already served as commander of the Shenyang MR. Before the war began, the Chinese government had already evacuated 300,000 inhabitants from exposed border areas in Heilongjiang and Xinjiang and put the entire Northern Front on maximum alert, as a precaution against a possible Soviet strike. After a week of fighting in the south, the tension in the north eased when a Soviet attack appeared increasingly unlikely.

Since the war was being fought in the south, the arrangement for the Southern Front was more important and complicated. Xu Shiyou (commander of the Guangzhou MR) was appointed commander; Yang Dezhi (new commander of the Kunming MR) was the deputy commander; Zhang Tingfa (commander of the air force) was the chief of staff. The Southern Front was divided into the Eastern and Western Wings. The Eastern Wing covered Guangxi and Guangdong provinces under Xu Shiyou. The Western Wing, covering Yunnan, was under Yang Dezhi. The air force was commanded by Zhang Tingfa. The South Sea Fleet deployed into the Zhanjiang-Hainan area.

Drawing from several MRs, the Chinese assembled approximately 31 divisions (330,000 men, which equated to about 10 percent of total ground force strength) and 1,200 tanks on the border. There were 948 aircraft stationed at 15 air bases in Yunnan, Guangxi, Guangdong, and Hainan, many of which deployed to these areas from elsewhere China.

At 5:00 a.m. on February 17, a Chinese force of approximately 100,000 men launched an extremely powerful artillery shelling, followed by tank units and waves of troops. The key targets were Lao Cai, Cao Bang, and Lang Son (Figure 12).

Advancing rapidly at the outset, the Chinese forces soon met with difficulties. The rugged terrain of the mountainous border area was unfavorable to the movement of division-sized forces using trucks and other motor vehicles. The Chinese, lacking modern logistic equipment, were forced to rely on old trucks, horses, donkeys, and laborers for the movement of supplies. In addition, there were

RANDMR580-12

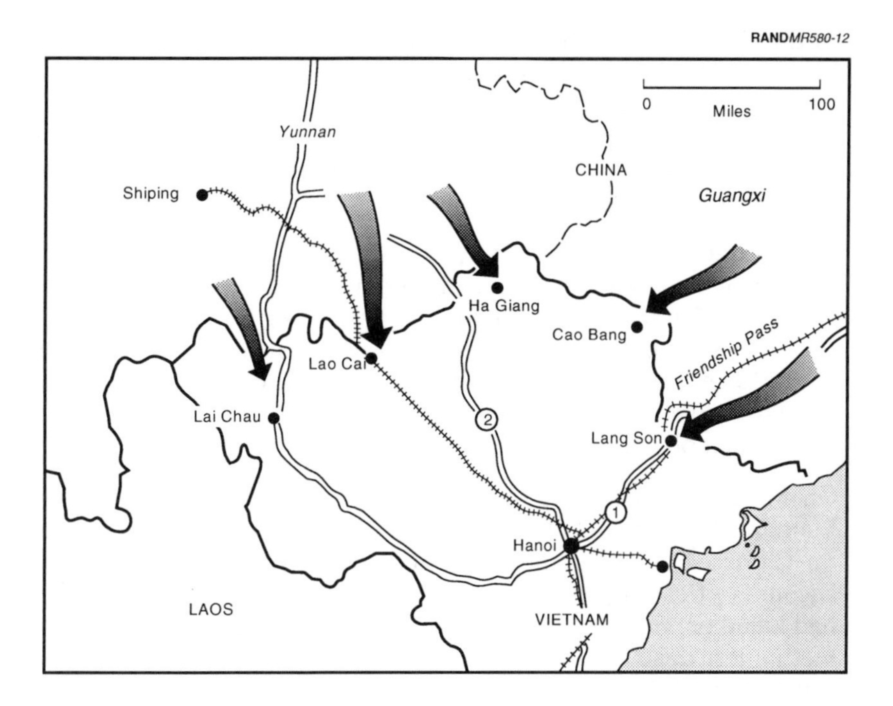

Figure 12—1979 Sino-Vietnam Border Conflict

tremendous communication problems between units because of equipment deficiencies. The PLA also had organizational problems because there was no rank system, so soldiers from different units had difficulties determining who was in charge at each level.

The Vietnamese employed local troops and militia along the border area for the fighting, while assembling their regular army in the plain south of Cao Bang and Lang Son. The purpose was twofold: to weaken the Chinese forces in the border fighting and to prepare for a major battle with the weakened Chinese in the plain. Meanwhile, the Chinese were reportedly under orders not to advance more than 50 km into Vietnam to avoid a major battle on the plain. In addition, the PLA reserved more than half of its forces inside China as replacement units.

At the end of the first period of fighting (February 17–26), the development of the war became relatively clear: The Chinese had taken several border cities while displaying no intention to advance to Hanoi; the war would continue for ten more days or so; and the Soviet Union would not intervene in the conflict. Meanwhile, casualties were extremely high.

The second period (February 27 to March 5), was centered on the capture of the strategic city of Lang Son, which was 10 miles from the Friendship Pass and 85 miles from Hanoi. Lang Son faces a rugged region in the north and an open plain in the south. It is a difficult city to take but is a useful location from which to launch a major drive toward Hanoi, and the Chinese encountered heavy losses in securing their objective.

On March 5, Beijing announced the withdrawal of the PLA from Vietnam. Over the next 12 days, the PLA leapfrogged its units back to the Chinese border. As the war ended, there were several conflicting accounts of casualties. Hanoi claimed that the Vietnamese forces had killed or wounded 42,000 Chinese, while Beijing claimed 50,000 Vietnamese dead or wounded, compared with 20,000 on the Chinese side (Chen, 1987, p. 114).

PLAAF Involvement

As discussed above, the PLAAF's operational capabilities had declined seriously over the previous decade and a half.[10] The military reforms launched during the Third Party Plenum came too late to affect PLA capabilities in a substantial way. The PLAAF had been so decimated during China's protracted internal upheavals that it simply was not prepared mentally or operationally for the border conflict with Vietnam.

Although the PLAAF deployed over 700 aircraft to the border area, neither the PLAAF or the Vietnamese Air Force flew missions in direct support of their ground troops (Li, 1981, pp. 33–35).[11] According

---

[10]The material in this subsection draws from Allen (1991), pp. 18-3, 18-4.

[11]The PLAAF deployed F-5, F-6, and F-7 fighters, plus Il-28 bombers, to the border. At that time, the Vietnamese Air Force was equipped with MiG-21s and MiG-23s, plus

to the PLA General Staff, "the Vietnamese Air Force did not dare start anything during the border conflict, which the Chinese limited to a certain area, time frame, and goals, because the PLAAF was able to maintain air superiority." (Allen, 1991; Chengdu, 1982.) The air force also cites its "deterrent capability" as the primary reason the Vietnamese Air Force did not become involved in the conflict. These statements belie the fact that no air combat took place, probably because neither side wanted to use its air forces, which would only have escalated the conflict.

According to PLAAF statistics, on the first day of the conflict, the air force flew 567 sorties using 170 groups of aircraft—many of which were helicopters and transport flights. Altogether, the air force reportedly flew 8,500 sorties, using 3,131 groups of aircraft. Transport aircraft performed a very crucial function, flying 228 sorties, carrying 1,465 troops and 151 tons of materiel (China Today, 1989a, p. 638). These figures most likely represent all activity over a two to three month period, including area familiarization, flights during the 30-day conflict, and postconflict sorties. Given a total of 700 aircraft deployed to the border area, this is only about 12 sorties per aircraft over a minimum of 60 days—about one sortie every five days.[12] Thus, the low sortie rates achieved in the conflicts with Taiwan during the late 1950s had not been improved upon and probably reflected continuing problems in support functions, which were further exacerbated by the effects of the Cultural Revolution. According to PLAAF data, maintenance personnel achieved a 97.5-percent readiness rate and a 99.7-percent takeoff rate for aircraft—probably not a difficult feat with such a low sortie rate.

The PLAAF was probably not capable of providing direct fire support for the ground troops or of gaining air superiority over the battle area. As a result, the PLAAF restricted its missions to fighter reconnaissance and early-warning missions along the border, helicopter rescue missions to pick up wounded soldiers, and air transport missions. The PLAAF did not fly any ground attack aircraft or bomber sorties during the conflict. Later PLAAF analysis of the conflict criti-

---

U.S. F-5As and A-37s left over from the war. The Vietnamese also had SA-2, SA-3, SA-6, and SA-7 SAMs plus the formidable ZSU-57-2 self-propelled AAA.

[12]In contrast, USAF aircraft were envisioned to fly up to three sorties a day in a European conflict.

cized the lack of effective reconnaissance and early-warning capabilities and identified these areas for improvement. However, the air force did use the conflict as a reason to build, repair, or acquire new equipment or facilities as far north as the Shenyang MR, which they had not been able to do during the Cultural Revolution.

PLAAF Preparations for the Conflict

A review of the key preparation and operational aspects of the conflict reveals why the PLAAF was not capable of conducting successful combat operations over Vietnam and provides insights into potential future PLAAF operations. The PLAAF began its preparations in the Guangxi Autonomous Region and Yunnan Province opposite the Vietnamese border about 45 days prior to the first day of operations, including establishing a command structure; preparing airfields to receive aircraft, AAA, SAMs, and troops; and delivering propaganda designed to get the troops and local populace ready for the war.

The Guangzhou MR air force commander (and future PLAAF Commander), Wang Hai, was placed in charge of PLAAF troops in the Guangxi operations area. The Kunming MRAF command post director, Hou Shujun, was placed in charge of PLAAF troops in the Yunnan operations area. Each operations area was further divided into several operational routes, and a combined command post was established at one strategically located airfield within each operational route to command and coordinate all matters among different branches, aircraft types, etc., within that district. The Guangzhou MRAF headquarters also established a forward command post at an unidentified location, which worked closely with the 7th Air Corps at Nanning as the unified authority for the PLAAF's participation in the conflict.

As one of its first missions, the PLAAF identified the need to educate the troops in Guangxi and Yunnan about the reasons for the upcoming operations and the need to motivate them to work all out preparing for the influx of additional troops. Upon receiving the combat readiness alert, the PLAAF's political commissar system provided all of the troops in the region with intensive education by having them study the Military Commission's and HqAF's orders and relevant newspaper articles. In addition, three simple principles were put forth—everything is subordinate to war; resolutely carry out orders; and hard work comes first.

One of the most important tasks prior to the conflict was to prepare the airfields in Guangxi for the influx of over 20,000 PLAAF aviation, SAM, and AAA troops and over 700 aircraft of different types. Since the Vietnamese Air Force was equipped with a limited number of MiG-21Bis, the PLAAF deployed some units equipped with F-7s to front-line airfields in Guangxi and Yunnan; however, the PLAAF's F-7s were having major problems and the entire program was in jeopardy at the time.

Before and during the conflict, the PLAAF's logistics organizations had two primary missions—to support housing for those troops already stationed in Guangxi and to prepare housing, food, water, and electricity for the incoming troops. These organizations issued about 10,000 mobile beds, over 32,000 m of water pipe, and 200 km of electric cable; built 43,000 m^2 of bamboo sheds; and repaired over 23,000 m^2 of old housing. In addition, the air force used vehicles and its boat troops to transport mobile housing with the troops to Tianyang. During the conflict, the Nanning Wuxu field station dispatched over 16,500 vehicles to provide support for portions of one aviation regiment and one independent air group.

The logistics organizations also had to acquire and supply enough fuel for the incoming aircraft. Based on initial estimates of the amount of fuel required, the PLAAF's fuel supply was totally inadequate, and several depots were almost empty. Therefore, during the preparation period, fuel depots at all of the region's airfields were filled. This included the depot at Tianyang, which relied on water transport for its fuel supply. Some of the airfields did not have rail spurs, so vehicles had to bring in all the fuel. In addition, all of the combat readiness tanks available throughout the MR and some from outside the MR were quickly transferred to the front-line airfields. These expanded the amount of aviation kerosene by over 50 percent. By the time the conflict began, the amount of fuel supplied to all the Guangxi airfields was 4.3 times the normal amount.

Supplying fuel during peacetime in China was difficult enough, but it proved even more difficult during wartime. Because some airfields, such as Ningming, are close to the border, their fuel storage was partially underground, and the rail lines supplying the bases were overscheduled. As a result, the PLAAF was concerned that the Vietnamese might destroy or disrupt fuel supplies. Because of this situation, the PLAAF took about 45 days to build over 50 km of semipermanent fuel pipes to three different airfields.

Since the air force did not fly any actual combat missions during the conflict, only about one-fourth of the fuel estimated for combat was used, and the difficulties with fuel consumption were fewer than expected. However, several organizational and facilities problems were highlighted. For example, the fuel depot capacity at the PLAAF's airfields was too small, and there was no way to support several types of aircraft or the sustained combat use of fuel for several batches of aircraft. In addition, the refueling equipment was deemed backwards and incompatible.

Once the conflict began, the air force flew numerous sorties along the border, but found that their on-station time was severely limited due to the distance they had to fly and the limited range of the F-6s.[13] On the other hand, the air force flew a large number of helicopter sorties to transport wounded soldiers to Nanning. Since the nearest point was 110 km and the farthest was 280 km, each helicopter trip took 2 to 4 hours. During most sorties, the helicopters could not turn off their engines or refuel at the pickup points. Altogether, the helicopters picked up 628 wounded soldiers from front-line field hospitals and transferred them to the rear (Allen, 1991, pp. 18-3, 18-4).

Conclusions

Overall, the 1979 border conflict was a wake-up call for the PLA. Following the devastating years of the Cultural Revolution, the PLAAF took advantage of the conflict to begin rebuilding its logistics and operational infrastructure throughout China. The conflict also helped launch Wang Hai into the PLAAF commander's position in 1985. In addition, the air force began rotating units to the border region after the conflict for several months at a time for area familiar-

---

[13]No statistics are available about the actual number of sorties flown near the border.

ization. These rotations helped sow the seeds of the PLAAF's rapid-deployment concept, to be discussed later.

THE NORTH CHINA EXERCISE: 1981

Shortly after the 1979 border conflict with Vietnam, the Military Commission ordered each of the three PLA general departments—general staff, general political, and general logistics—to provide a detailed report by midsummer describing the actions taken in preparation for and during the conflict.[14] In addition to these analyses showing how poorly the PLA performed against the Vietnamese, the PLA had the opportunity to watch how the Soviets quickly invaded Afghanistan in December 1979. By this time, Deng Xiaoping had further consolidated his military power, culminating in his appointment as Chairman of the Military Commission in June 1981.

As a result of these events, the PLA began organizing a large-scale exercise to take place in the Zhangjiakou area of the Beijing MR, September 14–18, 1981 (Figure 13). The purpose of the exercise was to test PLA changes in readiness since the Vietnam border conflict and as a show of force for the Soviets. The PLAAF's participation in the exercise provides further insights into how the air force would prepare for eventual combat.[15]

Altogether, PLAAF units that participated in the exercise included 12 aviation divisions, three independent regiments, one airborne division, 476 aircraft and 30,000 troops. From mid-March to July 15, the air force conducted the following five phases of preparations prior to the exercise:

- The PLAAF established an exercise command group, consisting of a deputy commander and deputy political commissar, plus the

---

[14]The material in this subsection draws from China Today (1989a), pp. 639–642. Unless otherwise indicated, quotations herein are from that publication.

[15]While the PLAAF has participated in numerous small-scale exercises, the official history only mentions two major exercises. The first was an antilanding exercise conducted on the Liaodong Peninsula, November 4–13, 1955, in which 428 PLAAF aircraft of all types participated. The second and last large-scale exercise conducted was the 1981 Zhangjiakou exercise.

RAND MR580-13

Figure 13—1981 North China Exercise

Beijing MRAF commander, deputy commander, and chief of staff.

- The PLAAF assessed the terrain, selected airborne and aircraft landing sites, and built live-fire and bombing ranges.
- The PLAAF studied the use of firepower.
- The PLAAF organized training exercises that included 20,600 sorties, covering 15,810 hours, with each pilot flying an average of 32 hours and 55 minutes—for an average of 8 hours per month. From July 16 to September 5, aviation troops practiced

arriving at the appointed time, tactical movement, and coordination, and flew an additional 6,194 sorties, covering 6,348 hours.

- Maintenance units conducted five major aircraft inspections, changed 371 engines, conducted intermediate repair and inspection on 349 aircraft, and modified 196 aircraft. Radar units deployed 84 radars and set up a radar net. Communications units set up additional communications hubs, established 19 radio network links, and temporarily installed 157 local and new landline links. The weather sections analyzed 8 to 10 years of weather data for the area and used 105 weather stations. The navigation department organized over 20,000 pieces of data to select over 100 routes.

After six months of preparation, the exercise took place between September 14 and 18. An official PLAAF history described the results of the exercise (China Today, 1989a, pp. 639–642):

> Fighter, ground attack and bomber aircraft flew out of 10 airfields, reaching their targets within 3.9 seconds of the estimated times. They conducted 30 regiment-size operations, using 114 groups with 838 sorties to perform live bombing, strafing, airborne troop drops, air assault landings, and mine laying. The fighters arrived over the exercise area on time to conduct patrols, gain air superiority, and fly cover for the ground troops. Ground attack aircraft conducted live fire or simulated attacks against 13 ground targets, hitting their targets 98.3 percent of the time with rockets and 90 percent with guns. Bombers arrived over their targets and hit them 100 percent of the time. B-5's (Il-28s) laid 864 antitank mines over the battle field at five second intervals. Reconnaissance aircraft completed their missions relatively well. Transports conducted large formation airborne troop drops and air drops on time and on target. Helicopters conducted paratroop insertions, mine laying, rescue, material transport, courier duties, as well as simulated armed helicopter attacks. Airborne troops conducted 1,191 jumps and 107 insertions by transports and helicopters.

As with the Vietnam border conflict, the PLAAF recognized deficiencies in its airborne reconnaissance capability during the exercise. It is also instructive that the pilots did not fly any additional hours and that there was no indication of training (or a capability) for high-tempo operations.

In the aftermath of the exercise, the PLA began to reevaluate its strategy and doctrine and to change its organizational structure. The war against Vietnam and the North China exercises had vividly imparted the incapacities of the armed forces and the imperative need to undertake major, long-term institutional change. This change encompassed an extremely wide array of issues that the PLAAF faced, and continues to face, in planning for the future. To assess these challenges more fully, we need to turn our attention to the air force's efforts to develop strategies and capabilities that will lead it into the next century.

Chapter Six

THE PLAAF'S SEARCH FOR AIRPOWER STRATEGY: TOWARD THE 21st CENTURY

In the course of its long history, the Chinese air force has endeavored to undertake an exceptionally broad array of organizational missions. The first operational mission assigned to the PLAAF in 1949 was the air defense of Beijing and Shanghai against Nationalist air raids. This mission was expanded during the Korean War to include northeast China. Although the PLAAF states that its secondary mission is support to the ground forces, it has never successfully carried out direct support to the ground troops and officially states that it can only support them indirectly in the future. Published PLAAF sources also refer to informal, secondary missions, such as assisting socialist construction, providing air services for disaster relief and air rescues, and artificial rainmaking support for farmers.[1]

By referring to the five branches of the air force, it is possible to understand more fully the scope of these missions. The PLAAF's branches are aviation, AAA, SAMs, radar, and communications. As noted previously, the aviation branch, which includes fighters, ground attack aircraft, bombers, transports, and reconnaissance aircraft, is the air force's main arm. The PLA's airborne troops belong to the air force, but are not considered a branch. The PLAAF

[1] *Shijie Junshi Nianjian* [World Military Yearbook], was published by PLA Press, Beijing, in 1985, 1987, 1989, 1990, 1991, 1992. Each yearbook provided progressively greater detail about the PLA's organizational structure.

also has logistics units, research institutes, hospitals, and sanitariums as part of its organizational structure.[2]

The PLAAF's brief description of its mission—the defense of China's air and land—is instructive. The terseness may be symptomatic of the traditional Chinese "forbidden zone" mentality regarding military matters. But it also appears to reflect a longer-term problem involving the nascent formulation of Chinese airpower strategy and concepts.[3] There was little in the doctrine of People's War that compelled a serious definition of the role of airpower. In the absence of broader air force statements about the PLAAF's missions, the only real clue to the range of air force responsibilities must be deduced from the functions of its operational branches. In the case of the PLAAF, the goal of air defense includes not only aerial combat but also responsibility for the ground-based air defense of China (i.e., SAMs and AAA). Many Western militaries regard airborne forces as being part of the ground forces because the air force only provides transportation. This is not the case in the PLAAF, which has all of these missions.

During the period of military reform, the PLA has published two internal studies that provide valuable insight into the air force's search for strategy. (It is possible that there is a more extensive internal literature on future air force strategy, but the studies cited below were the principal studies available for this research. Given that these analyses range very broadly over the various dimensions of strategy, their utility for this research is self-evident.) The first study was prepared in 1982 as part of the PLA's overall reorganization into group armies and the attempt to define "the campaign to defend group army field positions" (Chengdu Military Region Campaign Training Office, 1982).[4] The study spelled out in detail the various command relationships and what the PLAAF's role should be in this campaign, including the air force's dual responsibilities of defending China's airspace and supporting the ground forces.

---

[2]PLAAF histories do not consistently treat the airborne forces as a sixth branch (*junzhong*) of the air force. The air force's Logistics Department has its own water transport craft to ship fuel to units along the Yangzi River and coast.

[3]PLAAF literature concentrates on strategy (*zhanlue*) and campaigns (*zhanyi*), and does not discuss doctrine (*shiyong yuanze*).

[4]For a detailed translation see Section 3 of Allen (1991).

The second study, a 300-page PLAAF book entitled *Air Force Operations Research*, provides an extensive review of the air force's operational strategy (Teng and Jiang, 1990). The first third of the book reviews the history of airpower and the organization of foreign air forces, including the United States and Soviet Union. The last two-thirds of the book, however, provides a relatively detailed analysis of the PLAAF's capabilities, laying down a prescription for the future in four areas—strategy, campaigns, operations, and development. In addition, throughout the book, the editors discuss the use of airpower in air campaigns, such as the Falklands War, the various Israeli-Arab conflicts, the USAF raid on Libya, the Soviet invasions of Czechoslovakia and Afghanistan, and the U.S. Rolling Thunder and Linebacker campaigns in Vietnam. The major limitation with both studies, as with other comparable Chinese writings, is that they do not clearly differentiate between the current equipment and capabilities of the air force and the equipment and capabilities it aspires to develop or acquire, but which at present it conspicuously lacks. But these studies demonstrate the PLAAF's awareness of the disparity between its capabilities and its aspirations; it is this gap that the air force is presently seeking to narrow.

Teng and Jiang (1990) was published earlier in the same year that U.S. and allied forces began deploying to Saudi Arabia prior to Operation Desert Storm. The Gulf War dramatically illustrated the potentially decisive role of airpower in modern combat—and the distances the PLAAF had to go to modernize. While the study laid out a lengthy set of deficiencies, rectifying these problems does not appear feasible over the short term and quite possibly for much longer. In doctrinal terms, the PLAAF is also far behind. Offensive counter-air operations, close air support, battlefield interdiction, and sophisticated airborne command and control systems are simply not part of the PLAAF tradition and experience. Neither has the development of an air campaign to complement the ground campaign been part of the PLA's standard campaign planning process.

LACK OF MISSION STATEMENTS

The PLAAF remains virtually silent about the different means of employing airpower within the framework of China's active defense strategy. The employment of airpower in almost any country is far from a settled matter. In many Western countries, for example, mission statements and doctrine represent institutional and operational efforts to contain the debate within acceptable parameters. In some respects, mission statements are descriptions of jobs or responsibilities. By defining the scope of operations, military services concurrently limit and protect their "turf."

The PLAAF has not faced many of the pressures that have compelled numerous air forces to prepare detailed mission statements. For example, there was no existing PLA air arm before 1949; hence, there were none of the doctrinal and operational disputes that existed during the early years of U.S. and British military aviation. There were no air assets to be divided between the PLA and PLAAF.[5] Even existing air bases and equipment in 1949 belonged to the defeated Nationalist and Japanese armies.

Equally important was the defensive nature of the doctrine of People's War: There was no need for a strategic projection of air or sea power. For nearly four decades, the dominance of this doctrine effectively dampened any internal air force pressure to define the role of airpower more fully. Finally, the laggard pace of technological development in Chinese military aviation has retarded broader consideration of airpower options.

As a result, until quite recently, the PLAAF did not have specific mission statements regarding different air combat missions (i.e., strategic air defense, close air support, interdiction, strategic bombing, tactical or strategic airlift).[6] The PLAAF, for example, did not formally define its concept of direct ground support until 1982, but this concept received virtually no mention in the volume published in

---

[5]Naval aviation was not created until early 1950s. FBIS (1986), p. K20.

[6]In terms of air transport, one Chinese analyst described the problem as follows: "Due to historical reasons China's military transport departments have not managed military air transport for a fairly long time." Changing this practice involved "a new task," as well as departing from "the previous practice of just concentrating on railway and water transport." The issue of air transport was first addressed in a report to the director of the PLA's General Logistics Department in early 1985. Regulations were not put into effect until March 1989. Prior to that time, "the military used civil transport plans to carry out its air transport tasks. It lacked unified rules and regulations and was characterized by considerable arbitrariness in such areas as working out transport plans and time limits." Despite these changes, the analyst made no reference to a specific doctrine for tactical or strategic airlift (Hong, 1989, pp. 41–43).

1990. Moreover, there still is no formal doctrine for strategic air defense, and the issue of military airlift was not addressed in PLA regulations until 1989.

With the exception of naval aviation, the PLAAF has never had any competitors for air-related resources or missions. If anything, the air defense charter of the PLAAF was sufficiently broad that it was able to expand the scope of its functions to areas not universally associated with airpower. Thus, the PLA Air Defense Force was merged into the air force in 1957, and the responsibility for SAMs was added the following year. The PLAAF has had the charter for airborne forces (paratroops) since 1950. The extent to which PLAAF officers sought to define specific airpower missions during the 1950s and 1960s is unknown, although the air force did launch a prodigious effort during those years to consolidate and compile extensive publications that represented China's cumulative aviation experience.

However, the PLAAF did not become responsible for ground-based strategic missiles with nuclear warheads. That mission was assigned to an independent fourth service—the second artillery.[7] But the second artillery nomenclature had some of its roots in the PLAAF. For example, the PLAAF routinely refers to its antiaircraft artillery as "first artillery" and its SAM units as "second artillery." In addition, the PLAAF's SAM school is still informally referred to as the Second Artillery School, which has led to some confusion among Westerners with the real second artillery's school.[8]

The lack of specificity in Chinese air force roles and missions is telling. It was not until the early 1980s that the PLAAF began to emphasize the formal compilation of mission statements. Military reform in China has tended to stress internal organizational and structural changes versus equipment modernization. Since the early

---

[7]At least one of the early PLAAF deputy commanders became the minister of the 7th Ministry of Machine Industries (Astronautics), which was responsible for producing China's strategic missiles.

[8]In September 1958, the Special Weapons School (*Tezhong Wuqi Xuexiao*) was organized in Baoding. It was called the 15th Aviation School. This school was responsible for training personnel from all services to do maintenance work on surface-to-surface, surface-to-air and shore-to-ship missiles. In 1963, this school became primarily responsible for training only SAM maintenance and construction personnel and commanders.

1950s, the PLA has struggled with converting the guerrilla forces of a revolutionary political party into a regular army of the state. PLA writers have acknowledged that the armed forces have long operated without clearly defined responsibilities. In this regard, the PLA was much like other large Chinese ministries. Military mission statements have therefore become the PLA's equivalent of the written responsibility codes or contracts that reformers are promoting in the civilian sector. They are more than empty slogans, since they define a long-term path for military development.

Turf questions have also become more a part of the fabric of China's defense establishment. As the PLAAF has matured, mission statements have helped define responsibilities and justify allocation of resources.[9] For example, PLA ground forces took control of almost all the air force's helicopters in 1988 and formed the Army Aviation Corps to provide direct support to the newly formed group armies.[10] This illustrates the continuing dominance of the army in the Chinese military establishment.

The 1979 Sino-Vietnamese border conflict also compelled PLA and PLAAF commanders to address questions regarding joint operations and the appropriate role of airpower. Debate over these issues was also accelerated by the unprecedented economic constraints facing Chinese military forces in the 1980s. This situation resulted not so much from unanticipated budget shortages as it did from conscious CCP policy decisions. Initial PLA efforts to develop the equivalent of a policy, planning, and budgeting system visibly revealed the effort to

---

[9]Turf battles, of course, are not a unique phenomenon within the PLA or PLAAF. Normally, these disagreements are not publicly aired. A recent but still opaque question of turf involved the transfer of PLAAF tactical airlift helicopters to the ground force's army aviation corps (*lujun hangkong bing* or *luhang*) in the late 1980s. It is unclear whether the PLAAF wanted to retain the tactical airlift mission—which involved the small but modern fleet of Sikorsky Blackhawk helicopters—or give it away. It is equally unclear whether PLA ground force commanders felt they could do a better job satisfying tactical airlift requirements than the PLAAF, or if the army ground forces were forced to accept the mission.

[10]On one day, all the helicopters belonged to the air force. On the next day, they belonged to the army, and all the pilots and maintenance and associated personnel put on army uniforms. In addition, an Army Aviation Bureau was established within the General Staff Department and given total responsibility for Army Aviation Corps matters. "China Sets Up Army Air Arm to Increase Modernized Combat Effectiveness" (1989), p. 40.

link strategy, resources, and missions (Liu and Wang, 1987, p. 126; Wang and Dong, 1987, pp. 239–251; Wang, 1987, p. 233).

PLAAF STRATEGY

As an arm of the PLA, the air force has traditionally conducted its combat operations as a series of campaigns within the PLA's overall campaign. The air force describes a campaign as "using from one to many aviation, air defense, or airborne units to carry out a series of combined battles according to a general battle plan to achieve a specified strategic or campaign objective in a specified time." (Teng and Jiang 1990, p. 152.)

This chapter will discuss future air force campaigns as part of the air force's rapid-reaction strategy, including air defense campaigns, air attack campaigns, independent campaigns, air-ground combined campaigns, and counteramphibious assault campaigns. The basic concept of an air force campaign is "active initiative," which means to turn a passive posture into an active posture and to turn defense into an offense. As part of the air force's rapid-reaction strategy, active initiative complements the PLA's basic strategy of active defense described in Chapter Two (Teng and Jiang 1990, pp. 160–162).

The PLAAF's View of Itself

PLAAF writings continue to reveal a huge discrepancy between what the PLAAF perceives itself to be and what it really is. Teng and Jiang (1990), for example, notes that the air force is not an independent service, but it would like very much to be. The air force's weapons are not "relatively modern" compared with those of its neighbors. The air force has conducted its air defense role but has not truly "supported the ground forces" and currently does not conduct training to support the navy. The study also notes that it is doubtful that the air force can "influence and change strategic conditions." These sentiments, when compared to the more mature doctrines of independent Western air forces, illustrate the great distance that the PLAAF must traverse to better define its role in support of China's national security interests.

But the sentiments expressed in the document indicate some glimmerings of independent thinking. Indeed, the essence of the whole book is that the PLAAF needs to develop its own strategy and not rely solely on the PLA's strategy as its own. As noted in Teng and Jiang (1990), p. 147:

> Since it was formally established in 1949, the PLAAF has become an independent service and has developed using the army as its base. The air force has already changed from a single type aircraft branch, to a multi-branch combined service, with relatively modern weapons. Over the past few decades, the air force did a fairly good job of completing its missions by shooting down 3,700 aircraft and formed its own military studies system.
>
> However, because the air force was relatively weak and small in the past, the air force's use during combat was mainly to support the ground forces. Therefore, the air force had to use the ground force's victory as its victory, so it had a subordinate position during war. Furthermore, because of this, the air force only had campaign and tactical concepts, it did not form a strategic concept.
>
> Today, however, the air force is already fairly modernized, so that its missions go beyond just supporting the army and navy. For example, it can carry out independent combat missions in the air, on land, and at sea—especially in future "air-land battles," where the combined campaign has different phases, different battlefields, different times, and the three services can all conduct operations in their own sphere.
>
> As the air force continues to develop, its functions in modern warfare will continue to increase. It not only can influence and change campaign and battle conditions, but can influence and change strategic conditions. Therefore, the air force must establish a strategy in order to be able to direct its development and operational use.

Studies prepared at the behest of the PLAAF leadership take pride in the air force's accomplishments, but they also impart a recognition that it remains ill prepared for the future. On the one hand, the air force is extremely proud of the fact that (according to official Chinese data) it has shot down 1,474 and damaged 2,344 aircraft of all types since 1949 and established a positive kill ratio during the Korean War and the 1958 Taiwan Strait crisis. Whether or not these figures are accurate is largely irrelevant. The important point is that they tend to take on a reality of their own and may lead to miscalculations on the part of the Chinese military and civilian leadership. This is extremely important when it comes to evaluating the will, not the capability, to use airpower.[11]

Since 1985, the PLAAF has sought to define the principles for a formal air defense strategy, but has not been able to fully implement such a strategy. One of the main reasons for this gap in achievement is that various dimensions in the strategy presume capabilities the PLAAF still lacks given the lack of proper equipment, training, and organizational structure. Thus, the PLAAF has backed away from many of the tasks laid down for it in the early 1980s (e.g., providing support to group armies). Furthermore, the PLAAF is still not able to carry out effectively most of the missions it has prescribed in supporting the ground forces. To address these shortcomings, the PLAAF and aviation ministry have laid out ambitious plans to modernize the air force and have embarked on a concerted attempt to develop or acquire weapon systems that will provide the air force with a small, powerful force capable of carrying out some, if not all, of the prescribed missions in a small-scale border conflict after the year 2000. The prospects for achieving this goal are analyzed in Chapter Eight.

SEARCHING FOR AN AIR DEFENSE STRATEGY

Although the PLAAF has conducted its primary mission of air defense for 45 years, the air force still does not have a formalized air defense strategy and probably will not have one in the foreseeable future. The reason for this is that the air force is hampered by an inadequate command and control system, obsolete air defense systems, and an

---

[11]For example, a review of PLAAF combat operations since 1949 shows that the Chinese leadership has not hesitated to use the air force for air defense and "to support ground and naval forces" during the Korean War, the Yijiangshan Campaign, and the 1958 Taiwan Strait crisis. During the 1979 border conflict with Vietnam, Chinese documents state that "the air force sent large groups of aircraft to fly along the Chinese side of the border to maintain air superiority, forcing the Vietnamese to not dare use its aviation troops, thus implementing its deterrent objective." The PLAAF's airborne troops were also used domestically in Wuhan (July 1967) during the Cultural Revolution and during the 1989 Tiananmen crackdown.

inability to improve the situation in the near future. While authoritative military research organizations, such as the Academy of Military Science and the Chinese National Defense University, have been responsible for several major studies on changes in PLA doctrine and strategy over the past decade, the PLAAF's Command College in Beijing has been in charge of revising the air force's air defense strategy.[12]

Articles published by the Command College have focused on a wide range of air defense issues, including building a credible air defense force capable of deterring and then, if necessary, resisting any attack on China, and then conducting a defensive counterattack against enemy installations. By 1990, the air force began formulating an air defense rapid-reaction strategy that incorporates these three concepts, to cope with local wars. The biggest problem with this strategy, however, is that China currently lacks, and will continue to lack, the necessary weapon and support systems needed to conduct rapid-reaction operations effectively.

Deterrence

While PLAAF leaders believe that the air force's "deterrent capability" is an objective reality, there are several different views within the air force on this issue.[13] Those who believe that the PLAAF's equipment is backward, limited in power, and not equal to that of many other small and medium-size countries say that the air force's deterrent capability is not real. On the other hand, there are those who believe the PLAAF has already demonstrated its deterrent capability, and they advocate several measures to enhance its future deterrent.

---

[12]Three specific articles show the air force's continuing struggle to develop an air defense strategy. In late 1988, the PLAAF's Surface-to-Air Missile and Antiaircraft Artillery Applied Research Center published an article entitled "First Exploration of an Air Defense Strategy," which addressed the need for an air defense strategy. Teng and Jiang (1990) laid out in detail the need for a rapid-reaction force strategy as part of the PLA's overall active defense strategy. Finally, the *Liberation Army Daily* carried an article in February 1991 entitled "Formulate a Guiding Ideology on Active Air Defense."

[13]None of the studies or articles written by the PLAAF and cited in this study identify a specific country as the threat. For example, the articles discussing deterrence do not specify any specific country such as Vietnam, the former Soviet Union, India, Taiwan, or the United States. The term is used in a generic sense.

Some air force leaders contend that China must make known its existing deterrent strength, including its bomber, airborne, and defense forces. For attack purposes, the air force regards its current B-6 bombers and A-5 ground attack aircraft as a strategic attack force, although how these aging aircraft would fare in combat is questionable. The PLAAF further states that strengthening the airborne forces by increasing their strategic reach and quick mobility capability could also be used as a deterrent.

More important (as highlighted in Teng and Jiang, 1990), there is a growing belief that China should also show its determination to use military force to caution potential adversaries against taking military measures that the PRC would deem a challenge to Chinese interests. This could be done in several ways. One way is to claim territory held by another country but also claimed by China, and to assert China's sovereignty over sea and airspace more fully. For example, China could conduct airborne reconnaissance flights over the Vietnamese-occupied islands in the Spratlys, and could announce that China will use those islands or sea areas as bomb ranges. A second means would be to conduct military exercises and publicize them more fully.

Rapid-Reaction Strategy

As discussed in Chapter Two, the PLA began forming a rapid-reaction force consisting of "fist" units in the late 1980s. The rapid-reaction strategy is based on the premises that China will only be engaged in local wars for the foreseeable future, that the PLA must strike to end the war quickly and meet the political objectives, and that cost is a big factor as equipment becomes more expensive to use and replace. China would conduct any future wars as part of its active defense strategy, which consists of three phases: strategic defense, strategic stalemate, and strategic counterattack. Based on this strategy, some air force leaders firmly believe that their intelligence, mobility, and attack capabilities will be sufficient to allow them to react appropriately to any situation, including gaining air superiority, supporting the ground forces, and conducting counterattacks against targets inside the enemy's borders.

As part of the rapid-reaction strategy, Teng and Jiang (1990) stated that the air force plans to establish a rapid-reaction force within each theater of operations. Specifically, this entails establishing one fighter aviation division in each battle area. Each division would have three fighter regiments dispersed along the main attack routes, plus one ground attack regiment, one bomber regiment, one airborne early warning (AEW) aircraft, one electronic countermeasures aircraft, and reconnaissance aircraft special troops—these can change depending on the battle situation.

But the PLAAF understands the challenges it faces. The major problem is that the PLAAF leadership clearly admits that its air defense force is inferior to that of the United States and most of its neighbors and that China simply cannot spend the money needed to upgrade its air defense capabilities rapidly. Although the air force will be able to upgrade its weapon systems gradually, it will still lag behind its potential adversaries, especially in reconnaissance, mobility, firepower, and command and control.

Defining Future Air Defense Campaigns

According to Teng and Jiang (1990), the air force recognizes that air defense will become an increasingly difficult challenge as its potential enemies acquire more advanced aircraft that can attack from many directions at low altitudes under cover of electronic jamming. Consequently, the differences in weapon systems will affect the way each side wages its campaigns. Based on the characteristics and goals of the campaign, the PLAAF has divided its campaigns into defensive campaigns and attack campaigns, which can further be divided into independent air force campaigns and an air force campaign within a joint campaign.

As part of a rapid-reaction strategy, the PLAAF has classified its requirements for a successful air defense campaign into three types: (1) small campaigns involving air defense of a strategic position, (2) large campaigns involving air defense of a battle are, and (3) larger campaigns involving air defense of many battle areas.

The air force realizes that it cannot yet conduct an effective air defense campaign, because it does not have a reliable air defense intelligence network (particularly, AEW aircraft), a unified command and control system, capable defensive weapon systems, or a modern logistics and maintenance system. More specifically, the PLAAF lacks good early warning radars, early warning satellites, and automated intelligence handling and transmission facilities.

Intelligence Collection

Having analyzed various foreign air campaigns, the PLAAF identified its inability to detect low-altitude penetrators using electronic countermeasures as a major problem for future wars. The air force currently has no AEW capability, only a rudimentary airborne reconnaissance capability, and virtually no use of satellites to provide intelligence. If the PLAAF wants to conduct air defense successfully in the future, Teng and Jiang (1990) states that the air force must focus on these weaknesses, as well as build more and better radars to provide better low-altitude coverage. The air force must also deploy a mix of frequency-agile radars at different locations and distances. The study also states that many more observation posts must be established by mobilizing the militia and masses to form a huge observation net. These must be furnished with modern observation and communications equipment. For example, the air force cites the case in which an observation post gave the alarm in 1962 that led to a AAA unit shooting down a Nationalist RF-101 over Fuzhou airfield within two minutes and 25 seconds of first being sighted.

Command and Control

One of the biggest problems the air force has consistently identified in its air defense operations is the lack of a unified air defense command and a unified air defense plan. The problem is that each service has its own independent air defense structure, and it is extremely difficult to coordinate all of the different elements, even within a single service, under a single air defense plan.

Therefore, the air force has proposed that there should be a unified, multilevel command structure capable of controlling all air defense units within a specific scope. First, there should be a national-level unified command structure. Second, each large battle area should have a unified command structure. Third, there should be a unified command structure in charge of each defensive area.

This issue of "turf" is one of the biggest problems that the PLAAF faces, and one that will probably preclude any significant movement toward an integrated air defense system. For example, the PLAAF has proposed that the air force take primary responsibility as the unified commander for air defense, using one of two methods. One method would be to integrate appropriate army and navy air defense representatives into the PLAAF operations structure at each level. Another method would be to have the army and navy representatives stay with their own units, but to have the PLAAF coordinate command and control through radio communications. Either way, the air force wants to be the central air defense authority. There is very little chance this will happen given the overall lack of coordination among the services, let alone within each service.

"Light Front, Heavy Rear" Strategy

The PLAAF's primary air defense responsibilities are to protect China's airfields, national political and economic centers, heavy troop concentrations, important military facilities, and transportation systems.[14] As a result, most fighter airfields and virtually all of the SAMs have been concentrated around China's large cities—most of which are located at least 200 km from the nearest national border.

Therefore, as part of the rapid-reaction strategy, the PLAAF has focused on the concept of deploying its air defense forces according to the principle of "light at the front and heavy at the rear" along with the principle of "deploying in three rings." Using this concept, the air force would organize its SAM and AAA troops into a combined high, medium and low altitude and a far, medium, and short distance air defense net. The air force must also set up many intercept lines and organize the aviation troops into a layered intercept, especially along the enemy's main routes. This concept is not much different from the existing system, except that the air force realizes it must develop a better command and control system.

In deciding how to deploy its own forces, the PLAAF postulates dividing the battle area into three tiers, using the front line of enemy air-

---

[14] The following material draws from Teng and Jiang (1990), pp. 186–187. The Chinese for "light front, heavy rear" is *qian qing hou zhong*.

fields as the baseline. The first tier extends to a radius of 500 km from the baseline, within which the notional enemy will mainly use its fighters and fighter-bombers. The second tier extends another 500 km, where the enemy will primarily use its fighter-bombers and bombers. The third tier extends beyond 1,000 km, where the enemy will mainly use its long-range strategic bombers.

In using the "light front, heavy rear" concept, the air force believes it will have to deal with the two most important problems. The first problem is that the PLAAF's aircraft currently do not have the capability to fly to the border from their home bases, loiter for any length of time, conduct an intercept, and return home again. This problem was exemplified during the 1979 border war with Vietnam. In addition, the PLAAF believes that, during any sudden attack on China, it must be able to scramble all of its first-tier aircraft to meet the attack and prevent the incoming aircraft from striking any airfields.

The second problem is that the most likely anticipated adversaries—the United States and Russia—have aircraft capable of conducting deep strikes into the heart of China. Therefore, the PLAAF believes it should station most of its air defense weapon systems in the second and third tiers so they can intercept any longer-range aircraft as they converge on key targets. Furthermore, the attacking aircraft may not have the proper escorts at those distances, and the PLAAF's early warning radars might be able to give enough advance notice of an attack for the air defense systems to be ready.

Deploying in Three Rings

In conjunction with the "front light, rear heavy" principle, Teng and Jiang (1990) states that the air force should use the principle of "deploying in three rings."[15] Under this principle, the air force states that it should organize a small quantity of its interceptors, AAA, and SAMs as a combined air defense force into "three dimensional, in-depth, overlapping" firepower rings. Each weapon system would be assigned a specific airspace to defend—high, medium, or low. In-depth rings means assigning each weapon system a specific distance

[15]The following material draws from Teng and Jiang (1990), p. 187. The Chinese for "deploying in three rings" is *san lianhuan bushu.*

from the target to defend—distant, medium, or close. Overlapping rings means organizing each weapon system into left, middle, or right firepower rings facing the most likely avenue of approach. The three elements of the ring should be deployed as follows:[16]

- Interceptor units should be stationed at airfields on the left and right wings along the front tier and in depth, so that they can begin intercepting enemy aircraft as they cross the border and can continue to intercept them as they approach the target.
- The PLAAF's SAMs should be organized into fan-shaped rings, where they can operate independently and can concentrate firepower against attacking aircraft before they reach their bomb-release points.
- The PLAAF's AAA should be deployed into firepower rings in front of SAM emplacements, between SAM units, and between AAA and SAM units, to make up for blind spots.

Air-to-Ground Coordination

One of the biggest problems the air force has historically identified is the inability for the interceptor, SAM, and AAA units to coordinate among themselves and with the army and navy. While the operational area for SAMs and AAA is fixed, the aircraft must pass through them on their way to or from an intercept zone. Therefore, the air force is extremely concerned that the ground-based units will erroneously shoot down their own aircraft.

As a result, the air force identified several solutions to this problem, including separating the operational airspace by altitude and distance, identifying friendly ingress and egress flight corridors, providing the aircraft and ground-based air defense units with identification friend or foe (IFF) to identify hostile targets, specifying certain times for each weapon system to fire, and identifying fire zones by altitude separation. Yet another solution would be to have the fighter units and appropriate ground-based air defense units estab-

---

[16]The army has its own organic AAA and SAM (Chinese-produced SA-7s) units, which are not included in the three rings. The air force would encounter these units only in direct support of the ground forces.

lish a direct communication net to immediately notify the air force of special situations.

The air force concluded, however, that it will not be easy to organize or coordinate among the branches or the other services using the methods of separating combat routes, targets, times, or altitudes. Therefore, it advocates continued use of the existing method of separating the operational air space. This naturally will limit the effectiveness of the air defense network.

Aircraft Dispersal, Camouflage, and Concealment

Increasing "passive" defenses is an important way to enhance combat capabilities. For example, the air force has begun to focus on dispersing its aircraft and to devote increased attention to camouflage and concealment. In September 1989, three F-8 interceptors and one Il-14 transport used the Shenyang-Dalian highway as a dispersal runway for the first time ever. The F-8s landed singly and took off quickly in a three-ship formation.

In addition, the PLAAF has developed an extensive system of cave shelters for its aircraft, but many airfields do not have any hardened facilities at all. Therefore, the air force began building some hardened shelters at a few key bases in the early 1980s (more than a decade after other air forces had begun constructing such shelters in the wake of the devastating Israeli attack against Arab airbases in the 1967 Middle East conflict). Of particular note is the airfield at Nanning, which was a key airbase during the 1979 border conflict with Vietnam. In the early 1980s, the PLAAF built several hardened shelters at Nanning, but aligned them on the north side of the runway with the doors directly facing any attacking aircraft coming from the south.

The air force also identified enemy airborne troops as a major threat and states that the best time to attack these forces is when they are massing at the airfield and waiting to depart or when they are en route to their targets. The key, however, is to have reliable, timely intelligence information and to be ready to take advantage of any combat opportunity. Once airborne forces have landed, the PLAAF should use its bombers and ground attack aircraft to further harass enemy forces before they are able to gain a secure foothold.

GROUND AND NAVAL SUPPORT

One of the most difficult problems confronting the air force is defining its role in support of the ground forces. Air force policy has divided this mission into two types: direct support and indirect support. The air force defines direct support as attacking enemy targets close to the front positions of the ground forces or enemy targets directly threatening to influence the ground forces. In U.S. and NATO parlance, these missions would be labeled close air support and battlefield air interdiction. Indirect support consists of transporting supplies to friendly forces and of attacking targets that are relatively far from the ground forces. In the West, the latter missions would be considered interdiction and strategic attack.

Chengdu (1982), for example, placed heavy emphasis on the PLAAF providing "close" air support to ground forces. However, the study acknowledged the tremendous difficulties involved in coordinating between ground and air forces. It also noted that the PLAAF had concluded during the Korean War that it was not capable of providing direct support to the ground forces.

While the army reorganized along group army lines and several small scale joint exercises were conducted to test the concept, the PLAAF had backed away almost completely from the idea of close air support by 1990. The reasons for this continued to be the lack of an adequate command and control system, lack of coordination between the army and air force, and an inadequate reconnaissance capability. For example, Chengdu (1982) called for the air force to assign full-time FACs to army units at the division level, but the services were still arguing about how to do this in 1990. Chengdu (1982) also called for an elaborate system of real-time strike requests by the army, but this was not implemented due to lack of an adequate command and control system.

The PLAAF's 1990 study on air defense (Teng and Jiang, 1990) concluded, again, that direct support is extremely difficult and that the air force should focus on indirect support. However, the study spent considerable time proposing counterattacks against attacking forces within China's borders and against forces within the enemy's borders. The studies provided an opportunity for the air force to begin looking more realistically at its capabilities and limitations, but much of what was in the analysis was still based on what the PLAAF could do *if* it modernized its equipment and command and control systems, rather than *what* it is capable of doing now or in the near future.

According to PLAAF strategists, there are three key elements in supporting the ground forces: (1) gaining air superiority, (2) attacking enemy airfields, and (3) coordinating with ground force units to destroy airborne troops. Since the PLAAF acknowledges that its airpower is relatively weak, it plans to use aerial combat as the primary method and attacking enemy airfields as the alternate method.

The PLAAF optimistically states that it will be able to gain air superiority over the battle area within China's borders. However, Teng and Jiang (1990) also admits that the air force will have difficulty shooting down enemy bombers with their self-defense capabilities and fighter bombers with their high speed and good agility. Under certain circumstances, the PLAAF believes its aircraft can use air-to-air missiles to attack and to avoid bombers' self-defense firepower. The PLAAF's fighters plan to intercept the enemy's aircraft (which the PLAAF estimates will be flying at 6,000 to 8,000 meters at Mach 0.8 to 0.9) before they can drop their bombs, or at the least force them into dropping their bombs early to protect themselves.

In addition to gaining air superiority, the PLAAF has laid out three scenarios in which China should conduct attacks against enemy airfields and installations. The first is in response to another country invading China, thus directly threatening China's security and territorial integrity. The second is to teach a lesson and severely punish anyone who is threatening China's peace and security. The third is a border war involving strikes against a neighboring country that has the possibility of starting a local war with a neighboring state aligned with China. This is similar to the Korean and Vietnam wars in regard to U.S. involvement.

If the Chinese leadership decides to become involved in any of these types of conflicts, the PLAAF has determined that it will conduct attacks on enemy airfields when (1) the enemy is returning to base after an attack; (2) the enemy is preparing to attack again; (3) the enemy has dispersed its aircraft; (4) the enemy has come out in full force, and the rear is empty; (5) enemy aircraft are mostly parked outside; (6) enemy aircraft are changing airfields, and their fuel is low; and (7) enemy pilots are asleep or resting at night. After attacking an airfield, the PLAAF plans either to use a few interceptors or ground attack aircraft to select the appropriate time to conduct blocking actions against the enemy's airfield or to use a few ground attack aircraft, in coordination with local forces and the militia, to attack the enemy's important radar stations and communication facilities in order to destroy and disrupt the enemy's operations command. Again, however, objective reality clashes with PLAAF desires. The PLAAF offensive force is only a small proportion of the overall force (which is primarily dedicated to air defense) and, moreover, is extremely limited in capability.

The air force also anticipates development of a capability for a counteramphibious assault campaign. In the view of PLAAF strategists, the ideal situation is for the air force to attack the flotilla before it arrives. Once the enemy has landed, the air force will be used primarily to strike rear-echelon targets, including sea transport.[17] The 1990 internal assessment (Teng and Jiang, 1990) concludes that, if the air force wants to be successful in its counteramphibious assault mission, it must improve its sortie-generation capabilities, along with its operational readiness rate and wartime maintenance capabilities, and it must emphasize the "resting of people not aircraft." The authors assert that the air force should also practice flying at low altitudes to attack naval vessels, recognizing that the enemy's AEW aircraft will probably pick them up before they arrive. But these steps presuppose the establishment of a combined command with the Chinese navy. There is little to suggest that any significant measures are under way in this regard, demonstrating yet again the distance the Chinese must traverse to emerge as a more credible, modernized military force.

---

[17]According to Teng and Jiang (1990), the number of aircraft used depends on the size of the flotilla and landing force. For example, a large landing ship that is 100 m long by 15 m wide and displaces 3,400 tons can carry 39 tanks. To sink that ship, the air force would only have to fly 20 sorties (if high-explosive and accurate guided weapons are used, the number of sorties is even smaller). This is an average of 0.5 aircraft to destroy one tank. However, attacking the tanks after they have landed will need an average of four to eight sorties to destroy one tank.

A PRESCRIPTION FOR THE FUTURE

Teng and Jiang (1990), like internal Chinese analyses before it, concluded that the PLAAF must improve its weapons and equipment in a rational way and must upgrade its training if it is to build a credible rapid-reaction force. Other air forces have incorporated new technologies and equipment (such as AEW and jamming) into their inventories. China at present lacks many of these capabilities, and it is seeking ways to compensate for these deficiencies.

If China relies on developing these capabilities exclusively through indigenous effort, it will take many years to satisfy the PLAAF's needs. Although self-reliance in designing and developing new equipment remains a strategy goal, the air force has little alternative to selective acquisition of much-needed components and subsystems. Given this strategy, the air force will seek to modernize its equipment according to the criteria of "new, quality, modify, and introduce":

- *New* means that the PLAAF will use the newest weapons and equipment already in its inventory.
- *Quality* means that the PLAAF will focus on acquisition and employment of weapons and equipment that provide meaningful military capability and possess a high operational rate. It also means maintaining aircraft and engines to extend their service lives. This objective should be geared to reaching an operational ready rate of over 95 percent, so that Chinese forces can react on a moment's notice.
- *Modify* means using new technology and materials to upgrade existing equipment, thus giving it new life. For example, the air force will seek to adopt modern electronics technology to its weapon and communication systems. Designing and developing a new aircraft from the "ground up" is not a feasible option for the air force and would consume vast amounts of capital.
- *Introduce* means acquiring and integrating advanced weapons and equipment from abroad. The air force must face the reality that the technology gap will cost lives during a modern war. While it is not feasible for an air force rapid-reaction force to rely exclusively on new equipment, it is possible to introduce modern

systems selectively. The highest priorities are the acquisition of small numbers of highly capable combat aircraft and early warning aircraft.

The air force will also concentrate its deployment of modern equipment based on the size of the threat among the theaters of operations. In this manner, it can be ready to form quickly for battle and can also organize its training more easily. The air force should also avoid trying to give every unit the same equipment, which will only dissipate its strength where it will be most needed.

When deciding which weapons and equipment to modernize, the air force states it must focus on modernizing six combat capabilities: air superiority, ground attack, transporting troops and supplies, AEW and reconnaissance, electronic countermeasures, and maintenance and logistics. Thus, the air force leadership appears to recognize clearly the complex demands that await it.

Because of budget limitations, the air force recognizes the need to be logical and systematic in specifying the sequence of development for weapons and equipment. Therefore, the air force has devised the following general guidelines for proportionally developing its force, although no precise percentages or numbers have been specified:

- Fighter aircraft must have the highest priority.
- The proportion allocated for ground attack aircraft must be larger than that for bombers, since ground attack aircraft with a refueling capability could be used against rear-echelon targets.
- There must be a certain proportion of bombers, especially strategic bombers.
- Reconnaissance aircraft, jamming aircraft, and AEW aircraft must be supplied in relevant proportions.
- Development of transport aircraft, which have a strategic capability of moving troops and supplies, cannot be slowed down.
- Aerial refueling must constitute a certain proportion of combat aircraft as a force multiplier.
- China must pay attention to developing helicopters, especially armed helicopters, for the army and navy.

- The air force must develop ground-based weapon systems, particularly air defense missiles, radar, and communication systems.

Without question, this is a highly daunting list, and reconciling these resource allocation decisions will preoccupy air force planners for many years to come.

CONCLUSIONS

Developing skills in planning and employing joint forces in an integrated campaign is difficult even for those armed forces with considerable experience and tradition in joint warfare. For the Chinese armed forces, integrating airpower into campaign planning and execution presents a formidable new challenge. Although the air force has put forth a tremendous amount of time and effort compiling data and preparing various studies on airpower, the three biggest problems it has faced and will continue to face are the lack of modern equipment, which limits the way it can train and fight; the lack of coordination within and among the services; and the restrictive nature of the air force's training regime, which reflects the way it will fight.

There is no doubt that the size of China's air force alone acts as a deterrent at a psychological level to some of its neighbors. However, an analysis of the air force as a whole shows that it will most likely not be able to change its way of operating in the near future. The air force clearly recognizes that its equipment is inferior and lags behind its more advanced neighbors, but budgetary and institutional limitations will continue to constrain its ability to modernize.

The most realistic dimension of the air force's internal assessments is the PLAAF's use of the four links of "new, quality, modify, and introduce." The F-7 development program (to be discussed further in Chapter Eight) illustrates how the air force has implemented this policy. For example, the PLAAF has made good progress replacing its aging F-6s with "new" F-7s. The air force has sought to enhance quality by upgrading units with 10 to 20 new aircraft at a time. Although many units purport to have an operational ready rate of 95 percent, this claim does not reflect the fact that each aircraft only logs about 100 hours annually (barely three hours per week) and that most of this is navigation. The aviation ministry has "modified" the F-7 with foreign equipment, such as the Marconi head-up display.

However, the air force cannot afford to purchase large quantities of foreign components with which to upgrade domestically produced equipment. The air force has purchased 26 Russian-made Su-27s and several Il-76 transports, probably as part of its rapid-reaction force. However, these aircraft must be returned to the production plant for any major overhaul, and the PLAAF most likely will not fly the aircraft to its full capabilities because of a restrictive training regime.[18] Furthermore, the airborne forces have not been used except for internal purposes since the Korean War.

In addition, the air force remains preoccupied with air defense of China's major cities. This preoccupation is reflected in the historical mission and placement of the airfields, the location of SAM (SA-2) sites, and the deployment of air defense radar sites around the major cities.[19] Given the air force's strategy of "front light, rear heavy," it is unlikely the air force can justify building new airfields near the country's borders simply to have them destroyed by the first wave of enemy aircraft. Furthermore, the farther an airfield is from the border, the less likely any existing aircraft will be able to reach the border and conduct any lengthy operations before running out of fuel. In addition, the flaw in the "deploying in three rings" concept is that the air force still fears that its own ground-based air defense units will shoot down its own aircraft as they traverse the area. This will become even more complicated when the air force begins flying in closer proximity to army and naval units.

Given that the air force has decided that it cannot conduct direct support for ground forces and still have air defense as its primary mission, there is little likelihood that it will expend significant funds on new bombers and ground attack aircraft in the near future. Furthermore, there is little probability that the air force and army will agree on who should be trained as FAC's, and until this happens the air force will not have any FACs assigned to army units to coordinate joint exercises.

---

[18]For example, fighter pilots conduct scripted, tightly controlled GCI against mostly nonmaneuvering targets during exercises. There is little to no room for pilot initiative.

[19]Many of the airfields in China's major cities are joint civil-military fields, and the trend is continuing this way. In these cases, the air force has its aircraft at one end of the runway or on the other side of the airfield away from the civilian terminal. Examples of this are at Kunming and Xian.

While the air force has a relatively decent airborne signals intelligence capability, it does not have a good airborne photographic reconnaissance capability. Its prospects for acquiring such capabilities in the near to mid term remain highly problematic. This will hamper any strategic and tactical planning for attacks on enemy forces and enemy airfields. Any intelligence network is tied into the command and control system, which is only beginning to be automated. However, turf battles between the services and the lack of modern telecommunication equipment will limit the modernization of the command and control system.

Finally, although the air force has identified a counteramphibious mission, the PLAAF does not train over water and is therefore not prepared to conduct counteramphibious operations. This would remain the responsibility of naval aviation. The air force has identified what it will take to be effective in any future war, and it has developed a set of embryonic concepts for implementing these ideas in warfare. But it does not possess the equipment or structure to be able to execute its strategy according to its own preferences. Its transition to an effective role employing the full array of needed capabilities is likely to prove a protracted process that will preoccupy the PLAAF leadership well into the next century.

Chapter Seven

PLAAF EDUCATION AND TRAINING

Some of the essential building blocks of the PLAAF's institutional development will continue to be based on pilot education and training. Without requisite attention to such needs, the PLAAF cannot expect to ensure the recruitment and development of air force manpower.

The PLAAF currently has 26 schools and academies and has placed much greater emphasis on education over the past decade. Officers are trained on hands-on operations, such as aircraft maintenance, and perform many of the functions airmen or noncommissioned officers (NCOs) do in the USAF. New enlisted conscripts are trained at various training regiments and groups throughout China. As part of the overall restructuring of the education and training system, pilot training has progressed from a three-phase process—basic flight school, flying academy, and operational unit training—to a four-phase process, whereby the pilots attend "transition training" for one year between the academy and the operational unit.

Although the air force has set the goal of upgrading its operational pilot training, the biggest problems are aging, obsolete aircraft and a strictly regimented training environment. Pilots simply do not fly the same number of hours as their Western counterparts and mostly fly navigation flights. Furthermore, while some simulators are in use, they are quite rudimentary and are not standardized throughout the air force. In addition, while the air force has emphasized joint and combined training, this is still undertaken at a very basic level and mostly involves interbranch training within the air force itself.

PLAAF SCHOOLS AND ACADEMIES

Unlike the USAF, the PLAAF does not have a single air force academy. Presently, there are 10 flying academies and 16 other PLAAF schools and academies (AAA, SAM, communications, engineering, logistics, medical, navigation, political, radar, weather, NCO, and two maintenance technical training schools), for a total of 26—most of which are four-year institutions. Throughout the PLA as a whole, there are slightly more than 100 education and training institutions—down about 12 percent from the early 1980s and from a high of nearly 160 in the early 1960s (Editorial Group of the Changsha Military Engineering Academy, 1988, p. 107; FBIS, 1984, p. K14).

Conscript basic and technical training is conducted at various training regiments and groups throughout China. The total number of PLAAF schools and academies has changed considerably over the years, expanding and contracting routinely in reaction to policy changes regarding training objectives or war preparations. For example, there were as many as 17 flight schools during the Cultural Revolution, when Minister of Defense Lin Biao and PLAAF Commander Wu Faxian were advocating a doctrine of imminent war.

In response to new operational concepts in the 1980s, the senior PLAAF leadership joined other services in placing a greater emphasis on officer training and education.[1] Qualitative improvements were introduced for academic education, flight training, and joint exercise training. Academic excellence was increasingly stressed in the PLAAF, as it was throughout the military. To support this objective, the PLAAF closed some schools to consolidate resources and upgraded many schools into academies. For the first time, new pilots were expected to graduate from PLAAF academies with college degrees. Seven PLAAF academies also began in 1985 to confer masters degrees in technical fields.[2] Since the PLAAF does not have an NCO

---

[1]To emphasize the focus on training, the Commandant of the PLAAF Command College, Lt Gen Yang Zhenyu, became one of four deputy commanders at Headquarters Air Force in 1993. Another of the deputy commanders, Lt Gen Lin Hu, was previously a deputy commandant at the PLAAF Command College, and the current commander, Lt Gen Yu Zhenwu, was director of the Training Department at Headquarters Air Force.

[2]The 8th and 9th Flying Schools were abolished, and the 11th Flying School was changed to the Test Flight and Training Center. The SAM, Weather, Political, Radar,

corps like the USAF, officers are trained for hands-on operations. For example, maintenance officer cadets at the PLAAF's Engineering College and Maintenance Technical Training Schools complete from 2 to 4 years of hands-on training on aircraft maintenance, and once they are assigned to an operational unit, they conduct much of the actual aircraft maintenance. The same is true for the other schools and subsequent jobs in the operational units.

The organization of PLAAF training and education is currently based on the PLA's "5-3" tier system. This system consists of five tiers of specialized or technical training and education for officers: secondary specialized, specialized college or equivalent, university or equivalent, masters degree program, and doctorate program. There also is a three-tier system of professional military education for officers (i.e., primary command and leadership training, intermediate command and leadership training, and higher command education).

THE TRAINING PROCESS

Every March, the air force selects about 3,000 qualified high school students for pilot training, of whom about 1,300 graduate. In the past, the PLAAF has also recruited a small number of civilian college graduates (age 20–22); however, the best success rate for training pilots has been with the high school graduates, since the college graduates were not as motivated and willing to spend the amount of time required to acquire requisite skills.

Historically, fighter and ground attack pilot training was a three-phase process: basic flight school (20 months), flying academy (28 months), and operational unit training (4–5 years) (China Today, 1989a, pp. 503–504).[3] Beginning in 1986, however, the PLAAF began

---

and Communications Engineering academies, as well as the Engineering and Air Force Command colleges, have begun awarding masters degrees.

[3]By 1991, there were three operational transition training bases. Once all seven bases are established, the goal is to eventually eliminate the need for an operational fighter division to dedicate one of its three regiments to training, and to consolidate some of the flight training schools. For example, the PLAAF abolished three flight training schools after July 1986. Initial pilot training now lasts for four years as an undergraduate and is divided into two distinct parts. The first part (20 months) is held at one of two basic flying schools. The second part, which consists of three phases (28 months), is conducted at one of the ten flying academies. Graduates receive a degree in military

to experiment with an additional fourth phase. For graduates of fighter and ground attack flying programs, phase three became a one-year aircraft "conversion program" at newly organized "transition training bases." Phase four, or proficiency development, became a slightly truncated version of the old operational training in units (now three to four years). The program was formalized in July 1988 when the Military Commission authorized each MRAF to establish a transition training base.[4]

PLAAF pilots do not fly as many hours as their Western counterparts. For example, bomber pilots fly an average of 80 hours per year; fighter pilots fly 100 to 110 hours; and A-5 ground attack pilots fly up to 150 hours. To help build esprit de corps, the air force began awarding four pilot ratings in 1986—special, first, second, and third grade—after the pilots complete their initial and upgrade training at an operational unit. The criteria include time-on-station, flying hours, flying in weather, and special missions. Of the 10,000 pilots in the entire PLAAF in 1989, 7 percent of the total and 15 to 20 percent of the fighter pilots were special grade. In addition, the PLAAF began awarding aircrew ratings to navigators, communications and gunnery personnel, and instructor pilots.

According to a December 1991 report, 70 percent of the PLAAF's pilots were qualified as all-weather pilots, which is called "flying under four different weather conditions"—simple daytime weather conditions, complex daytime weather conditions, simple night weather conditions, and complex night weather conditions. Training also included low-altitude flying, minimum-altitude flying, air combat, high-altitude air acrobatics, and transregional movement. Some 80 percent of flight combat regiments had purportedly taken part in multiservice and multiarm tactical exercises in 1991 (BBC, 1991).

---

science and are commissioned second lieutenants. They are also given the AEP of a deputy company commander (*fulianji*). Actual flight training (155 hours) begins at a flying academy where students train in the CJ-6. They get an additional 130 hours in the F-5.

[4]Training at the "transition training bases" (*gaizhuang xunlian jidi*) lasts for one year (100 to 120 flying hours). The pilots begin flying the F-5 for basic airmanship, then transition to the F-6 or F-7. Upon graduation, the pilots are expected to be capable of flying in "three weather conditions" (i.e., day and night visual flight rules [VFR], and day instrument flight rules [IFR]). Thereafter annual flying hours vary according to the type of aircraft: bombers (80 hours), fighters (100–110 hours) and the A-5 ground attack aircraft (150 hours). (China Today, 1989a, pp. 503–504.)

The PLAAF has also established age limits for the various types of pilots: 43 to 45 for fighter and ground attack pilots (the average age is 28); 48 to 50 for bomber pilots; and 55 for transport pilots. Once a pilot has reached the mandatory age or fails to meet medical qualifications, his flying is terminated. One of the most common problems cited, however, is that the PLAAF does not have a mechanism to absorb these pilots into nonflying jobs once they leave the cockpit. The reason for this, as mentioned above, is that most officers are involved in hands-on operations or are in management positions where they have had years of experience.

JOINT AND COMBINED TRAINING

The increasing emphasis on joint and combined operations in the 1980s led to additional training changes. One initiative was the creation of greater combat reality in flight training. Since 1982, each MRAF has formed one to three "blue force units" that serve as enemy or aggressor squadrons. The PLAAF Flight Test and Training Center, located in Cangzhou, Hebei province, also formed an F-7 and F-8 interceptor unit to fly as aggressors during air defense exercises throughout China. The problem, however, is the absence of realistic training as they use nonmaneuvering, obsolete aircraft in tightly scripted scenarios with strict GCI.

PLAAF histories often referred to "mixed" or "combined" military actions—even in the 1950s. In reality, it is doubtful that joint or combined operations were ever raised to a doctrinal or conceptual level until perhaps the early 1980s. Combined arms training for the PLA more often than not involves combining the arms within a service. In the case of the air force, each of the seven MRAFs has begun since 1985 to establish a tactical training area. These training areas are specifically designed for the five PLAAF branches to train together. In 1986 the different services also addressed joint training (i.e., involving different services). Some MRAFs and air corps formed joint tactical training areas in conjunction with MR ground forces. However, as noted in Chapter Six, the air force does not have any personnel permanently assigned to army units as liaison officers or FACs, and only assigns them there during exercises.

SIMULATOR TRAINING

Development of aircraft simulators used for aircraft engineering development and pilot training in China has corresponded to the technological sophistication of China's aircraft.[5] The first simple simulator for MiG-15 training came from Russia during the Korean War. This simulator had no visual system and was primarily a procedural trainer. Later, during the 1950s, a Tu-2 bomber simulator was imported from Russia. This training device included a point-light visual display to depict targets. Additional Russian simulators followed. These were simple cockpit devices useful primarily for emergency and procedural training.

The first Chinese-built simulator was developed in 1964 for the MiG-19. This simulator, used mainly for engineering development, used an actual MiG-19 aircraft connected to analog computers to simulate instrument and control inputs and responses. In 1965, China produced its first flight-control simulator. This simulator was used over the years in developments related to F-6, F-7, F-8, F-12, and A-5 aircraft.

During the 1980s, China began a simulator development program, which resulted in development of an F-8 simulator. This simulator included a simple visual system with a sky-earth projected horizon and a separate projected target image. In 1987, an F-7 simulator on a six-degree motion base and a three-channel, computer-generated image was built. This reflects the latest currently available simulator technology now being used by military pilots in China. However, use of this simulator is not widespread at the unit level.

With the importation of more-sophisticated simulators in recent years for use by China's airline pilots, knowledge and appreciation of currently available simulation technology is growing. While the military would like to have improved simulators, including high-quality visual systems, budget limitations and priorities have resulted in continued reliance on what can be produced within China.

---

[5]The information for this section was provided by Donald P. Brown of Evans & Sutherland.

CONTINUING TRAINING DEFICIENCIES

The air force has emphasized that improved training—especially "training for the way you fight"—is a key to establishing its rapid-reaction force. Therefore, according to the PLAAF's internal studies, training time should be increased about 50 percent; the content of the training should project combat objectives; and training targets should focus on difficult missions. But to date, these lofty goals have not been realized. For example, the following list from the 1990 study showing "what the air force should do" is a good indicator of what the air force cannot do (Teng and Jiang, 1990, pp. 279–282):

- Conduct combat training at night and under VFR conditions, especially under poor weather conditions.
- Conduct two- and four-ship attack training against low-altitude targets.
- Conduct mobility training, including frequent scramble exercises, "intertheater" air-raid combat training, and massing aircraft for defense or for a strike.
- Conduct combined combat training among the various air defense branches and services.
- Conduct dissimilar aircraft and simulator training.

However, while military technology and weapon development is extremely important to building a more credible capability, the air force still stresses that the decisive factor in winning or losing future wars is people. Therefore, the air force plans to pay more attention to developing commanders, pilots, and technical personnel, along with acquiring the proper weapons and equipment.

Finally, the air force has identified maintenance training as a focal point. According to PLAAF data, the flight safety record remains among the highest in the world (BBC, 1991b). However, as noted in Chapter Six, this safety record is misleading, since the aircraft are only flown about 2 to 3 hours per week, most of which is navigation flights.

These considerations impart the extent of the challenge the PLAAF continues to face in its transition to a 21st century fighting force.

Perhaps the largest challenges, however, are in the realm of China's defense industrial structure, for without modern airpower, the air force cannot possibly expect to carry out a demanding set of roles and missions. We therefore need to turn our attention to the PLAAF force structure and its prospects for modernization over the coming decade.

Chapter Eight

PLAAF FORCE STRUCTURE TRENDS

Since the PRC's establishment, China claims to have developed and manufactured more than 10,000 fighter planes comprising over 60 models with which to equip the PLAAF and the navy (Zhu, 1991). According to the IISS *Military Balance* for 1994–1995, the air force is currently the world's third-largest air arm, with approximately 4,000 fighters, 400 A-5 ground attack aircraft, and 120 B-6 bombers organized into 45 air divisions. In addition, naval aviation has about 600 fighters, 100 A-5 ground attack aircraft, and 25 B-6 bombers organized into nine air divisions.[1]

Although large in total numbers, the PLAAF's current force consists predominantly of obsolete aircraft. Other than the 26 Su-27s acquired from Russia in 1992, virtually every aircraft in the Chinese inventory is based on 1950s and 1960s technology. Except for about half of the 600 F-7, 150 F-8 fighters, and 150 B-6 bombers, all these aircraft are well over a decade old. This stands in great contrast to the PLAAF's world-class inventory at the end of the 1950s.[2]

The analysis presented below indicates that the air force has no immediate hope for significant improvement. Modernization of the

[1]IISS (1994–1995), pp. 172–173, and discussions with PLAAF officials.

[2]Although the Chinese use the "J" (Jian) designator for their fighters (J-6, J-7, J-8), "Q" (Qiang) for ground attack aircraft, and "H" (Hongzha) for bombers, Western publications refer to these aircraft using "F," "A," and "B" designators, respectively. For purposes of this study, the Western designators will normally be used; however, the Chinese designators "Z" (zhi) for helicopters and "Y" (Yun) for transports will be used for those aircraft, since the Chinese designators are routinely used in Western publications.

PLAAF has been thwarted by the rigid industrial policies and political turmoil that have characterized the Chinese economy over the years. Although China has embarked on an ambitious effort to modernize the air force along the lines of a rapid-reaction force, it will be very difficult to achieve this goal over the next decade.

The two most important factors explaining these difficulties are the shortage of funds to purchase aircraft and associated systems (e.g., command and control, reconnaissance, and communications), even on a small scale, and the restrictive nature of the PLAAF's organization, training, and operational structure. Another key factor is the character of the Chinese aviation industry, which is ill-postured to help modernize its defense production capabilities, combined with the diversion of scarce resources to civilian production. The air force's existing inventory of combat aircraft is therefore expected to decline as increasing numbers of aircraft reach their service-life limits without sufficient numbers of replacement aircraft to take their place. Although there is no reason to believe the Chinese are seeking "one for one" replacements for old aircraft, the forecast for introducing significant numbers of modern aircraft in the near to mid term seems problematic.

CAN THE PLAAF AFFORD TO MODERNIZE?

Although China's official defense budget has grown appreciably since the late 1980s, many Chinese officials insist that the bulk of these increases is intended to compensate for the inflationary pressures of recent years. Despite rapid economic growth, galloping inflation and budget constraints could limit China's military purchasing power and may stall weapon modernization programs. Training and unit readiness could also suffer, given inadequate facilities and the diversion of personnel and assets to money-making enterprises. To compensate for the lack of funds, and to continue to feed and clothe its personnel properly, the Chinese government ordered the PLA in 1991 to start new commercial business activities and enlarge those already under way. A government-mandated shift from military to civilian production would also exacerbate PLA supply problems in the event of a future armed conflict. (An estimated 80 percent of China's defense manufacturing is being shifted to commercial products to help revive the national economy and improve living standards.[3])

Airpower is a capital-intensive form of military power, and modernization requires a substantial, sustained commitment of funds. Although there has been real growth in Chinese defense expenditure during the 1990s, inflation has limited the effects of defense budget increases evident since 1989. Thus, the Chinese have yet to recover fully from the defense cuts of the 1980s, when the military's share of the state budget had fallen to historic lows (Kaye, 1994, p. 80).[4] According to outside analysts, China's urban inflation rate was estimated at 33 percent in 1989, 30 percent in 1992, and 20 percent in 1994.[5] Inflationary pressures have thus continued to impinge on the PLA's actual purchasing power, even as the Chinese feel impelled to increase their acquisitions of advanced foreign equipment.

Making estimates of Chinese military expenditure is an uncertain business at best, and no specific figures are available on the amount allocated to the air force. In dollar amounts, the official defense budget increased by more than 12 percent annually, to 32.5 billion yuan (US$6.2 billion) in 1991 and 36.4 billion yuan (US$6.8 billion) in 1992. These increases accelerated further in 1993 (42.5 billion yuan) and 1994 (52.04 billion yuan). However, the official defense budget excludes numerous defense-related expenditures, such as funds for the defense industry and for research and development. The PLA also earns substantial income from its own production activities and arms sales abroad; some of this income has very likely been allocated to acquisition of more advanced foreign weapon systems.

---

[3]"Inflation, Budget Constraints Force Deep Reductions in Spending Power, Modernization for China's Military" (1991).

[4]It should be noted, however, that the much smaller percentages of recent years reflect a vastly larger economic base.

[5]Official inflation estimates sometimes reflect about half the real inflation in China. In 1989, the government's announced inflation rate was 17.8 percent, while actual inflation was closer to 33 percent, and inflation in China's top 35 cities was 30 percent in 1992, but was reduced to about 20 percent in 1993 and 1994. The increase in 1992 was fueled by sharp rises in food costs, caused by a decline in grain acreage and Beijing's attempts to appease the countryside with higher farm prices. (Huus, 1994, p. 44; Zielenziger, 1994, p. 59.)

Calculated according to NATO methods, analysts estimate China's 1991 and 1992 defense budget at somewhere between 70 and 80 billion yuan (US$13.4 to 15.3 billion), or two to three times what was officially admitted.[6] Weapon procurement, however, accounted for only 20 to 25 percent of the defense budget, or 6.5 to 8 billion yuan (US$1.25 to 1.53 billion), in 1992 (Hu, 1992). In March 1993, Beijing announced an increase in its defense budget to 42.5 billion yuan (US$7.4 billion), up 8.8 percent in real terms from its 1992 expenditure. Using Western estimates, this means that China may have spent as much as US$22 billion on military forces in 1992 (less than one-tenth of the U.S. defense budget) (Ackerman and Dunn, 1993, p. 57). It is important to bear in mind, however, that these budget data reflect a very different wage and cost structure. It would be highly inappropriate to make comparisons between Chinese and U.S. defense budgets in view of these differences.

In March 1994, the government announced plans to hike defense spending by about 22 percent to 52.04 billion yuan (US$5.9 billion) in 1994, with expectations that double-digit increases will continue through the remainder of this decade.[7] Despite the large increase in percentage terms—greater than that planned for agriculture, science, or education—China's military leaders are still left with less money than they had in 1993. The reasons also reflect changes in current conversion practices. Sweeping financial reforms introduced in January 1994 eliminated the former two-tiered exchange rate, effectively devaluing the yuan by about 33 percent against major world currencies (Reuters, 1994). The PLAAF buys F-7s for between $2 and 3 million each today, while an Su-27 costs more than $35 million. Even if more advanced Russian aircraft could be produced in China, the price would not fall by a factor of 10. Under prevailing circumstances, therefore, there is no prospect to purchase more modern combat aircraft in significant quantities.

---

[6]For a more extended discussion, see Acharya and Evans (1994).

[7]In March 1995, Beijing disclosed that the defense budget for 1995 had reached 63 billion yuan, an increase of 21 percent over the initial allocation for 1994 and 14.6 percent over the final expenditure for 1994. The Chinese insisted that the preponderance of these increases was intended to cope with inflation.

FIGHTER PROCUREMENT

Examination of the fighter inventory provides a useful illustration of the development of the Chinese aviation industry and the evolution of Chinese industrial policy. The PLAAF and naval aviation are integrated into the overall air defense network and fly the same types of fighter aircraft. The estimated number of fighters in each service is shown in Figure 14 (Cohen and Forsberg, 1993). Total naval aviation fighters represent between 10 and 15 percent of the air force total. These percentages would change appreciably only if the air force were to decide to reduce the size of its force posture in the coming years, without naval aviation making equivalent compensatory cuts.

At the time of the establishment of the PRC in 1949, the PLAAF inventory consisted of a variety of captured Japanese and Nationalist aircraft. Large-scale Soviet aid began to flow into China in the early 1950s, with aircraft and training high on the list of priorities. During the Korean War, Soviet assistance enabled a major enhancement of the PLAAF's capabilities in both quantitative and qualitative terms.

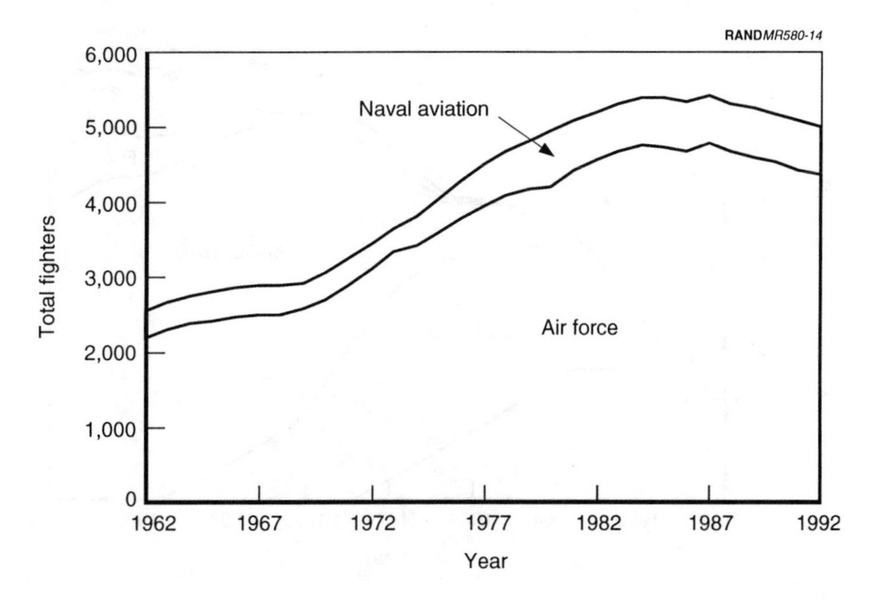

Figure 14—PLAAF–Naval Air Force Inventory, 1962–1992

By the war's end, the air force had deployed a full complement of attack aircraft, bombers, and transport planes.

Figure 15 depicts the total Chinese jet fighter inventory for the air force and naval aviation. The Chinese inventory increased steadily from the early 1950s—with a pause during the Cultural Revolution—to reach a peak in the mid-1980s. Since that time, the total combat inventory has declined, as aircraft have reached the end of their service lives. The figure reflects the dominant position of the F-6 fighter, which constitutes the majority of the PLAAF force structure. The size of the air force is largely dependent upon the future of this fighter and the rate at which replacement systems can be brought into the inventory. By comparison, the United States began introducing fourth-generation fighters (the F-14, F-15, F-16, and F-18) in the mid-1970s, whereas the Chinese are only now starting to operate equivalent systems (such as the Su-27) some two decades later.

But there are qualitative as well as quantitative constraints on Chinese military aviation. The Chinese method of operating their

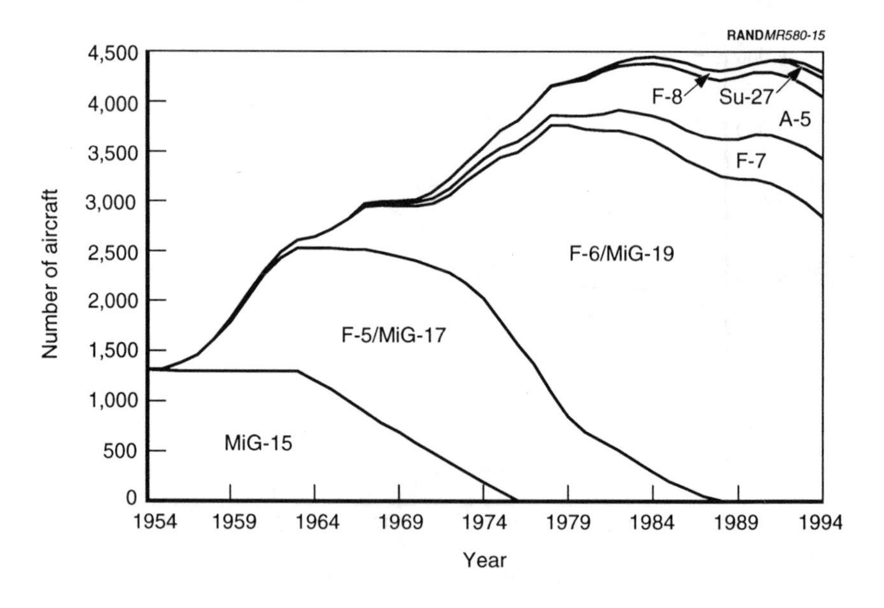

Figure 15—Chinese Jet Fighter Inventory, 1954–1994

aircraft does not employ multimission tasking. This means that whatever ground attack capability might be resident in the F-6 is not exploited, since it is assigned to interceptor units. Similar limitations apply to all F-7s and F-8s assigned to these duties. Thus, virtually all PLAAF attack capability derives from A-5 units and bombers. This limited capability is consistent with low levels of readiness and training across the air force as a whole. A high level of training activity is required for U.S. multirole pilots, even with the sophisticated systems that they have to assist them. Changes to the PLAAF single-mission orientation would require major shifts in Chinese training, logistics, and doctrine to develop, maintain, and exploit the resulting advances.

All of China's successful fighters have been acquired or produced with some assistance from the Soviet Union or, subsequently, Russia. Detailed descriptions of acquisition timelines and modifications for each aircraft can be found in Appendix E. The net result of more than four decades of external assistance, political upheaval, and reverse engineering is that China has an air force consisting of old aircraft of limited combat utility, with a very limited quantity of modern aircraft and weapons. The PLAAF's prospects for modernization will depend on the ability of the Chinese to overcome the major constraints that presently limit their defense acquisitions, as discussed below.

CHINA'S DEFENSE INDUSTRIAL INFRASTRUCTURE

From the air force's perspective, the aviation industry has not been able to produce affordable, modern equipment in a timely manner to meet the air force's needs. At the same time, the aviation ministry contends that it can produce reliable, affordable aircraft for the air force, although it will take time to develop new platforms or to modify existing systems.[8] The ministry, with some justification, contends that the air force is not currently capable of flying or maintaining sophisticated foreign aircraft. For example, the PLA purchased 24 Sikorsky S-70C-II Black Hawk helicopters in the early 1980s, but by

---

[8]This information is based on the lead author's discussions with numerous aviation ministry, factory, and air force officials.

mid-1993, two had crashed and only six of the remaining aircraft were airworthy because of maintenance problems.[9]

As a result of the love-hate relationship between the air force and the aviation ministry, in 1990 PLAAF adopted the four links of "new, quality, modify, and introduce" to accelerate its acquisition of new equipment for its rapid-reaction strategy (Teng and Jiang, 1990, p. 278). Some of these links were already in use, but the renewed access to the Russian market created new opportunities.

Self-reliance has been the goal of every Chinese aircraft procurement program since the 1950s. The question is how to reconcile this objective with the PLAAF's imperative need for aircraft modernization. China's aviation industry remains determined to establish its own production base by acquiring specific foreign technologies in small quantities, which it seeks to incorporate into indigenously developed weapon systems. The Chinese have purchased an extensive number of foreign systems over the years, which have provided defense R&D personnel with important insight into current design trends (Table 4). But access to these technologies does not mean that they can be indigenously produced in significant quantities or incorporated successfully into Chinese weapon systems. Modernization will clearly be a long-term process. Although China has recently acquired some badly needed Russian equipment, hard currency shortages will continue to prevent large-scale purchases of foreign-made military aircraft and related weapon systems.[10]

Even if ample hard currency were available to the PLAAF, a strategy favoring external purchases is strongly opposed by China's aviation industry. Domestic critics in China stress the experience with the Soviet Union in the 1950s and with the United States in the late 1980s

---

[9]Discussion with knowledgeable sources close to the helicopter program.

[10]Although the Chinese aviation industry has produced for export the F-7M and A-5M with Western avionics, the PLAAF has not been interested in purchasing large numbers of these aircraft. One major reason is that the Aviation Ministry requires the air force to pay hard currency for the foreign equipment on the aircraft. This requirement substantially increases the unit cost of each aircraft. The PLAAF receives *renminbi* procurement funds from the GSD, but the foreign currency costs must be made up by the air force. The PLAAF naturally wants to pay for the entire aircraft in *renminbi*, which would mean a net loss for MAS factories.

Table 4

Chinese Weapon Purchases

System	Year	Origin
Aircraft		
MiG-15	1950	Russia
Il-28	1952	Russia
MiG-17	1955	Russia
AN-2	1956	Russia
Tu-16	1957	Russia
MiG-19	1959	Russia
MiG-21	1961	Russia
MiG-23	1978	Egypt
Beech Super King Air	1984	United States
MD-80	1986	United States
Su-27	1992	Russia
Il-76	1993	Russia
Missiles		
K-5 ALKALI	1958	Russia
SA-2	1959	Russia
AA-2 ATOLL	1961	Russia
AA-8 APHID	1970s	Russia
SA-7	—	Russia
Rafael Python III	1980s	Israel
Matra Magic I	1980s	France
Crotale	—	France
AA-10 ALAMO	1991	Russia
AA-11 ARCHER	1991	Russia
SA-10	1993	Russia

(when existing defense programs were cancelled or severely curtailed) as examples of the dangers of dependence on foreign suppliers for defense equipment. Despite such criticisms, the Chinese have frequently had no recourse but to "go abroad" to address pressing defense needs.

The historical record shows all programs based on foreign systems have been structured along similar lines. Initially, a small number of complete prototypes, along with a number of knocked-down kits, are imported for assembly and testing in China. These are followed by full imported parts sets, then assembly using an increasing domestic parts content, ultimately reaching full manufacturing capability of the specific aircraft or weapon system. As full manufacturing capability is reached, plans are made for modified versions to meet specific Chinese requirements. This long chain of events begins with a current aircraft, but ultimately results in domestic manufacture of an obsolete system. Contemporary procurement policies show some recognition of this problem, but the Chinese have not been able to solve it.

At the same time, purely domestic development programs have had little success. Poor requirement definition, limited industrial capability, and lengthy development cycles have all contributed to poor results. The aviation ministry designs and builds all military aircraft produced in China. Since the air force has not been able to identify its requirements to the satisfaction of the aviation ministry, interminable meetings take place between the two sides to clarify and review what the air force really wants and needs. The ministry is likely to build what can be domestically designed and manufactured, rather than incur the technical risks and development costs to provide an aircraft with superior combat capabilities. Internal rivalries within the aviation industry have also impeded timely development.

THE CHINESE WEAPON DEVELOPMENT CYCLE

China's rapid economic growth during the 1980s and 1990s has led many observers to project commensurate increases in military procurement. However, many of the factories in China that were built for military production are now being used by military and civilian industrial firms to manufacture consumer goods for domestic use and export and are not available to manufacture military hardware on a scale comparable to that of the past. In addition, traditional programmatic limitations remain in place for military procurement. The military must work within the five-year planning cycle used by the Chinese government, although exceptions can be made depending upon the situation. Weapon systems must be justified to gain a place in the medium- to long-term plan (i.e., beyond five years) and the program must progress through a five-phase development plan to keep its place in the annual planning process. It has been argued that the two determining factors in any Chinese weapon development program are high-level interest and money—without the first, the second will not be forthcoming.

The PLAAF receives its funds in a variety of forms. It gets "fenced" money to buy specific items, such as aircraft. It gets "constrained funds" over which it has some control, and discretionary funds to spend as needed. It also earns money through commercial enterprises, such as hotels, charter airlines, factories, and equipment sales.[11] This has allowed the PLAAF to add money earned through foreign exchange to its procurement accounts. It cannot move money allocated by the state to different programs (e.g., cancel an aircraft order), but it can enhance its buys with foreign equipment and features that must be bought in hard currency (e.g., add foreign equipment to the aircraft under order).

It is also ironic that the military earns much of its foreign exchange in competition with industry. Polytechnologies Inc. is the import-export arm of the GSD and has a PLAAF component, which can sell military equipment directly from the military inventory. China National Aerotechnology Import & Export Corporation represents the aviation ministry and sells newly manufactured equipment. This places the military and the aviation ministry in direct competition for sales, servicing, training, and equipment overhaul. Polytechnologies Inc. has, on occasion, used its position to order new equipment for overseas delivery, in the same order with PLA production, and used the foreign exchange to pay for foreign-made equipment for its models.

The design, development, and testing of new aircraft involves a lengthy process. Chinese aviation historians claim that the Cultural Revolution extended some development cycles well beyond ten years. During the Cultural Revolution, demands were placed on aviation engineers to develop aircraft in two or three years. If China is now developing new fighter aircraft, the factories and institutes will still have to go through several time-intensive phases.

---

[11]In 1984, the PLAAF organized several of its transport aircraft into a public-owned enterprise known as China United Airlines (CUA/*Zhongguo Lianhe Hangkong Gongsi*) to operate charter passenger and cargo flights to supplement CAAC, China's only official carrier at that time. CUA pays less than 4 percent of its income for taxes to the state. About 86 percent goes for operating costs, and the final 10 percent is profit. In 1988, CUA operated seven days a week and had 24 fixed routes connecting 23 different cities, utilizing both civilian and military airfields. All flights originate at the PLAAF's Beijing Nanyuan airfield each day and terminate back there by sunset. CUA also manages hotels, passenger services, catering, and souvenir outlets.

The five-phase development cycle for an aircraft in China consists of the theoretical evaluation, program definition, engineering development, design finalization, and production finalization phases. For domestic production programs, the air force and the Commission for Science, Technology and Industry for National Defense (COSTIND) are involved during all five phases. To initiate the theoretical evaluation, the air force submits a report to three organizations—the GSD, COSTIND, and the Military Commission—requesting a weapon system. If the report is approved, the program is put in the medium-long term or annual plan. For the program definition phase, the PLAAF submits a request for proposal to the appropriate ministries and/or foreign companies. Once the program is defined, the PLAAF and the contracting ministry do a joint report to the GSD and COSTIND. The design phase takes at least four to five years. The test flight phase, involving four to five prototypes, takes another four to five years, depending on the design. Once aircraft development reaches finalization, the training of pilots and maintenance personnel can take six to twelve months. Depending on the type of aircraft, it could take another six to twelve months to produce enough (10–15) aircraft to begin equipping the initial units. Finally, according to one *Liberation Army Daily* article, it took one PLAAF unit three years to become operational after the initial F-8 fighters began to arrive. These phases are shown in Figure 16, using previous and current programs as examples.

When all needed manufacturing technology has been provided, the Chinese have been able to set up facilities and begin production rapidly. The three years needed for F-5 production was fast by any standard. This was preceded by a three-and-a-half-year effort to prepare for MiG-15 production that could be added to the three years shown for F-5 preparations. Even when this is done, the accomplishment is still impressive. The F-6 effort was stretched out by the Great Leap Forward and the Sino-Soviet split, but was not lengthy considering the complexity of the aircraft. Subsequent aircraft, which have required substantial domestic engineering and development, have had much longer development cycles. If China attempts to buy pieces of modern production processes, and bridges any gaps with domestic engineers, major delays can be anticipated in the introduction of future aircraft types.

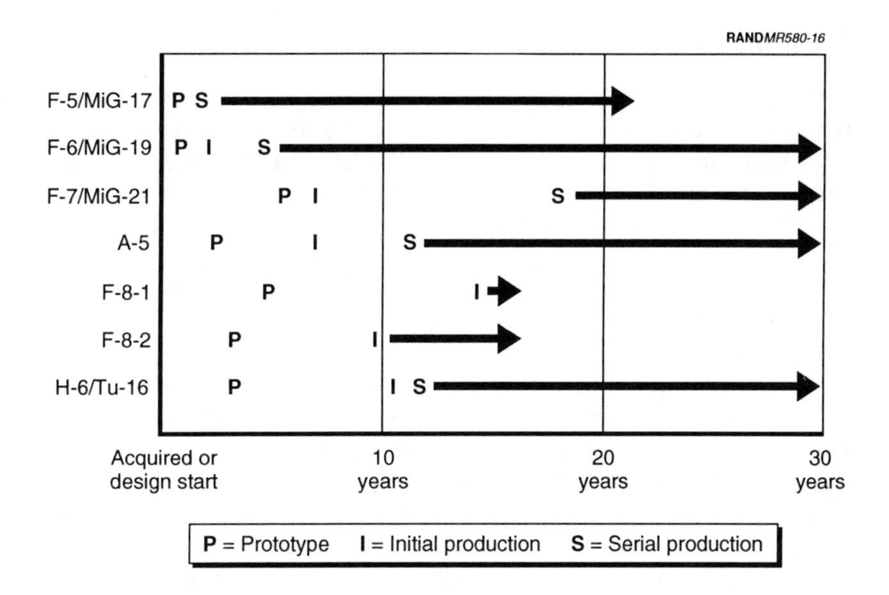

Figure 16—PRC Aircraft Development

CURRENT PROGRAMS

China has seen many of its development efforts fail to provide the aircraft needed to maintain a modern force. In 1971, during the Cultural Revolution, the air force ordered development of 27 different types of aircraft (Duan, 1989, p. 71). This effort resulted in no new aircraft and great disruption of existing programs. Later failures can be traced to poor requirement definition, extended development time, and inadequate design capability. For example, the F-12 was designed to be a lightweight, short-takeoff-and-landing supersonic fighter. It began development in 1969 and was terminated after the completion of six aircraft and the initial flight tests in 1975, because of its inadequate thrust and firepower and ever-changing air force requirements. Several current programs—the F-7, Super-7, F-8-2, B-7/FB-7, and K-8/L-8—provide good examples of the problems China will have in developing and producing a new aircraft, with or without foreign assistance.

F-7 Program

Although modernization of the F-7 has continued in various forms for over a decade, it has consistently had major problems. In one of its original forms, the F-7 modernization program was based on the integration of Western subsystems that were embargoed following the 1989 Tiananmen incident. Despite many efforts, the PRC was incapable of even replacing the Western electronic subsystems installed in the Pakistani F-7Ps. The F-7Ms sold to Iran were not compatible with the advanced missiles carried by the Pakistani Air Force F-7Ps. Moreover, a major aspect of the original upgrade program, called Saber-2, was the adaptation of a U.S. jet engine (GE 404) to a redesigned F-7 airframe with side inlets and a Western fire control system, thus drastically improving its performance (BBC, 1993a). In the late 1970s, Harlan Jencks, a leading specialist on Chinese military affairs, described the F-6 as "the most highly perfected, obsolescent aircraft in the world." There is little doubt that the F-7, which has taken the F-6's place, can be described in much the same way.

Some possible long-term solutions emerged in the aftermath of the 1991 Gulf War. Chinese experts reportedly studied with great care the Iraqi aircraft that landed in Iran and identified several components and subsystems they can reverse-engineer and adapt for integration into their own aircraft. In addition, Iran reportedly agreed in January 1993 to transfer several Iraqi aircraft to China. These aircraft will be used to support the programs beneficial for both Iran and Pakistan. In the first phase, the Chinese will purportedly adapt the MiG-29's R-33 engine for use in the F-7 derivative. In addition, Chinese engineers will study the various advanced Soviet and Western subsystems installed in the Iraqi MiG-21s, which were done locally in Iraq. Pakistan has also reportedly negotiated the acquisition of electronic systems and their production technology in Western Europe to support the F-7 program. Most important was the acquisition of radar technology in Italy in February 1993. These systems will be incorporated into Chinese and Pakistani F-7s (BBC, 1993a).

Super-7 Program

In addition to a modified F-7 program, the Chengdu Aircraft Company has for several years been developing an updated version of the F-7M, known as the Super-7 aircraft, with foreign assistance. Information on the Super-7 program was first disclosed in 1988. The project was conceived as a joint U.S.-China-Pakistan program, designed to use the General Electric F-404 engine. However, U.S. involvement ceased following imposition of restrictions on further U.S. military sales after the June 1989 Tiananmen incident. According to one official at the Chengdu Aircraft Company, despite sanctions, initial subsonic wind-tunnel tests of a fully configured Super-7 were under way in Chengdu in October 1989. A number of Western systems were to be incorporated in the aircraft, including the power plant, fire control systems, and missiles. A model of the Super-7 on display at the 1992 Farnborough Air Show was shown with an Italian Alenia Aspide missile, but no firm agreements had been reached on marketing the missile. According to literature accompanying the model, the Super-7 would be customized to meet any European or U.S. missile fit. Also on display on the Chinese stand was the GEC Ferranti Blue Hawk radar, a new low-cost venture designed for retrofit of A-4 and MiG-21-type aircraft but also capable of being fitted to the new Super-7. GEC Avionics of the United Kingdom is believed to have offered avionics for the aircraft. The Super-7 will supposedly incorporate new wing and tail structures, improved avionics and a higher endurance than the F-7M. TurboUnion, the European consortium comprising Rolls Royce, MTU, and Fiat Aviazione, also offered the Tornado GR1's RB199 turbofan for the single-engined Super-7.[12]

Other reports indicate that Russian Defense Minister General Pavel Grachev signed an agreement with China during a November 1993 visit to Beijing to develop the Super-7 jointly. Under the Sino-Russian agreement, the Super-7 will purportedly use the Russian AL-31F engine, currently used in the Su-27. According to Chinese aviation industry officials, the first flight for the Super-7 is scheduled for 1996, and the aircraft will be available for export in 1997. There are conflicting reports whether or not the PLAAF and/or naval aviation

---

[12]"First Flight Set for Super 7 in 1996" (1992), p. 9.

will acquire any of the aircraft. According to one report, the Super-7 is planned to enter Chinese service around the year 2000 as a replacement for the F-7. Meanwhile, according to a senior adviser at the Chengdu Aircraft Corporation, Tu Jida, the Super-7 will be manufactured for export and not for the PLAAF. As with the original modification program, Pakistan is also involved in the project and will be the launch export customer for the Super-7.[13]

F-8/Finback Program

The Shenyang Aircraft Corporation's F-8 and F-8-2 interceptor development programs are among China's most ambitious military R&D undertakings. The F-8, whose development lasted from 1964 to 1979, was first flight-tested in June 1969. Although the PLAAF began deploying the F-8 in the early 1980s, it was dissatisfied with the aircraft and still considered it an "operational test aircraft" as late as 1989. Therefore, the PLAAF established requirements to modify the F-8 as the F-8-2. The requirements that were given to the Ministry of Aviation Industry emphasized two primary needs: a new fire control system—including a larger radar antenna for an increased search and track capability—and a more powerful engine.[14] The first F-8-2 prototype flew in June 1984, and design flight testing was completed in October 1987.

However, China's aviation industry was still not able to satisfy the PLAAF's requirements fully. What ensued was a remarkable breakthrough in cooperation involving the U.S. government, the PLAAF, and the Chinese aviation ministry. After long negotiations, the parties concluded a foreign military sales (FMS) agreement under a

---

[13]Fink and Proctor (1989a), pp. 82–83, Agence France Presse (1993); "China Favors Russia over Rolls Royce" (1993).

[14]The senior author visited the Shenyang Aircraft Corporation eight times from 1987 to 1989. According to various articles in *Hangkong Shibao*, the F-8-2 incorporated 157 new or modified pieces of F-8 equipment from 1986 to 1989, which amounted to about one-third of all the F-8's equipment. Some of these modifications include the WP-13 engine, the FDSX-02 and FDSX-03 electronic antiskid brake system, the KJ-12 autopilot, the use of titanium alloy in 64 load-bearing areas, and a new radome. During the development process, 94 primary experiments were performed.

program known as "Peace Pearl" to upgrade the F-8-2's fire control system (Fink and Proctor, 1989b, p. 70).[15]

Following the June 1989 events in Tiananmen Square, the United States suspended arms sales to China. Chinese technicians were allowed to resume work on the program a few months later, but Beijing decided in May 1990 not to proceed beyond the development stage of the Peace Pearl program (Mann, 1990). The two F-8-2 prototypes and a mock-up delivered to the Peace Pearl prime contractor (Grumman Corporation) were subsequently shipped back to China in January 1993, along with four shipsets of avionics-upgrade kits.[16]

In spite of this setback, Chinese aviation industry officials continued development of their F-8-2 variant with a new domestic fire control system. PLAAF and PLA naval aviation maintenance personnel conducted three months' training on the F-8-2 at the Shenyang Aircraft Corporation from April to June 1990, and CCP General Secretary Jiang Zemin visited the F-8-2 production facility at Shenyang in October 1990 (Zhu, 1990). The first F-8-2s were finally deployed to a naval aviation unit in 1992.[17]

FB-7: A Viable Program?

The second aircraft that shows China's experience in developing an aircraft from scratch is the B-7/FB-7, which is under development at the Xian Aircraft Company for naval aviation.[18] If the aircraft is actually produced, not more than 20 aircraft are expected to be completed. Although the air force initially considered possible pur-

---

[15]From its outset in 1985 until its cancellation in May 1990, the Chinese F-8-2 development project actually consisted of two programs. One program was the integration of an American fire control system acquired through the "Peace Pearl" program. The second program involved the installation of a Chinese fire control system. Peace Pearl was a $502 million project funded solely by the PLAAF through a U.S. FMS program. The PRC–U.S. program originally called for modernizing 50 basic F-8-2 aircraft with a modified Westinghouse AN/APG 66 radar and fire control computer, a Litton LN-39 inertial navigation system, and a head-up display.

[16]"USA Cancels Defunct Chinese Contracts" (1993).

[17]Discussion with PLA official.

[18]The model of the aircraft shown at the Paris Air Show was designated the B-7. However, during discussions with PLAAF and aviation ministry officials in China, they all called it the FB-7, and jokingly called it the FB-4 after the U.S. F-4.

chases, it is not interested in acquiring any of the aircraft. This is probably even more the case since acquiring the Su-27s.[19]

The status of the B-7/FB-7 interdictor-strike aircraft at Xian remains in question because of technical difficulties and competition for funding, although some sources claim that at least two prototypes were flying as of late 1993. Given the aviation ministry's experience with other aircraft, at least five prototypes, including one for stress tests, will be required to complete a full test program. The test program began as early as 1988 and is not yet complete. A model of the B-7/FB-7 was first revealed at the Paris Air Show in September 1988, but had been under development for several years.

The tandem-seat B-7/FB-7 has a compound-sweep shoulder wing and four underwing stores stations, wingtip air-to-air missile launch rails, and internal 23 mm cannon and uses two "locally manufactured" (probably assembled) WS-6 reheated turbofans (Rolls Royce Spey Mk202), giving a maximum speed of around Mach 1.7. China originally acquired 50 Spey engines and production rights in 1975, but was unable to use them until the B-7/FB-7 was developed. It is not known just how many engines, if any, China produced or assembled beyond the original 50. However, by the time the Xian Aircraft Company began using them in the B-7/FB-7, they were no longer in production in the United Kingdom, and Rolls Royce had to scramble to secure some spare parts for them.

This program is also representative of how the Chinese deal with foreign experts assigned to assist with particular programs. For example, a Rolls Royce representative at Xian was never allowed to see the aircraft. If there was a question concerning the engine once it was in the aircraft, the Chinese would go to the representative's hotel room and ask some very general questions like "if this were to happen, how would you deal with it?"[20] As one military official stated, "The B-7/FB-7 program was originally an engine looking for an aircraft, but is now an aircraft looking for an engine." Negotiations over licensed production of the Turbo-Union RB.199 took place but were apparently unsuccessful.

---

[19]Based on the senior author's conversations with aviation ministry and PLAAF officials.

[20]Senior author's discussion with Rolls Royce representative.

K-8/L-8 Trainer

In the early 1980s, Pakistan and China established a joint venture to build a two-seat combat trainer designated L-8 by the Chinese and K-8 by the Pakistanis at the Nanchang Aircraft Manufacturing Corporation (NAMC). The L-8/K-8, powered by a Garrett TFE731-2A turbofan, is equipped with a Rockwell-Collins electronic flight instrumentation system, with two displays in the front and two in the rear cockpit. Martin-Baker is providing the Mk.10L ejection seats for the aircraft. The first prototype crashed in late 1989 just before it was to be shown to an international audience. The L-8/K-8 made its debut outside China at the Singapore Air Show in March 1992, although the aircraft did not fly because of a probable engine control problem. After the first prototype crashed, four additional prototypes were used to complete the flight-test program by early 1993. Three of the prototypes are involved in the flight-test program, with a fourth providing a ground test-rig.[21]

Reports indicate that a second assembly line was to be established by the end of 1994 at Pakistan's Kamra aircraft factory. Kamra currently produces about 45 percent of the aircraft and will start importing aircraft assemblies from Nanchang for final assembly in Pakistan. Pakistan took delivery of the first six of 75 aircraft in October 1994.[22] While the Chinese aviation ministry has stated that the PLAAF will require more than 200, the air force has continued to resist ordering any of these aircraft. The L-8/K-8 is reportedly intended to provide final training for PLAAF pilots for the Shenyang F-5 attack aircraft, and intermediate training for pilots converting to the F-7 and F-8 fighters. The L-8/K-8 also has a secondary combat role and is fitted with four underwing hardpoints that can carry a mix of bombs, unguided rockets, and air-to-air missiles. In addition, Bangladesh and Sri Lanka have expressed interest in purchasing the aircraft.[23]

---

[21]"K-8 Makes International Debut" (1992); "Pakistan is Expected to Confirm the First K-8 Order" (1992).

[22]Discussion with industry representative, November 1994.

[23]"K-8 Makes International Debut" (1992); "Pakistan is Expected to Confirm the First K-8 Order" (1992).

NEW PROGRAMS FOR THE NEXT DECADE: MYTH OR REALITY?

Of the five factories that currently design or produce combat aircraft (Shenyang, F-8; Chengdu, F-7 and F-10; Guizhou, FT-7; Nanchang, A-5; and Xian, B-6 and FB-7), the only real design competition exists between Shenyang and Chengdu. Besides the F-8-2, the only new combat aircraft undergoing flight testing is the naval aviation's FB-7 (also identified as the B-7) ground attack aircraft at Xian. Comparing the time it has taken to complete development of past aircraft—including the F-8 and F-8-2—and given the likely diversion of funds to purchasing foreign aircraft, the FB-7 will not be ready for deployment until at least the late 1990s—and even then in small numbers (not more than 20). If other aircraft are being designed, past experience suggests it will be well into the next decade before they are ready for deployment.

The situation is further complicated by frequent Chinese and Western articles stating that China's aviation industry is developing new fighter aircraft, but it is not clear whether any of these programs actually exist today (O'Lone, 1987, 1989). For example, in January 1994, China's official Xinhua news agency reported that China plans to design and produce advanced jet fighters by 2000. In the article, the head of the state-owned aviation industry, Zhu Yuli, stated (Reuters, 1994a):

> China's goal is to build not only an indigenous fighter, but also advanced turbojet engines and military helicopters. By the year 2000, China will be able to design and produce its own advanced fighter planes for the People's Liberation Army. China will also build a complete research and production system for advanced helicopters and be able to design and produce turbojet engines for military planes. In the field of transports, the Yun-7, Yun-8 and Yun-12 series will be further improved, the target of designing and producing large passenger planes will be reached and the civil aircraft industry will be gradually formed.

The Chengdu Aircraft Factory has been actively, but unsuccessfully, involved in trying to develop a new fighter for about 15 years. The program apparently began as the F-9, a canard-equipped supersonic aircraft that began development in 1970 and was canceled after prototype construction in 1979, without ever flying. The original F-9 program apparently evolved into the F-10 or "New Fighter" program.

According to a USAF estimate, the F-10 fighter, which is based on the Israeli Lavi, is likely to be produced sometime after the year 2000 and appears to be the focus of current development efforts at introducing a new multirole combat aircraft into the Chinese airpower inventory.[24] Although attempts to produce such a markedly more capable Chinese fighter have failed in the past, those efforts did not involve pervasive foreign assistance and use of foreign dual-use technologies characteristic of the F-10 program.[25]

According to a March 1995 account in *Aviation Week and Space Technology*, the Chengdu Aircraft Corporation is nearing completion of an initial prototype of the F-10, incorporating design features analogous to some found in the F-16, while also utilizing technologies first developed in the Israeli Lavi. Current estimates project an initial flight test "in the next year or two" and an "initial operating capability in 10 years." (Fulghum, 1995, p. 26.) However, it remains unclear at this point what specific technologies or systems Israel has provided to China for such a project. Most accounts suggest that technology transfer has focused principally on avionics and radar, with China still seeking to acquire Russian engines to serve as the powerplant for the F-10.

The results of the F-10 program will reveal a great deal about whether the Chinese are yet capable of configuring their R&D process in a manner that will enable them to maximize emergent opportunities to acquire advanced defense technology from abroad. However, it is far too early to conclude that the Chinese system will be able to overcome the pervasive legacies of the "old" R&D system.

---

[24]For further details, consult "Mainland Researches and Develops Jian-10 Fighters Modeled on Israel's Lavi" (1994); Mann (1994).

[25]Based on discussions with Headquarters USAF/INX, August 1994. It is the authors' view that the F-10, if produced at all, will not be deployed until at least the year 2002. Given the Chinese track record for the F-8-2 and FB-7, they simply cannot speed up the development cycle, which will take about eight years between the first test flight and final deployment to an operational unit.

RUSSIA AND THE PLAAF

Following the Tiananmen incident in 1989 and the subsequent collapse of the Soviet Union, China turned to Russia for assistance in modernizing its forces. In July 1990 (just two months after China decided not to proceed with the Sino-U.S. Peace Pearl FMS program), Military Commission Vice-Chairman Liu Huaqing and Aviation Minister Lin Zongtang led a delegation to Russia to visit a MiG-29 production facility and to discuss the possible purchase of MiG-29s and Su-27s.[26]

The transaction was delayed amid the uncertainties surrounding the August 1990 failed coup in Moscow but was finally completed in March 1991. China reportedly paid more than US$1 billion for 26 Su-27s and related armament, missiles, logistics, and pilot training.[27] The Su-27 is one of the most modern, capable fighter aircraft in the world. It has a state-of-the-art weapon system and is capable of using a wide variety of air-to-air and air-to-ground ordnance. The aircraft are equipped with AA-10 ALAMO and AA-11 ARCHER air-to-air missiles and are currently stationed at the PLAAF's 3rd Air Division at Wuhu airfield, 250 km west of Shanghai, in south-central China. According to the Chinese paper *Cheng Ming* in Hong Kong, PLAAF fighter pilots at the lieutenant level entered a 12- to 18-month training course in Russia, beginning in June 1991. Prior to the departure of these Chinese pilots, some Russian pilots visited Chinese training sites and considered the quality of China's pilots to be rather inferior (BBC, 1991a).

The consummation of the Su-27 sale and a host of activities in the wake of Boris Yeltsin's December 1992 trip to Beijing generated widespread expectations in the West and in East Asia of a rapid infusion of advanced Russian military hardware into the Chinese military system, and the air force in particular. Over the next two years, China took possession of a more extensive array of advanced defense equipment from abroad than at any time since the late 1950s. During Yeltsin's trip to Beijing, the Russian president said that China

---

[26]Cheung (1990), p. 30; "Command of the Skies" (1991, pp. 8–9).

[27]Of this, 35 percent of China's payment is in hard currency and the remainder in barter goods (Mann, 1992).

had ordered US$1.2 billion in Russian equipment in 1992 alone (Ackerman and Dunn, 1993, p. 57). By early 1994, in addition to the Su-27 Flankers, the Chinese had purchased ten Il-76 Mainstay transports, which are now located at the PLAAF's 13th Air Division near Wuhan to support the air force's airborne troops; at least 24 Mi-17 Hip helicopters assigned to the army aviation corps[28]; and 100 (four batteries) SA-10 Grumble (S-300) SAMs for the PLAAF's units responsible for the defense of Beijing (Mecham, 1993).

But it was soon evident that there were severe impediments to sustained, large-scale purchases of Russian equipment. The anticipated delivery of a second batch (24) of Su-27 aircraft, which had reportedly been awaiting delivery from the Komsomolsk production facility since 1993, was instead subject to repeated delays.[29] Some observers believed that the second set of aircraft would be assigned to naval aviation units on Hainan Island for use over the South China Sea, but these aircraft remained undelivered in early 1995. In an April 1995 discussion with a group of knowledgeable military researchers, these individuals informed one of the authors that the PLAAF had been severely chastened by the prohibitive logistics and maintenance costs associated with the Su-27.[30] These researchers also reported that the weight and performance characteristics of the aircraft had exacted an unanticipated toll on runways constructed for much less demanding aircraft. Based on these admissions, it seemed far from certain that the PLAAF had yet realized a meaningful enhancement of its air power capabilities from the Su-27 purchases.

However, it is also possible that the Chinese were unprepared to proceed with additional aircraft purchases unless the Russian aviation industry consents to more forthcoming arrangements on either coassembly or coproduction. A March 1995 Russian television report suggested increased Chinese pressure for licensing of Su-27 technology for transfer to China (Ostankino TV, 1995). In May 1995, industry sources reported that China had reached agreement on the long-

---

[28]Numerous open sources and discussions with Chinese and foreign military personnel.

[29]"U.S., French Fighter Sales to Taiwan Nudge Mainland China Closer to Russia" (1993); discussion with Headquarters USAF/INX, August 1994.

[30]Jonathan Pollack, discussion with Chinese military researchers, Beijing, April 1995.

pending sale of the second set of Su-27s, with delivery anticipated during the remainder of 1995 and 1996. The sources also indicated an "agreement in principle" on licensed production of the Su-27 in Shenyang, although it seemed very likely that negotiations over the terms of such transfer would continue for some time.[31]

But the spate of rumored or reported sales of a wide array of advanced Russian aviation systems repeatedly if uncritically cited in various publications (especially between 1992 and 1994) fueled expectations that have subsequently proven unfounded or unrealistic. Although there may be partial credibility to some of these reports, many have been discredited, even if citations in the professional literature continue to imply or assert that these transactions are still under way. Many of these reported "acquisitions" and "negotiations" must be regarded as highly speculative and must be treated accordingly.

For example, the following information has been reported in various Western and Asian media in recent years:

- In late 1992, China was reportedly seeking to procure 50 to 90 MiG-31 Foxhounds, many to be produced in China. One specialist on Chinese military affairs (Chongpin Lin) has claimed that the MiG-31 deal may be much larger than is now projected, with a Guizhou factory expected to produce 600 aircraft, 400 of which would be sent back to Russia. China was also purportedly discussing purchases of four or more Tu-22M Backfire bombers and two Kamov Ka-27 Helix ASW helicopters.[32] None of these sales have been consummated as of the spring of 1995.
- A separate press report claimed that the PLAAF was to take possession of 24 MiG-31s by April 1995, even while also negotiating for licensed manufacture of up to 150 of the aircraft over the next eight years with the help of a 1,500-strong Russian expatriate workforce.[33] The Chinese purchase of MiG-31 fighters was purportedly to be accompanied by Russian engineers who would

[31]"'Made in China' Deal Is Forged for Su-27s" (1995).

[32]"China's Military Aircraft Inventory," (1992), p. 48.

[33]"U.S., French Fighter Sales to Taiwan Nudge Mainland China Closer to Russia" (1993).

help to revitalize an outdated factory in southern China (presumably in Guizhou). According to one analyst, the intent was not to produce MiG-31s as much as it is a first step toward a new manufacturing capability (Mecham, 1993). Despite such elaborate claims, no reports of purchases or technology transfer of the Foxhound have appeared for over two years, casting considerable doubt on the credibility of these claims.

- According to a Japanese press report in early 1995, a prototype of a next-generation Chinese fighter aircraft powered by an improved version of the RD-33 engine used in the MiG-29 was first flight-tested in Shenyang in October 1994. The report further claimed that Russian technicians had provided vital technical assistance in provision of the new engine (Hamamoto, 1995).
- Another Russian weapon that is a supposed candidate for procurement by China is the AS-15 air-launched cruise missile, which has a 3,000-km range and is capable of being launched by the PLAAF's B-6D bomber.[34] The status of any proposed transaction remains uncertain in the spring of 1995.
- Russia is also alleged to have agreed to provide China with the naval Su-27K version, which would facilitate China's drive to develop a blue-water navy (Mecham, 1993). As of May 1995, however, no such transactions have yet occurred.
- According to reports in Taiwan's *Lien Ho Pao* (United Evening News), Russia will produce the latest Sukhoi Su-33 and Su-35 fighters for China, in addition to the previous purchase of Su-27s.[35] No such transactions are known to have occurred.
- According to a Russian source in Beijing, as disclosed in the Japanese press, China in 1990 had supposedly reached agreement with Russia to introduce the newest Russian jet fighter (the Su-25) into the PLAAF. China reportedly planned to purchase about 20 Su-25s and to use them for the purpose of mastering new production technologies, thereby improving its production

---

[34]"U.S., French Fighter Sales to Taiwan Nudge Mainland China Closer to Russia" (1993).

[35]*Lian Ho Pao,* as cited in "US Defence Envoy's Trip Set to Boost Military Ties" (1993).

capability of fighter aircraft.[36] More than four years later, no sales of this aircraft have been disclosed.

- The PLAAF has plans to order an unspecified number of AN-124 military cargo transports.[37] These claims have proven more credible.

Although many of these reports derive from presumed or known Chinese explorations with Russian defense firms, the credibility of these claims in their totality is open to doubt. Some of this speculation has probably been stimulated by Russian arms suppliers or by sources in Taiwan. But different segments of the Chinese aviation industry (in particular the separate complexes of factories and facilities in Shenyang and in Chengdu that dominate Chinese fighter aviation) have also encouraged these reports. But the accuracy and reliability of these reports remain questionable, if only because the Chinese aviation industry is simply incapable either in budgetary, technological, or infrastructural terms to sustain aircraft acquisition programs of such scale, complexity, and diversity.

This flurry of reports nevertheless caused much concern among China's neighbors, and this also helped open the market for Russian weapons in Southeast Asia. For example, in mid-1994 Malaysia purchased some MiG-29s after several years of negotiations. However, several issues must be kept in mind when evaluating the potential contributions of the Russian aviation industry to any dramatic improvement in the PLAAF's capabilities:

- Russia faces a credibility problem in Asia. The USSR never enjoyed a good reputation for postsale product support, and since its breakup, the situation has deteriorated further. For example, the Indian Air Force, which has 43 ground attack and fighter squadrons using MiGs (from MiG-21s to MiG-29s), said in late 1992 that it was scrambling for spare parts to keep its MiGs operational (Mecham, 1993).
- As noted previously, the funds needed to conduct full-scale procurement of Russian equipment are not available to the Chinese.

---

[36]"PRC Plans to Purchase Soviet Su-25 Fighters" (1990), p. 6.

[37]"China Orders Il-76 Transports" (1993).

- At the same time, there may be a growing unease within Russia about the wisdom of widespread transfer of advanced Russian defense technologies to the Chinese.
- China has long stressed the importance of indigenous production, and the manufacturing sector would fiercely resist attempts to procure equipment from foreign sources on a major scale. Given the time lags required to develop the manufacturing infrastructure to build fighters, which will undoubtedly be lengthened by the advanced nature of an aircraft like the Su-27, China would be highly unlikely to be able to manufacture substantial numbers of these aircraft until well past the year 2000. If the Su-27, or any other Russian aircraft, is chosen to be the next standard Chinese fighter, a lengthy development cycle could again result in China building its air force around an aircraft that is old by the time it enters service in appreciable numbers.

China has little interest in procuring large numbers of foreign fighters. The Chinese ultimately want to be self-sufficient in equipment procurement; self-sufficiency continues to be the guiding principle of their modernization efforts. Most Chinese dealings with foreign suppliers have focused on obtaining critical technologies (e.g., avionics, system integration, turbofan engine production, composite construction, low-observable technology, etc.), which they would seek to incorporate into their own designs. Thus, China does not intend to sacrifice indigenous development and production for foreign fighter purchases. Even though it is likely to be ten years or more before China is able to field fighters comparable to today's state-of-the-art aircraft, the Chinese nevertheless remain committed to such a course of action.[38]

THE FIGHTER FORCE

Barring a major change in Chinese threat perceptions or an appreciable augmentation of the Chinese defense budget, the PLAAF should expect a continuation of current funding trends. With no new aircraft ready to enter production in the near future (i.e., the next 8–10 years) and the previously discussed budget constraints in place,

---

[38]Based on discussions with Headquarters USAF/INX, August 1994.

future procurement will likely continue in a manner consistent with recent practice. Fighter production for domestic use is shown in Figure 17.

In addition, as discussed earlier, much of the manufacturing capability that was used to achieve the pre-1980 levels of production is now employed in the production of civilian goods. This trend serves to reinforce the budget reductions evident during the 1980s. Using the service life estimates found in Table 5, Figure 18 provides a prediction of the Chinese fighter force (PLAAF and naval aviation).

The spreadsheet model that is the basis for Figure 18 can be found in Appendix F. China does not publish official figures on inventory and airframe life, making it necessary to estimate these numbers to project future inventories. By constructing a spreadsheet covering 1954 to 2005, inventory levels for all aircraft can be reviewed to ensure consistent trends in production, service life, and retirement. Cross-checking totals with numerous open sources provides some degree of confidence in the individual types and overall totals. When in-

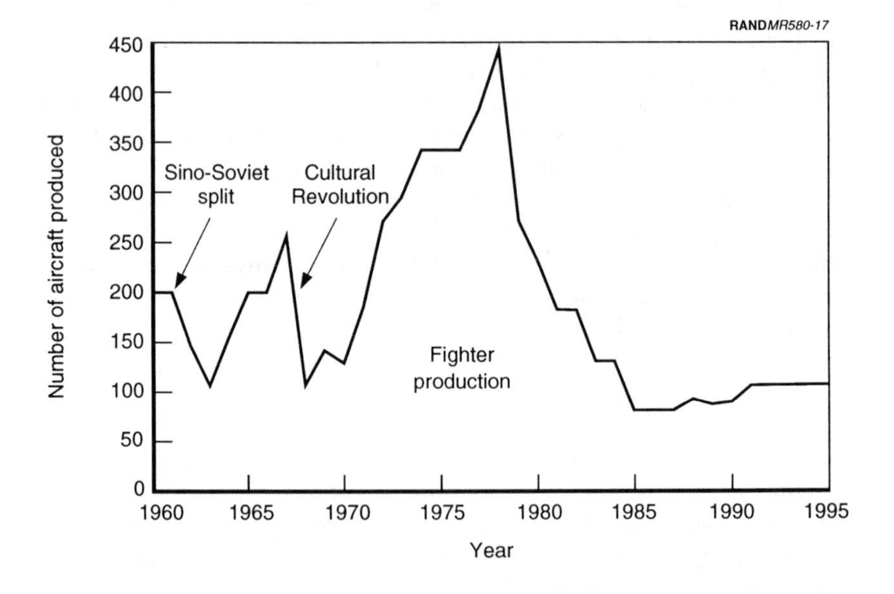

Figure 17—Chinese Jet Fighter Production, 1960–1995

Table 5

Chinese Fighter Force Projection

Aircraft	Assumed Service Life (years)	Number in 1994	Number in 2005
F-6	28	2,824	544
F-7	25	586	919
A-5	20	630	324
F-8	25	205	466
Su-27	30	26	70
FB-7	25	0	21
Totals		4,297	2,344

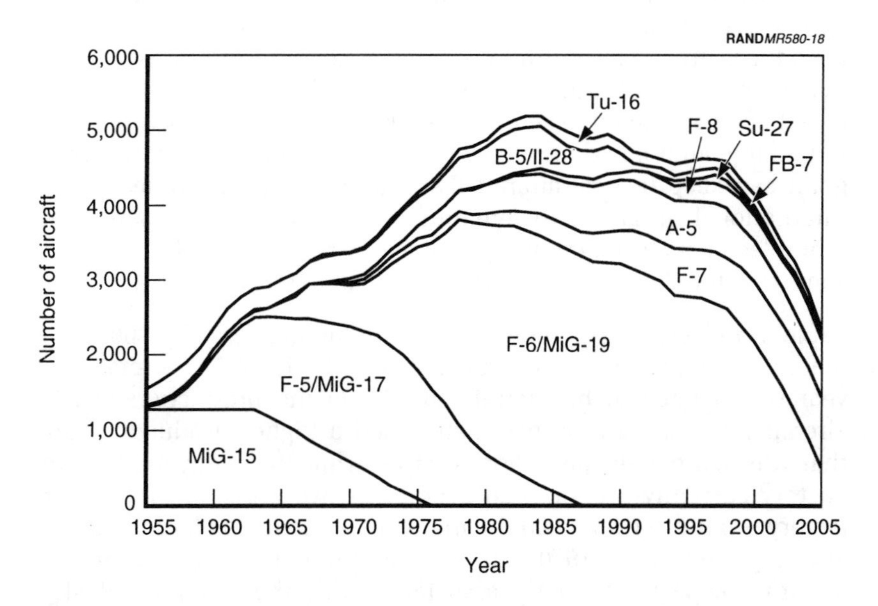

Figure 18—Chinese Jet Fighter Inventory, 1955–2005

consistencies between sources are encountered, they are resolved by smoothing the results over a number of years.[39]

---

[39]The most used source in this methodology is IISS's *The Military Balance*, issues from 1960 to 1993–1994. Issues of Aviation Advisory Services Limited's *International Air*

The service lives listed in Table 5 are a compromise between the useful airframe life, generally computed in hours, and the absolute age considered practical to keep a fighter flying. The low flight time experienced by Chinese pilots translates into low utilization rates for the aircraft, allowing them to be used for many years. If an average flight time of 100 hours per year were assumed, along with a 3,000-hour airframe life, then a 30-year service life would result. However, other aging processes affect the utility and reliability of aircraft. Corrosion is the primary enemy of old aircraft. The amount of corrosion present is highly dependent on where an aircraft has been stationed, and how it has been maintained and overhauled. Planes stationed near salt water, or in moist climates, are exposed to more-corrosive environments. Manufacturing and overhaul methods can introduce stress concentrations, and small imperfections in raw materials can greatly affect the useful service life. While these factors have been considered in setting these limits, the willingness to commit a large amount of resources to a rework and maintenance program can keep tactical aircraft flying longer than the times listed. International programs to remanufacture Northrop F-5s are good examples of such programs. But it seems highly improbable to assume that the Chinese are particularly adept at such tasks.

Table 5 projects a 45-percent drop in the fighter force by 2005. To maintain the present force structure, an additional 175 aircraft per year would need to be manufactured, placing production at 239 aircraft per year. China has maintained a higher production rate than this figure in the past. For example, while the Shenyang Aircraft Factory currently produces an average of two F-8s per month, the factory produced over 3,000 F-6 interceptors, reaching 50 per month at one period in the 1970s. It is unclear how much of the manufacturing capacity formerly associated with the aircraft industry could again be harnessed to produce aircraft and how efficiently it could produce modern high-technology aircraft. It is safe to say that, barring a substantial escalation in the external threat to China, the needed resources will not be available, thwarting large-scale modernization of the PLAAF during the next ten years.

Forces & Military Aircraft Directory dating from 1972 to 1991 were also frequently referenced. The major source for cross-checking was Cohen and Forsberg (1993).

Moreover, all of the aircraft that China is capable of manufacturing in large numbers are presently obsolete, such as the F-7 and F-8. Developing an indigenous capacity to produce more-advanced aircraft, such as the Su-27 or F-10, would take a substantial period of time and would entail an order-of-magnitude increase in aircraft price. In short, dramatic improvements in Chinese airpower capabilities are not going to take place over the near to mid term.

Finally, the Chinese appear unable to afford more than one full-scale primary fighter development program at any one time. But this does not mean that they will not continue to maintain R&D programs on other fighters. For example, a decision to produce the F-10 would very likely impede full realization of Chinese plans for coproduction of the Su-27. However, it is entirely possible that competing military aviation centers would seek to keep the prospect of other major sales alive, even if there were no realistic possibility of sustaining high rates of production of different modern aircraft on a simultaneous basis. Even assuming realization of a coproduction arrangement, the costs of any such transaction will remain very high, with full domestic content production of the aircraft and its associated weapon systems taking a decade or more. Irrespective of Chinese decisions on the F-10 or Su-27, the cost of full-scale production of either aircraft will also have a major effect on other programs, such as the FB-7.

THE BOMBER FORCE

Figure 19 provides an overview of the development of the Chinese bomber force, including both air force and naval aviation. Like the fighter force, it built up steadily—with a pause during the Cultural Revolution—to reach a peak in the mid-1980s. The aircraft are described in Appendix E. China has maintained a sizable force of bombers, but has never used them operationally. The earliest mission of the bomber fleet was as a deterrent against U.S. actions in the Korean War. Chinese bombers did not attack allied bases in the south, in return for the U.S. limiting its bombing to the Korean peninsula (Bueschel, 1968, p. 22). Following the war, deterrence against the Nationalists on Taiwan and against U.S. forces in Japan replaced the Korean mission. The Sino-Soviet split made deterrence a major factor in dealing with the Soviet Union. China demonstrated

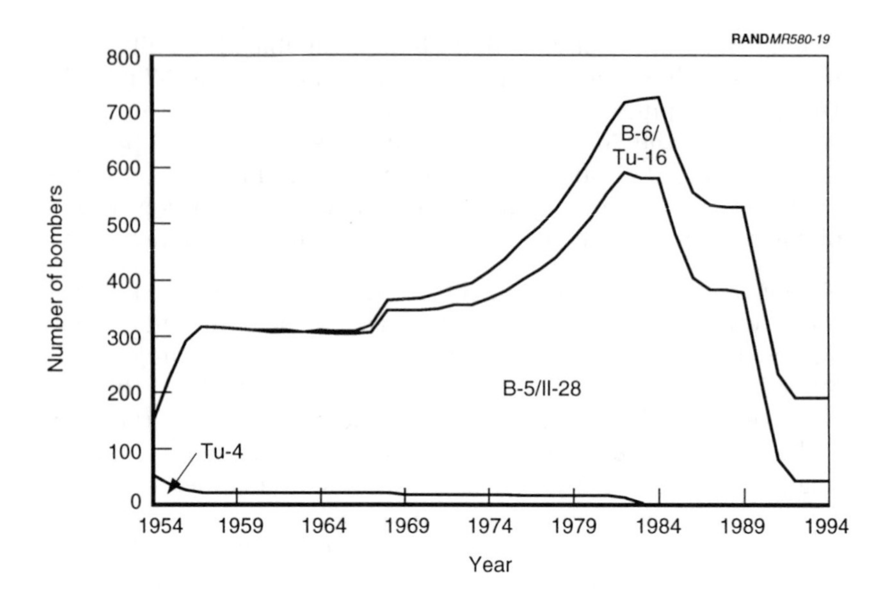

Figure 19—Chinese Bomber Inventory

an operational air-delivered atomic bomb in May 1965, strengthening this deterrent posture.

But the PLAAF has never demonstrated that it can effectively employ its strategic bomber force. The total bomber force inventory declined steeply from 1989 to 1991, given the retirement of the B-5 from air force service. This is a timely change in view of the aircraft's extremely limited bombing capability and the poor air force results in the 1979 Vietnam conflict. The fact that many of these aircraft were retired before reaching the ends of their useful lives and were not replaced is evidence that the PLAAF is serious about rationalizing its force structure and its missions.

Even so, the remainder of the bomber force consists of B-6s (Tu-16 Badgers), which are also of questionable value, especially when the pilot only receives an average of 80 hours of training per year. For example, the following article from the PLAAF's official magazine *Zhongguo Kongjun* is meant to praise the bomber force, but instead shows its real limitations:

> In September 1986, eight B-6 bombers from an air division in the Guangzhou MRAF participated in a seven hour inter-MRAF long range attack training exercise. The bombers first dropped bombs at a bomb range in Hunan Province, then flew through five provinces for over three hours to drop bombs at a bomb range in the northwest. Although the bombing results were good in Hunan, they were unsatisfactory in the northwest—it was a strange target, the sun was in their eyes, the target was difficult to find, and they were not on time over target, so they had to return home with those bombs. As a result, they only received a rating of two for this portion.
>
> In August 1987, another cell of eight bombers conducted a long range attack inspection based on a tactical scenario. The first target was hit during low level bombing, which was followed by a high altitude long distance navigation route with a direct run on a target range on another lake. Before entering a false enemy radar net, they rapidly descended to quietly close on the target. Following this, they used maximum climbing speed to conduct their bombing. However, before entering the bombing starting point, they met an unpredictable event. The number one target on an island in the middle of the lake could not be seen because the water had risen. By the time the first two aircraft discovered this, it was too late to switch to another target. The third aircraft quickly switched to target number six on a peninsula on the lake. The bombs were dropped and hit 15 meters from the center of the target, resulting in a rating of five."[40]

Moreover, the development of new generations of tactical ballistic missiles and the lessons of the 1991 Gulf War have prompted China to emphasize the employment of such capabilities for deep-strike operations, formerly conducted by bombers.[41] Naval aviation B-6Ds can be expected to continue to be important in sea control and sea strike roles, but the emphasis in deep-strike land-target bombardment will be on missiles. Tactical bombardment will continue to be performed by A-5 fighter bombers.

---

[40]*Zhongguo Kongjun* [China's Air Force], January 1989, pp. 41–43.

[41]"China Switches IRBMs to Conventional Role" (1994).

AIR TRANSPORT FORCES

China has always relied on ground transportation for logistics and personnel movement. As a land power of limited economic capability, it has relied on its internal lines of communication, establishing an effective rail transportation network. However, the speed required to deal with internal civil unrest and external threats has caused the PLAAF to be called into action several times to perform large-scale air transportation. In response to the 1950 Tibet action, Mao ordered the PLAAF to airdrop supplies. Total airdrop capability at that time was 12 C-46 and C-47 aircraft. During the 1979 Vietnam border war, transport aircraft flew 228 sorties carrying 1,465 troops and 151 tons of material. During the 1981 North China Exercise, the PLAAF conducted 1,191 parachute jumps and 107 insertions by transports and helicopters. These numbers are so small that it is hard to imagine air transport influencing the outcome of any major action. More recently, an Indian press report claimed that China transported a 10,000-man airborne division to Tibet in less than 48 hours in 1988, thereby demonstrating an enhanced rapid-reaction capability.[42] In addition, *Zhongguo Kongjun* reported that, following a three-and-one-half hour flight, an unidentified airborne unit conducted an airborne assault on an island in the South China Sea during October 1990, which was the first-ever landing on an island.[43]

In spite of these purported demonstrations of the effectiveness of air transportation, and the PLAAF's airborne forces mission, the PLAAF's only modern transports are 10 Il-76s and 25 Y-8s (AN-12), out of a force of 600 total transports. Most of the remainder are small piston-powered aircraft with high maintenance requirements and low cargo lift capability. Past practices have allowed the PLAAF access to commercial aircraft. This, along with a limited number of specialized military aircraft types, could provide a significant airlift capability. Commercial aviation is a rapidly growing segment of the economy, with 190 Western-designed jets in China as of September 1993.[44] Airbus Industry estimates that there will be 500 airliners sold

---

[42] *Indian Express*, December 29, 1992. Despite this claim, it is doubtful that 10,000 troops were involved in the exercise.

[43] *Zhongguo Kongjun* [China's Air Force], March 1992, p. 25.

[44] "Playing Catch-up" (1993), p. 65.

to China over the next 20 years.[45] Commercial aircraft can be used to transport personnel and light cargo, but their inability to move outsized cargo and vehicles could hinder attainment of PLAAF goals without appropriate investments in militarized transports. Also, civilian aircraft can be used to transport troops to the theater but have no capability for combat-zone air drops or landings.[46]

China has manufactured the Y-8, a version of the AN-12, since the early 1980s. While it is a capable design, the 25 available aircraft provide little wartime airlift capability. China's efforts to indigenously manufacture large jet aircraft without a foreign joint-venture partner have not yielded a usable product, forcing the PLAAF to look abroad for military airlift capability. The McDonnell Douglas MD-80 coproduction program has not provided the technology needed to allow the design and construction of large jet aircraft by the Chinese. Although MD-80s have been assembled in Shanghai since 1986, this has been kit assembly with a maximum of 25 percent non-U.S. content, of which only a small portion is Chinese.[47] Even if China had the ability to produce airliners, it is a far more complex problem to design and produce an effective combat aircraft.

According to an October 1993 *Jane's Defence Weekly* report, China has expanded its airborne forces to boost the rapid-response capabilities of the PLAAF. The three brigades of the PLAAF's 15th Airborne Army, headquartered in Kaifeng, Henan Province, are reportedly being upgraded to division-size elements. The 15th Airborne Army is the spearhead of the PLAAF's rapid-response forces and is expected to be among the first units to be called upon for military intervention. Elements of this unit were among those deployed to Beijing during the crackdown on prodemocracy activists in mid-1989. The 43rd Brigade, based in Kaifeng, is the first of these units to undergo expansion. Others are the 44th and 45th Brigades, based in Yingshan and Huangpi, Hubei Province, respectively. Military planners had decided that brigade-size forces are too small for their as-

---

[45]"1993 Forecasts—Part 7 of 7—Asia Pacific" (1992), p. 30.

[46]Many of the airports in the larger cities are joint civil-military airfields.

[47]Discussion with McDonnell Douglas representative. Negotiations for the original contract began in 1975 and were concluded in 1985 for a total of 25 MD-80s. This number was later increased to 35. Assembly of the first aircraft began in 1986. There will not be a point where the entire aircraft is made of Chinese-produced materials.

signed combat missions. Chinese brigades normally comprise about 3,000 to 4,000 troops, and divisions normally about 15,000.[48]

The mating of these larger brigades with the few Y-8 and Il-76 transports and appropriate civilian transports will allow the PLAAF airborne troops quick access to any internal trouble spots. Their ability to be delivered into combat on China's periphery has not been greatly enhanced, reflecting the true mission of these forces.

AERIAL REFUELING

Aerial refueling aircraft provide receiving aircraft with increased range and munition-carrying capability, and they add substantially to an air force's flexibility. The vast majority of China's fighter force is very short-ranged. Given China's limited transport force and problematic logistical structure, this consideration severely limits the mobility of PLAAF fighter units. In view of China's vast size, the PLAAF appears capable of providing point air defense around key targets, such as cities, but not providing an in-depth and flexible air defense for the country as a whole.

Tanker aircraft could greatly improve the PLAAF's defensive and offensive capabilities. *The New York Times* reported in August 1992 that China had acquired the technology to refuel its jet fighters in midair, an ability that would allow it to extend its power beyond China's borders. China, however, has never acknowledged obtaining the refueling technology, thought to have been acquired from Iran, Pakistan, or Israel (Kristoff, 1992).

According to Chinese and Western military officials, the PLAAF has equipped four of its combat aircraft with air refueling probe kits purchased from Iran. The kits are understood to have come from Iranian stocks purchased from the United States by the Shah. The Iranian refueling kit purchased by China is likely to be Beech refueling pods, along with "bolt on" probes provided by the United States for Iranian F-5 aircraft.[49] In addition, Israel's Bedek Aviation, the

[48]See Section 7 of Allen (1991) for the history and organization of the PLAAF's airborne forces.

[49]"Chinese Combat Refuelling Needs Tanker" (1991).

upgrade and refit side of Israel Aircraft Industries, has long promoted a package for converting transport aircraft to aerial tankers (Ackerman and Dunn, 1993, p. 59). The Chinese were also reported to be negotiating with Great Britain prior to the 1989 Tiananmen incident. The aviation ministry is believed to have converted a Yun-8 transport plane into an aerial refueling tanker, and it may also have similarly converted a B-6 into a test platform.

Foreign military experts believe that China faces huge obstacles in fully incorporating the refueling technology into its active inventory and doubt that the pilots could be counted on to refuel their fighters unless they have several years of practice. While the Su-27 has an aerial refueling capability, it is not known whether the Su-27s acquired by China are so equipped. China's B-6 bomber can also apparently be adapted for aerial refueling (Kristoff, 1992). According to Teng and Jiang (1990), the A-5 is the aircraft of choice, over the B-6, for aerial refueling.

One final note is the political aspect of providing pilots with enough fuel to be able to fly to Korea or Taiwan. The PLAAF has ample reason for concern about political reliability, especially concerning its pilots. According to Taiwan's Ministry of National Defense, 15 PLA pilots have defected to Taiwan in 12 military aircraft since 1958, not including several aircraft flown to South Korea in the 1980s. In May 1991, Taiwan ended its efforts to encourage Chinese military personnel to defect, canceling a program that offered defectors huge sums in gold. Previously, defecting PLAAF and naval aviation pilots, feted as "freedom seekers" and given high-paying jobs in Taiwan's air force, used to receive gold bars worth as much as $3 million. Taipei cut the rewards sharply in 1988, partly in response to public opinion, which was outraged when a defector complained his reward was not big enough. The most recent defector, a first lieutenant who flew an F-6 to Quemoy in 1989, received only $800,000 in gold (Reuters, 1991). According to one Hong Kong press report, the PLAAF and naval aviation have apparently tried to discourage pilots from defecting by installing antidefection devices on military aircraft so that they will "automatically crash" before they reach Taiwan (Lo, 1990). This suggests continued high levels of sensitivity about the loyalty of Chinese pilots.

AIRBORNE EARLY WARNING

The PLAAF has no AEW aircraft. Accordingly, the air defense capabilities of the force—its primary mission—will remain severely limited. Ground-based radars cannot provide adequate surveillance of such a vast nation as China, except at prohibitive cost. Accordingly, China's airspace could be penetrated by low-flying aircraft exploiting terrain masking and radar coverage limits. AEW aircraft do not suffer from these same constraints.

There have also been several unconfirmed reports about China's acquisition of an AEW capability. Based on the reported sighting in November 1993 of a photo of an Il-76 Airborne Early Warning and Control System (AWACS) with the PLA "August 1st (Ba Yi)" fin flash on it, the Taiwan newspaper *Lien Ho Pao* reported that China now has deployed an AWACS capability. The article stated that China imported 16 radar systems from the United Kingdom for Nimrod AWACS in 1990 and 1991. According to the report, China imported 10 Il-76 transports from Russia in 1993, of which Russia modified three into A-50 early warning aircraft (BBC, 1993b). Purchase of the Il-76 Mainstay AWACS has not been confirmed, but China is known to be looking at several options for acquiring some sort of AWACS capability. One of the options under study is the acquisition of a Russian radar and other equipment for fitting on a Chinese platform, with the Y-8 (AN-12 variant) military transport being considered (Ackerman and Dunn, 1993, p. 59). Such a capability, if acquired, would greatly improve Chinese air defense capabilities. However, the aircraft would have to be fully integrated into the air defense system, would have to be maintained adequately, and would have to be deployed and supported logistically, as needed.

MUNITIONS

Modern munitions are critical to enhancing the lethality of combat aircraft. The PLAAF posture in terms of air-to-air weapons is mixed. It possesses good short-range systems but until recently has been poorly equipped with modern radar-guided weapons. Information on stockpile levels is not available. For air-to-ground ordnance, however, the PLAAF is poorly equipped.

Air-to-Air Missiles

The Chinese discovered the linkage between aircraft weapons systems and air-to-air missiles on their first attempt to field a missile-equipped aircraft. The K-5 ALKALI missile, known as the PL-1 in China, was provided to China by the Soviets in November 1959. Although it was produced in trial lots in 1960, it was not approved for production until 1964. Two years of this time can be attributed to a poorly calibrated test radar, which was essential to the missile's beam rider guidance (Duan, 1989, p. 300). China had not fielded another radar-guided air-to-air missile since the PL-1 until the recently developed PL-10.

The PLAAF was the first air force in the world to feel the effectiveness of the IR-guided Sidewinder missile in combat. During the 1958 Taiwan Strait crisis, the PRC lost several MiG-17s to Sidewinder-equipped Nationalist F-86 Sabres. In 1959, two damaged Sidewinders were recovered from aircraft that managed to return after being hit (Zalonga, 1993). These were offered to the Soviets, who reverse-engineered them to create the ATOLL series and sold a manufacturing license to the Chinese along with MiG-21F-13s in 1962.

The Sino-Soviet split caused a disruption in the delivery of further hardware and technical support, causing the Chinese to reverse-engineer this missile, labeling it the PL-2. Range tests began in June 1964, and the PL-2 entered the inventory in 1967. The Chinese have continued to develop and deploy improved IR homing missiles, but did not successfully deploy any radar homing types until the late 1980s.[50]

---

[50]The PL-2B, incorporating an improved seeker and motor, began development in 1978 and was approved for production in December 1981. The PL-3 was another modification of the PL-2. It has larger control surfaces, a more powerful warhead, and an improved fuse. Its design began in 1965, and it was certified for production in 1980. Further Chinese IR missile developments produced the PL-5, an AIM-9G Sidewinder look-alike, in 1986. The PL-5B has an air-cooled seeker head for improved target discrimination and interchangeable IR and RF fuses with fragmenting and continuous-rod warheads. The PL-7 is a Matra Magic I look alike, produced in 1987. The PL-8 is reportedly a license-built Israeli Rafael Python 3, produced in air-to-air and surface-to-air models. The PL-8 has all-aspect engagement capability, an active laser fuse, and countermeasures capabilities. The PL-9 is apparently a development of the PL-5, with AIM-9P seeker technology incorporated. It is expected to be operational in 1995, as an

The PL-10 is projected to be an SAR homing missile with a design similar to the U.S. Sparrow on a much larger airframe. The PL-10 is an air-launched version of the Chinese-developed HQ-61 SAM. It is quite heavy (300 kg) for an air-to-air weapon. The PL-10 was developed to give the PLAAF an all weather air-to-air weapon to match the weapon system in the F-8-2 but appears very crude compared to the missiles available on the Su-27.

The Chinese are estimated to have bought the Su-27 with the AA-10 ARCHER and the AA-11 ALAMO air-to-air missiles. The aircraft has a very advanced weapon system that is capable of supporting more advanced weapons as they become available. The advances in the Su-27 and its weapon systems are worth examining to see the progress that it represents over current Chinese hardware.[51] The performance of the Slotback radar along with the AA-10 creates a formidable weapon system, which is among the best in the world in the medium-range environment. The match between the helmet-mounted sight and the AA-11 makes the Su-27 one of the world's most deadly close-in dogfighters.

If the Chinese could acquire the licenses and technologies needed to manufacture the Su-27 and its weapons, they would still be battling time and obsolescence. Their past efforts in aircraft production have no parallels to the complexity of producing an integrated aircraft and weapon system like the Su-27. It is unlikely the Chinese will be able to achieve an independent production capability in the near to mid

---

air-to-air and surface-to-air weapon. All of the IR-guided air-to-air missiles are similar in size and weight. They are carried on F-6, F-7, F-8, and A-5 aircraft.

[51]The AA-10 is available in six versions. The four versions commonly seen on the Su-27 are the AA-10a medium-range SAR, AA-10b medium-range IR, AA-10c long-range SAR, and AA-10d long-range IR. Two new versions were introduced in 1992: a long-range SAR missile with improved performance against low-flying and small targets and an active radar version, of unknown designation. All of the AA-10 missiles have a large 39-kg warhead with an active radar fuse. They are inertially guided for the initial phases of flight, with midcourse updates received from the launch-aircraft radar. The Su-27 can carry six AA-10s in a normal combat configuration, along with four AA-11 or other IR missiles. The AA-11 is assessed to be the most advanced short-range IR missile in service today. Its thrust vectoring and aerodynamic controls, combined with a wide-field-of-view seeker incorporating advanced countermeasures resistance and a large warhead, make it the standard of its class. When teamed with the helmet-mounted sight, radar, and IR capabilities of the Su-27, it is considered one of the most deadly systems in the air today. The AA-11 can be used on older aircraft, but without the helmet-mounted sight much of its capability would remain untapped.

term future (i.e., over the next five years). In the mid term (i.e., five to ten years), it is possible that a limited number of aircraft could be produced, but a true production capability would only emerge over the longer run (i.e., ten years and beyond). Furthermore, the PLAAF would have to restructure its concepts and approaches to pilot training and ground-based weapon control.

The net result of these factors is that, today, China primarily manufactures and fields IR missiles for air-to-air combat. A few modern systems are available, but not enough to change the character of the entire force. China will have to make major advances to produce complementary weapons and weapon systems that can compete with contemporary offerings from other countries. Until then, Chinese aircraft will face enormous odds in air-to-air combat.

Air-to-Surface Weapons

China manufactures a wide variety of free-fall bombs and rockets. Its only air-launched guided weapons are a helicopter-carried anti-tank missile and a number of antishipping missiles. China has no terminally guided bombs, rockets, or missiles for ground-attack aircraft in its inventory. This gap in equipment is consistent with the air defense mission that has received most of the PLAAF's attention, but it is a major deficiency for a modern air force.

The Chinese have a full family of general-purpose bombs, in 250; 500; and 1,000 kg sizes. Bombs designed for internal carriage on the B-5 (Il-28 Beagle) and the B-6 (Tu-16 Badger) are available in these sizes, as well as 1,500 and 3,000 kg. Cluster bombs are available with antipersonnel, antirunway, and sensor-fused anti-tank submunitions. Fuel air explosive bombs are available in 250 and 500 kg sizes. Rockets are manufactured in 57, 70, and 90 mm sizes with a variety of warheads. No laser, inertial, television, IR, or antiradiation guidance has been reported on any air-to-ground weapons.

The sole overland guided missile is an adaptation of the AT-3 Sagger missile, known as the H-8. The air-to-surface guided missiles in service, the C-601 and HY-4, are adaptations of the Soviet SS-N-2C Styx missile. The C-601 retains the Styx liquid-fueled rocket propulsion, while the HY-4 uses a turbojet. Both missiles use inertial midcourse guidance with active radar seekers for terminal guidance. Two

C-601s or HY-4s can be carried by the naval aviation's B-6 bomber. Two more antishipping missiles are under development. The YJ-1 is a solid-fueled missile similar to the AM-39 Exocet. The YJ-2 is somewhat larger, resembling a U.S. Harpoon missile. These are being marketed as the C-801 and C-802, respectively (Lenox, undated).

The total lack of precision-guided overland air-to-ground ordnance seen in the PLAAF is a glaring deficiency. Capabilities that could be reasonably expected include laser-guided bombs, guided anti-tank missiles, and possibly conventional stand-off missiles with terminal homing seekers. China does not have any tactical aircraft weapon systems capable of supporting such weapons and has little prospect of attaining a widespread capability in the near future. Foreign assistance will probably be required to achieve even a modest test and evaluation capability in a reasonable time frame. This gross deficiency will greatly inhibit China's effective application of airpower in all scenarios requiring strikes against land targets until it is corrected.

Surface-to-Air Missile Programs

The PLAAF is responsible for fielding and operating Chinese surface-based defenses. The deployment of SAM systems has been modest in comparison to the practices of the Soviet Union. The PLAAF has used its SAMs to defend population centers and military bases. There has never been an attempt to extend coverage to all of China, as was done in the USSR. China has primarily relied on reverse-engineered versions of the Soviet SA-2 missile and its associated radar and support systems. They have developed several indigenous SAM systems and variants (see Appendix G). In addition, their recent purchase of the SA-10 (S-300) system from Russia represents a major equipment upgrade, but not a change in operational philosophy.

China has shown no inclination to extend its SAM coverage beyond its traditional boundaries. Planned upgrades to its radar and missile systems will allow some additional defense against cruise missile and ballistic missile attack, but no substantial increase in coverage. The low number of modern SA-10 systems in country will keep China from risking them to defend border areas or armies in the field. The PLAAF's lack of an effective integrated air defense doctrine limits SAM usefulness in strategic and tactical air defense scenarios. This is a good example of all of the pieces that must be brought together to upgrade the effectiveness of the PLAAF in its primary mission area. Better missile systems and fighters will not help without a working identification friend or foe (IFF) system, an effective surveillance network, and a redundant command, control, communications, and intelligence system. All of these systems must be in place for the PLAAF to hope to do its job against an enemy equipped with a modern air force.

LOGISTICS AND MAINTENANCE LIMITATIONS

In addition to aircraft obsolescence and age problems, the air force also has logistics and maintenance limitations. Almost 100 percent of the air force's supplies are shipped by train, although the air force also has its own boat troops to ferry some supplies and fuel to bases along the coast and major rivers. Matters are made more difficult because not all spare parts are interchangeable. For example, because the rivets in each aircraft are hand drilled, the holes are not all in the same place. Therefore, when a subsystem, such as the radio, is pulled out to be repaired, the aircraft does not fly until that radio is replaced. In addition, pilots only fly one or two aircraft, and the members of bomber crews are fixed and do not switch around, which limits making efficient use of operational aircraft.[52]

Each base has a one-year supply of spare parts for each aircraft. This philosophy greatly limits the air force's mobility in case of a crisis. However, a number of supply depots are located around China. The PLAAF Logistics Department's air materiel organization at each level manages supply depots and warehouses and orders the supplies. Supply depots are organized on a three-tier structure—first-level depots are located in various military regions but are subordinate to HqAF; second-level depots are located in each military region and are subordinate to the MRAF headquarters; and third-level depots are located at and subordinate to operational units. First-level depots can either supply the second-level depots or send items directly to the unit if necessary.[53]

---

[52]The reason for this is that each regiment (25 aircraft) has three groups (eight aircraft each), which are further divided into three squadrons (two to three aircraft each).

[53]The Lanzhou MRAF does not have any first-level depots, but has second-level depots at Xian, Wulumuqi, and the He-Xi corridor.

At an aviation division or base, the field station is an independent logistics support unit under dual leadership of the air division and the MRAF headquarters' logistics department. It is responsible for organizing and supplying material and equipment and for providing continuous combined service support for operations and training. A field station at an airfield supporting two fighter regiments has about 930 personnel, including 170 officers and 760 airmen. Each airfield housing aircraft assigned to the division has its own field station.

The air force also has 21 major aircraft and engine repair facilities, employing over 40,000 personnel, to overhaul and repair aircraft and engines. With the exception of the F-8, which is sent back to the Shenyang Aircraft Factory for overhaul, the air force repairs and overhauls all of its own aircraft and engines. For example, the air force overhauled over 10,000 engines in 1989.[54]

As a general rule, the PLAAF's fighter engines require a major overhaul after 300 to 350 hours, a second overhaul after an additional 200 to 250 hours, and a third after an additional 150 hours. After that, the engines are scrapped. This is why pilots, who average only about 100 flying hours annually, are airborne within three minutes of starting their engines and shut them down before they reach the end of the runway and coast to the taxi apron upon landing.[55]

The conservative attitude and problems related to flying time are also reflected in the maintenance statistics commonly cited in PLAAF publications. For example, units are often cited for a 10 to 15 year accident-free record. This belies the fact that the air force's aircraft have numerous maintenance problems. For example, one PLAAF publication in 1989 described the situation where hydraulic-system malfunctions accounted for 25 to 50 percent of all fighter and ground attack aircraft malfunctions during the 1980s—accounting for 25 to 75 percent of all aircraft malfunctions. For the A-5, the air force spends 35 hours of maintenance for every one hour of flying time, and one PLAAF officer stated that the F-8 was down over 50 percent of the time due to radar malfunctions.

---

[54]Discussion during visit to PLAAF aircraft repair facilities.

[55]The senior author visited three repair facilities and about 10 air divisions/regiments and flying schools from 1987 to 1989.

CONCLUDING OBSERVATIONS

Even if its inventory problems are solved, China lacks several elements that are essential to an effective modern air force. The lack of AEW has been acknowledged in the open press, but there are no indications that aircraft to solve this problem have been ordered or are under construction. The complete lack of precision-guided weapons greatly compromises Chinese offensive capabilities. The acknowledged deficiencies in reconnaissance show few if any signs of improvement, with no significant capability for active or lethal electronic countermeasures in or projected for deployment.

Over the next ten years, there is little hope for the PLAAF to be more than a homeland air defense force with a very limited power-projection capability against a credible foe. To assess China's options in this overall context, we need to review the findings of our study and to consider the implications for China's future airpower goals.

Chapter Nine

CONCLUSIONS AND IMPLICATIONS

As the Chinese air force approaches its half-century mark as a military institution, it faces daunting challenges in fulfilling its role in defending and securing China's national interests. Having emerged rapidly in the 1950s as one of the world's largest air forces, the PLAAF went into a period of upheaval and decline that severely set back its development during the next two decades. It has only been during the reform era launched by Deng Xiaoping that the air force has been able to renew its quest for modernization and combat effectiveness.

As the Deng era draws to a close, however, the PLAAF's pursuit of institutional renewal remains highly incomplete. The air force leadership can take understandable satisfaction from the reconstitution of its officer corps, from the greatly enhanced emphasis on military professionalism, and from its newly realized opportunities for defining a set of longer-term interests and goals. But many of its core objectives still remain unfulfilled, and the prognosis for the next decade is far from certain. In this concluding section, we will examine the PLAAF's primary areas of "unfinished business" and will briefly assess the prospects for addressing these deficiencies in the years to come.

The air force faces five basic challenges in seeking to emerge as a more credible institution and combat force over the next decade and beyond. In simplified form, these are the challenges of (1) leadership and strategy, (2) manpower, (3) technology and infrastructure, (4) budget, and (5) competition. Each warrants brief review.

LEADERSHIP AND STRATEGY

The PLAAF has made undeniable headway in developing and promoting a senior officer corps committed to professional military goals. Even though clearly subordinate to the higher-level military leadership structure, this corps has enabled the air force to develop concepts of operations appropriate to its designated defense responsibilities. As noted previously, however, the PLAAF still operates under severe political constraints. Its primary mission remains air defense, and the vast bulk of its force structure is dedicated to this mission. But the PLAAF remains reluctant or unwilling to put forward more assertively a set of strategic concepts that would be appropriate to a fuller range of defense responsibilities—even under existing doctrinal constraints. These inhibitions will continue to limit opportunities for defining its future equipment requirements and for engaging effectively with other levels of the PLA hierarchy in building a more integrated national defense force that cuts across the Chinese military system as a whole. For example, although PLA writings refer increasingly to combined warfare operations and the like, measures undertaken to date in this regard (including by the PLAAF) seem very limited.

Thus, it will be incumbent on emerging leadership generations in the air force (1) to think in more comprehensive and innovative fashion about the prospective role of airpower in fulfilling China's national security goals, (2) to identify a set of equipment requirements associated with such tasks, and (3) to integrate these capabilities much more fully. Despite the lip service given to these tasks, it is clear that this process has a long way to go. It must appropriately begin with senior officers willing to sanction the exploration of uncharted territory, and who are then able to pursue institutional interests in relation to a larger policymaking process. The initial indications of the development of a more autonomous airpower strategy during the 1980s and early 1990s suggest that a more institutionally defined set of concepts and policies will emerge over the next decade but that this process will remain protracted. Success in these efforts will be critical if the PLAAF is to be able to present a more coherent sense of its longer-term institutional goals than has heretofore been the case.

MANPOWER

The PLAAF cannot possibly hope to realize more ambitious goals if it does not recruit, integrate, and train new generations of officers and support personnel capable of implementing more innovative airpower strategies. These needs will be true at all levels of the air force. As noted throughout this study, the PLA has long stressed the role of man in combat, particularly to compensate for equipment deficiencies. But the PLAAF does not fully prepare its pilots to fly in combat. Although part of this shortcoming can be explained by a three-decade hiatus in air force combat experience, other factors are also at work. PLAAF pilots do not receive nearly as much training time as their Western counterparts, and much of this training is not especially demanding. Many of these limitations are explained by serious logistic constraints, as well. The air force remains severely deficient in night combat and poor-weather flying, low-altitude attack tactics, mobility, and experience in flying against dissimilar aircraft.

Matters are rendered worse by the rigid structure imposed upon the pilots, such as strict GCI and the lack of initiative, which will continue to restrict the air force's advancement. For example, one foreign air force attaché in Beijing who was an F-6 pilot himself has stated that the "PLAAF never flies its aircraft to the edge of the envelope, so they will never know what the aircraft's capabilities really are." Recent reports of an increased accident rate—which some observers believe may have contributed to Cao Shuangming's unexpectedly early departure from PLAAF command—hardly seem likely to encourage efforts to truly test the potential of current or future aircraft. Unless the air force is better able to inculcate a philosophy that encourages its pilots to demonstrate their abilities more fully and unless it is prepared to allocate resources at all levels to accomplish these tasks, it is highly doubtful that even a more technologically advanced air force will translate into a more meaningful combat capability. The air force leadership must begin to address these shortcomings in the coming decade.

TECHNOLOGY AND INFRASTRUCTURE

The PLAAF's problems in acquiring, developing, and mastering advanced technology remain prodigious. As discussed in Chapter Eight, the air force lacks a clear concept and direction through which to shape its priorities and programs and to pursue them with a measure of consistency. These difficulties are rooted heavily in the absence of a coordinated R&D process that can define initial tasks, mobilize the requisite resources, and induce effective collaboration across the R&D process as a whole. A system committed to vertical integration is thereby far less able to achieve the lateral connections and relationships that remain vital to development and dissemination of new products and processes. As a result, Chinese aerospace R&D has long frittered away budgetary resources along unproductive or highly duplicative paths, with very little to show for its efforts.

Many of these problems are rooted in the inherent dilemmas of China's desire for technological autonomy, as manifested by the aviation industry, and the service's desire for acquiring new and improved equipment at as early a date as possible. Put simply, the defense industries are prepared to sacrifice near-term combat capabilities for longer-term independence from external sources of supply. Despite the convictions of the aviation ministry, it is poorly organized to make optimum use of its extant assets. A highly "stovepiped" R&D process, with each actor accustomed to maximum autonomy from rival factories and facilities within China, imposes enormous inefficiencies on the process as a whole. Thus, the presumed key to successful R&D management in the aviation sector would be whether a given undertaking is defined as a *zhong dian zhi yi* (literally, focal point) project. This designation would equate to very high level endorsement of a given project, the provision of the requisite funds for such an endeavor, and the capability of central leadership to cut off unproductive activities that can only drain scarce resources away from higher-priority projects.

The inability or unwillingness of the aviation industry to tackle these problems underscores the daunting challenges that China continues to face in the rational allocation of defense resources. Unless and until the leadership demonstrates a genuine determination to address these problems, it is no surprise that China (despite a vast ongoing scientific and engineering effort) continues to realize such modest accomplishments. At the same time, despite China's increased access to advanced aircraft technology from Russia and other potential suppliers, it is far from certain that the Chinese will prove fully able to maximize these opportunities within their own R&D process. This is the challenge of integration, synthesis, and high-level coordination that can only happen when defense programs are adequately funded and effectively led. This is a level of accomplishment and organization that the Chinese aviation industry has yet to achieve.

BUDGET

The PLAAF's problems are also financial. It is difficult to understate the scale of resources that would be required for the air force to make an effective transition to a credible, modernized force structure. This is even truer in relation to efforts to enhance China's indigenous design and production capability for newer generations of combat aircraft. Given the diverse range of newer airpower technologies that the aviation industry is seeking to incorporate in its weapon systems, it will cost significantly more for China to develop an indigenous manufacturing capability than it would to buy "off the shelf" items. But given the scale of China's airpower needs, the latter course is also not cost-effective.

Some of Taiwan's difficulties in designing and building its indigenous defense fighter highlight many of the problems that the PRC also confronts.[1] Serious design flaws and related problems in specialized manufacture have continued to plague the aircraft—even though the program has benefitted from excellent access to advanced U.S. engineering and technical assistance and has large numbers of highly skilled engineers from Taiwan associated with it. Problems related to engine development have proven especially acute, resulting in an airframe too heavy for the power plant. As a consequence of these multiple problems, costs for the aircraft have skyrocketed, with final "flyaway" costs estimated between $50 and 60 million per aircraft. Despite Taiwan's abundant financial resources, the final production run for the indigenous defense fighter will be

[1]For additional details, see Baum (1995).

approximately 130 aircraft, or roughly half of what was envisioned when the program began more than a decade ago. Comparable problems have repeatedly plagued PRC aviation projects in the past. Unless the Chinese are able to develop an engine appropriate to a new airframe, they face the prospect of yet another underpowered aircraft in the future. Given that the collaboration with Israel does not extend to engine development, Russia would therefore become the only plausible supplier for such a program.

In view of the scale of China's airpower requirements, it is likely to face far more acute budgetary pressures than those on Taiwan, in an environment where planners have far less to allocate. Indeed, if we examine China's aircraft priorities in recent years, there seems to be a general pattern of shifting from one potential project to another, but a very limited ability to sustain separate full-scale programs on a simultaneous basis. Thus, following the cancellation of the Peace Pearl program in May 1990, senior Chinese officials almost immediately explored the possibilities of more active weapon sale or technology transfer relationships with Russia and Israel. The initial purchase of 26 Su-27s in 1992 appeared to presage a much fuller military supply relationship with Russia, but by the end of 1994, the Chinese appeared to be moving ahead more vigorously to complete an agreement for manufacture of a new aircraft based mainly on the Israeli Lavi. If subsequent reports of an agreement in principle on licensed production of the Su-27 prove credible, it remains to be seen whether China would be able to realize fully the seeming opportunities for production of the F-10.

This pattern suggests an obvious conclusion: Although the aviation ministry and the air force would clearly like to pursue a range of programs simultaneously, the foreign exchange allocated to these activities will not permit full-scale pursuit of multiple activities. The reality of a constrained budgetary environment is likely to continue to impinge on China's future airpower development for the indefinite future. On this basis, Chinese military aviation is likely to give off multiple (and potentially contradictory) signals for some time to come, very likely with less to show for its efforts.

COMPETITION

The underlying element of budgetary stringency concerns the competing impulses that are at work within the defense sector. Air force planners are not alone in lobbying for development of more modern systems; in varying degrees, all the services are seeking to make their best case. We still know little about the inner workings of the Chinese defense decisionmaking process.[2] However, in comparison to its peers in strategic nuclear policy, in the ground forces, and in the naval forces, the Chinese air force does not appear especially advantaged. To a certain extent, this may reflect the inability of the air force to put forward a strategic concept that demonstrates persuasively the potential role of airpower, as compared to other defense priorities. Alternatively, this situation may simply reflect the lesser political clout of the air force leadership in the upper reaches of the PLA. In either case, it reinforces the belief that the defense modernization process is likely to remain one of incremental technological development and force enhancement, rather than a sudden breakthrough.[3] Given the scale of China's aircraft requirements and the still-large gap between the PLAAF's capabilities and those of the advanced airpower states, there can be no quick fix.

A SUMMING UP

This conclusion reinforces a judgment emphasized throughout this study: The Chinese air force today is the product of decisions and policies that have shaped it over decades, and the present force structure represents the ongoing legacy of the past. We should certainly expect the step-by-step enhancement of Chinese airpower capabilities, but the modernization process will be prolonged and subject to fits, starts, and reversals. Indeed, the protracted character of this process provides the PLAAF leadership a continuing opportunity to think through its longer-term requirements, as the air force inventory is steadily drawn down over the next decade.

---

[2]For an overall assessment reflecting the situation in the early 1990s, consult Pollack (1992), pp. 151–180.

[3]For a useful overview along these lines, consult Swaine (1994).

There seems little doubt that the air force faces a daunting battle in its efforts at modernization. Although the PLAAF will continue to replace older aircraft and to introduce more modern systems from abroad selectively, a comprehensive modernization process will only be possible over the longer term. Should China need to commit its air forces to battle again in the coming decade, leaders in Beijing will use their available assets, even if the present air force (and the air force that will continue to exist over the coming decade) is not judged equal to the task. In the longer run (i.e., over several decades), the PLAAF should begin to assemble more credible airpower capabilities with which to protect or assert its interests in East Asia. Until that time, the air force leadership has little alternative but to persist in a long-term effort to compensate for two lost decades and to undertake the patient effort of adapting and integrating modern airpower technology, without which the PLAAF cannot expect to emerge as a decisive factor in the regional or global air balance.

Appendix A

THE STRUCTURE OF THE PLA, PLAAF, AND NAVAL AVIATION

This appendix briefly describes the PLA's administrative and operations structure, as well as the interactions between the PLA, the PLAAF, and naval aviation (Wang, 1991, pp. 62–70).[1] China's military establishment is known simply as the PLA and is based on the five field armies that began forming in the 1920s. In other words, the PLA *is* the army, and the navy and air force are subordinate services to it. Generally speaking, although the PLAAF commander is one of approximately 20 full generals in the PLA, he is only equal in status to the commander of an army MR.[2] In addition, the PLA has a strategic rocket force, known as the second artillery, which lies somewhere between a service and a branch.[3]

---

[1]Information in this appendix on the organization of the PLA is based on a compilation of all the Military Yearbooks that have been published annually since 1985. The first edition in 1985 was very sparse on information on the PLA, but each edition since then has added further insights into the PLA's organization and way of operating. For detailed information on the PLAAF's history and organization, see Allen (1991).

[2]Lieutenant General Yu Zhenwu, appointed PLAAF commander in November 1994, has yet to receive a third star. If past practices continue to be followed, we would anticipate this change at the earliest appropriate moment.

[3]From an analytical viewpoint, the order in which organizations are listed in articles in Chinese military journals, such as *Jiefang Jun Bao* (*Liberation Army Daily*), reveals much about the way the PLA is organized. When listing various organizations, protocol order (i.e., the pecking order) is extremely important—much of which is based on the dates the organizations were originally formed. For example, articles on the PLA in general always list the army and its two subordinate services as "the army, navy, and air force," since the army was organized in August 1927, the navy in April 1949, and the air force in November 1949. Of particular note, the second artillery is almost never listed unless the article specifically addresses a strategic rocket forces issue. In addition, the PLA's annual military yearbook lists the dates the army, navy, and air force

The army component of the PLA is composed of eight branches: artillery, armor, engineering, communications, chemical defense, army aviation, and electronic warfare. The navy is divided into three fleets—North Sea, East Sea, and South Sea—and has five branches: surface warfare, submarines, naval aviation, shore defense, and marines. The air force is organized into five branches: aviation, antiaircraft artillery, SAMs, radar, and communications. The aviation branch, which includes fighters, ground attack aircraft, bombers, transports, and reconnaissance aircraft, is the PLAAF's main arm. The air force also has airborne troops and logistics units, as well as directly subordinate units, such as procuratorates, research institutes, hospitals, and schools.

The air force's aviation units are organized into divisions, regiments, groups, and squadrons, while the nonaviation units are organized into divisions, brigades, regiments, battalions, companies, platoons, and squads. The only exception is that the airborne troops are organized into an army (Wang, 1991).

The second artillery, which was formally established in 1965, does not have subordinate branches but is organized into missile launch units with supporting engineering, intelligence, reconnaissance, mapping, planning, meteorological, communications, chemical defense, and camouflage and concealment troops (Wang, 1991).

ADMINISTRATIVE ORGANIZATION

Administratively, the Military Commission of the Chinese Communist Party's Central Committee is the highest military policymaking body in the PRC.[4] The PLA itself consists of three equal

---

were formally established, but does not list a date for the second artillery or any of the services' branches.

[4]The terms CMC or Central Military Commission are commonly used erroneously for this organization. According to Chinese-English dictionaries published in China, three terms—*zhongyang junshi weiyuanhui, zhongyang junwei,* and *junwei*—are used interchangeably and mean the Military Commission of the Central Committee of the Chinese Communist Party. Although these terms have always been used in Chinese, Western publications have translated them differently, and, consequently, certain Chinese publications printed for outside consumption have followed the Western practice. For example, Western publications originally translated them as the Military Affairs Commission (MAC), but later changed to the Central Military Commission (CMC).

"general departments"—General Staff Department (GSD), General Political Department (GPD), and General Logistics Department (GLD)—and these departments are mirrored down to the lowest unit level throughout all services and branches of the PLA. While it is difficult to make an exact comparison with the U.S. Department of Defense, the Military Commission is a rough equivalent to the Office of the Secretary of Defense, and the three departments combined serve almost all of the functions of the Joint Chiefs of Staff and the Department of the Army (Figure 20). COSTIND, which is subordinate to both the Military Commission and to the State Council, is responsible for coordinating defense R&D, and serves an additional NASA-like function by managing and operating China's space program.

While some of the subordinate departments within GSD, GPD, and GLD have offices responsible for coordinating air force matters, Headquarters PLAAF basically serves the same administrative functions as Headquarters USAF.

The administrative structure within the navy, air force, and second artillery and all of their subordinate branches and units within the seven MRs is virtually a mirror image of the three general departments. The only difference is a change in their names to the headquarters, political, and logistics departments, respectively (Wang, 1991).

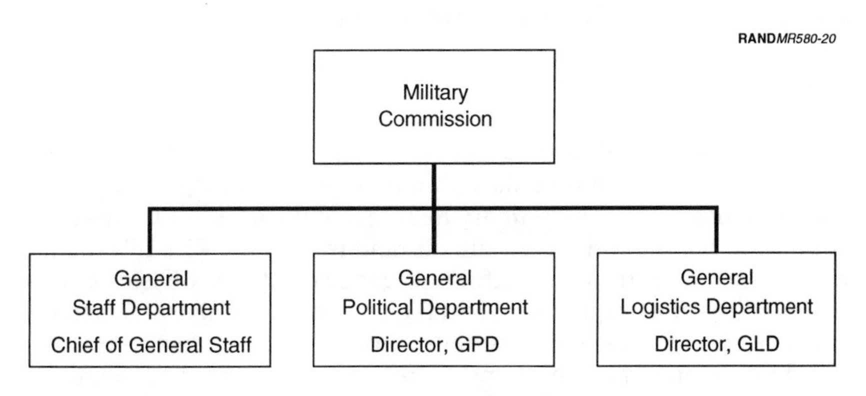

Figure 20—PLA Administrative Organization

In addition, the navy, air force, and second artillery have added first-level departments to handle special responsibilities. For example, the navy has three additional departments—equipment and technical department, equipment repair department, and naval aviation department. The air force added the aeronautical engineering department in 1976 to handle aircraft maintenance. The second artillery has a fourth technical and equipment department that is responsible for maintenance and systems acquisition (Wang, 1991).

COMMAND STAFF

Within the PLAAF, the command staff at every level from HqAF to the lowest level consists of the following personnel: commander, political commissar, one to four deputy commanders, one or two deputy political commissars, a chief of staff (who is the director of the headquarters department), a director of the political element, a director of the logistics element, and a director of the maintenance element. These officers constitute the air force's Party Standing Committee at each level in the chain of command.

PLAAF BRANCHES

As noted above, the PLAAF is organized into five branches—aviation, antiaircraft artillery, surface-to-air missiles, radar, and communications. Below is a brief description of each branch.

Aviation Troops

As one of the PLAAF's five branches, the Air Force's aviation troops consist of fighter, ground attack aircraft, bomber, transport, and reconnaissance units. The primary missions of the aviation troops are support to the ground forces and air defense. As the PLAAF's main arm, the aviation troop aircraft are organized into air divisions, air regiments, groups, squadrons, and flights. There are also associated logistics, maintenance, and support units, which are further organized into regiments, battalions, companies, platoons, and squads. Air divisions can be directly subordinate to HqAF, to an MRAF headquarters, to an air corps, or to a command post. There are also independent regiments and groups, which conduct specialized missions, such as operational test and evaluation of equipment, reconnaissance and surveying, troop transport, and reforestation. For the most part, these aircraft include reconnaissance fighters and Il-14 and Yun-5 transports.

A typical air division headquarters consists of the command staff and administrative organization. These organizations are responsible for combat and training, political training, supply, and maintenance support for the division. Each division and regiment has a Party committee and a standing committee, of which the political commissar is the secretary. The standing committee consists of the command staff, and the Party committee consists of the standing committee plus the commanders and political commissars of each subordinate regiment.

An air division normally has two to three flying regiments, and if the regiments are located at different airfields, each airfield has a field station for logistics support. Some flying academies have four regiments. The flying regiment, which has a set number of from 25 to 32 aircraft (but may actually have more or less assigned), is the basic organization for training and operations. Each regiment has three flying groups, which are numbered the first through the third, and one aircraft maintenance group. Each flying group has three flying squadrons.

The division has about an equal number of pilots and aircraft, and each pilot only flies the aircraft assigned to his squadron (two or three aircraft). The average pilot is a college graduate, with the degree usually earned at a PLAAF flying academy, and has no set commitment after completing pilot training. However, the PLAAF established age limits for its pilots in the 1980s: fighter and ground-attack pilots, 43–45 years; bomber pilots, 48–50 years; transport pilots, 55 years; helicopter pilots, 47–50 years; and female pilots, 48 years. The average age of fighter and ground-attack pilots is 28 years.

Antiaircraft Artillery and Surface-to-Air Missile Troops

Until the PLAAF (which consisted primarily of aviation troops) and the PLA Air Defense Force (which was mainly composed of AAA troops and radar troops) merged in 1957, they shared the air defense mission. In 1958, the PLAAF added SAM troops to its air defense mission. For historical and security reasons, AAA troops have sometimes been referred to as first artillery (*yipao*) and SAM troops as second artillery (*erpao*). Also for security reasons, SAMs became the responsibility of a separate HqAF technical department, instead of calling it a SAM department. The technical department was later merged into the AAA department.

The first organized AAA units were organized to protect Beijing, Tianjin, Nanjing, and Shanghai. As more cities were liberated, the PLA's eight field AAA regiments became responsible for their air defense. By the end of 1949, the PLA had purchased enough AAA from the Soviet Union to form 16 regiments located along eastern China from Shenyang to Changsha.

The PLAAF's SAM troops began with the first delivery of Soviet SAMs in October 1958. The first batch of SAMs was organized into three battalions, consisting of people borrowed from the AAA, radar, aviation maintenance, and searchlight troops, and was responsible for the air defense of Beijing. The first SAM division was formed on 1 April 1964 as the 4th Independent AAA Division. In September 1958, a special weapons school was organized in Baoding and called the 15th Aviation School. It was responsible for training all services on surface-to-surface, surface-to-air, and shore-to-ship missile maintenance. In 1963, however, this school became responsible only for training SAM commanders, maintenance, and construction.

Prior to the 1985 MR reorganization, AAA and SAM units were organized separately into divisions or independent regiments. Each independent regiment also had the status of a division. Each division had subordinate regiments, battalions, companies, platoons, and squads. Each independent regiment also had battalions, companies, platoons, and squads. Following the reorganization, however, the division level and subordinate regiments were abolished, and their AAA and SAM assets were merged into combined brigades, so that the chain of command now goes directly from the brigade to the battalion. Each brigade now has five or six battalions, including two or three AAA and two or three SAM battalions, plus their subordinate companies, platoons, and squads.

As for the remaining independent regiments, each SAM regiment has one to three battalions, and each battalion has six launchers plus various support companies, such as command and control, logistics, maintenance, and radar companies. Each AAA regiment has two or three battalions; each battalion has three to five companies (minimum of three); each company has three AAA squads plus support squads (vehicle, maintenance, logistics, etc.); each squad has three to six platoons; and each platoon has one AAA piece.

Since the late 1980s, the PLAAF has been in the process of restructuring its AAA and SAM forces by gradually turning over most of the AAA (37 and 57 mm) to the Army and by combining some of the remaining AAA regiments with SAM regiments into combined brigades (*huncheng lu*). So far, combined brigades have been noted in every MRAF except the Jinan MRAF. However, the Jinan MRAF does have at least one SAM regiment.

As part of the restructuring process, all active-duty SAM and AAA divisions have been abolished, and at least one SAM brigade without any AAA has been established in the Beijing MRAF and one in the Shenyang MRAF. In addition, some SAM regiments have still not been combined into brigades. The AAA units that are not being combined with SAMs or have not been turned over to the Army will be used for deployment purposes. Although there are no longer any active-duty AAA divisions, the PLAAF still has some reserve AAA divisions, which apparently are the only air force reserve units. The reserve division(s) took part in a live-fire exercise for the first time in September 1990.

Radar Troops

The first radar battalion was established in April 1950 in Nanjing, but was called a Telecommunications Group for security purposes. The second battalion was established in Shanghai as part of the Shanghai Air Defense Headquarters in May 1950. The first radar regiment was formed in 1955. The name "radar troops" became official, and the radar troops became a PLAAF branch in July 1957.

After the PLA Air Defense Force was established in December 1950, radar units were divided into two types. Those subordinate to the ADF were responsible for early warning, and those subordinate to the PLAAF were responsible for directly supporting aviation units. In 1959, radar sites were established as the basic unit, while regiments became the highest unit. At that time, the sites and regiments either had a reporting battalion headquarters or an administrative battalion headquarters between them, depending upon the situation. As a result, the radar organization had either a three-level (regiment-battalion-site) or a two-level (regiment-site) structure. In the early 1960s, this changed so that there was only a three-level structure.

Today, radar troops are organized into regiments, battalions, and companies or sites. Each regiment has various battalions, including one reporting battalion and up to 20 radar companies or sites. The regiments apparently have the status of independent regiments, and are therefore equal in status to a division. Each company or site has two or three radars and 20 personnel (officers and enlisted) assigned. For example, one company near the Sino-Soviet border reported 39,705 groups and 45,539 sorties in 1988.

Radar troop training takes place at the PLAAF Radar Academy in Wuhan or at various radar troop training groups. The Radar Academy had graduated over 7,800 cadets by the end of 1987, and there were 510 cadets in the 1989 and 500 in the 1990 graduating classes. Training is for three years, and the cadets must serve one year in a unit before they receive their commissions. In addition, over 1,200 technicians and platoon commanders had been trained at MRAF training units, such as the training group in the Chengdu MRAF, by the end of 1987.

Radar regiments are administratively subordinate to the radar division within the next higher headquarters level for day-to-day technical matters, to the operations division for operational matters, and to the training and logistics elements for those functions. When a radar unit tracks an aircraft, the unit passes the information up two separate chains of command. The first chain is to the command post at HqAF through the radar unit's next-higher command center, whether that next-higher level is the regiment, an MRAF headquarters, an air corps, or a command post, such as the Tangshan Command Post. At the same time that the information is going to HqAF, it is being sent directly to the GSD's command center.

Airborne Troops

In July 1950, the Military Commission established the PLAAF 1st Marine Brigade in Shanghai, thereby constituting the PLAAF's airborne troops for the first time. On August 1 of that year, the brigade's headquarters moved to Kaifeng, Henan Province, while Kaifeng and Zhengzhou, Henan Province, were designated as the brigade's training bases. This brigade eventually became an airborne division. Thereafter, the unit's designation changed several times, becoming the air force marine first division, the paratroops division, then the airborne division. In May 1961, the Military Commission changed the army's 15th Army, which had fought during the Korean War, into the PLAAF 15th Airborne Army and subordinated the PLAAF's original airborne division to this new army. Today, it is known as the PLAAF 15th Airborne Army. In October 1964, an aviation transport regiment was created to support the airborne troops. In December 1969, the first helicopter regiment was assigned to the airborne troops, and the number of personnel and equipment increased. In 1975, the airborne troops underwent a reduction in force, yet new types of weapons were introduced.

The airborne troops have various special units, including weapon controllers and reconnaissance, infantry, artillery, communications, engineering, chemical defense, and transportation soldiers. Today, the airborne troops have three brigades, which are further divided into battalions and companies as shown in Table A.1.

Paratroopers are recruited throughout China by special recruiting teams from the 44th Brigade. The new recruits are between the ages of 18 and 20. Most have at least a junior middle school education, but high school graduates are the goal. Recruits enlist for a mini-

Table A.1

Airborne Troop Locations

Brigade	City	Province	MR	Function
43rd	Kaifeng	Henan	Jinan	Combat
44th	Yingshan	Hubei	Guangzhou	Training
45th	Huangpi	Hubei	Guangzhou	Combat

mum of four years and may stay for up to six years. If recruits want to stay after six years, they must be selected as "leaders." Officers report for training at the brigade after having completed training at a military academy.

The airborne troops conduct training throughout China. For example, from July to August 1988, an airborne unit conducted training in the Kunlun Mountains and the Qinghai-Tibetan Plateau at 3,000 to 5,000 m. The training consisted of paradrops, reconnaissance, harassing attacks, taking and keeping strong points, and testing Chinese-produced parachutes.

Operationally, the 15th Airborne Army works closely with other PLAAF branches. For example, during the 1979 border conflict with Vietnam, three of the 15th Airborne Army's light artillery battalions were subordinated to the PLAAF'S 19th AAA Division's 55th Regiment at Ningming. The airborne troops have also been used for internal purposes. For example, they were used in Wuhan during the Cultural Revolution. In addition, they were also used as a spearhead during the military crackdown on demonstrators in Tiananmen Square in June 1989.

Communications Troops

PLAAF communications consists primarily of communications and navigation aids. Communications troops are organized into administrative elements, as well as regiments, battalions, stations, companies, teams, equipment repair factories, and equipment warehouses. The PLAAF Communications School was established in September 1957. Today, the Communications Engineering Academy in Xian is a four-year school, where cadets graduate with an undergraduate degree in military science. The 1990 freshman class had 1,300 cadets.

Each MRAF headquarters has a communications battalion and subordinate transmitter company. The battalion also has subordinate receiver companies, each of which has operator platoons. Each operator is networked to a receiver company at an air corps, air division, or supply station. Since 1955, all the radio operators (most of whom are women) have been enlisted troops.

OPERATIONAL ORGANIZATION

National Level

Besides being the highest military policymaking body, the Party's Military Commission is also responsible for making major operational decisions when necessary. While the 1982 Constitution established a Military Commission of the National People's Congress, it is composed of the same people as the Party's Military Commission and is seldom mentioned.

The Ministry of National Defense (MND) is subordinate to the Premier and to the State Council (the PRC's Cabinet). Although MND was a powerful organization during the 1950s and 1960s under Marshals Peng Dehuai and Lin Biao, it no longer has the same power. The ministry itself, with a staff of about 100 people today, is primarily responsible for protocol functions, such as meeting with the foreign military attaché corps and visiting military delegations, and its staff members are known as the "barbarian handlers." However, the current and previous two ministers, Chi Haotian, Qin Jiwei, and Zhang Aiping, have all wielded personal power because of their previous military positions and as members of the Party's Military Commission.

The PLAAF is under the leadership of the Party's Military Commission through the GSD. As a service arm, the air force's position in the chain of command is equal to that of the seven MRs.[5] Within the PLAAF, the chain of command is organized into four levels: HqAF, MRAF headquarters, air corps and command posts, and operational units (Figure 21).

The air force's operations nerve center is located at PLAAF headquarters in Beijing, where a new command center was completed in 1991.[6] According to a 1992 news report (BBC, 1992):

---

[5]The primary reason for this is that the air force is subordinate to the army. Although the PLAAF commander generally has the rank of general (three star), he only has the status of an MR commander.

[6]Of note, the HqAF compound houses the headquarters, political, and aero-engineering departments, but the fourth major department, logistics, is located a few miles away. This is generally the case throughout the PLA, since the logistics departments

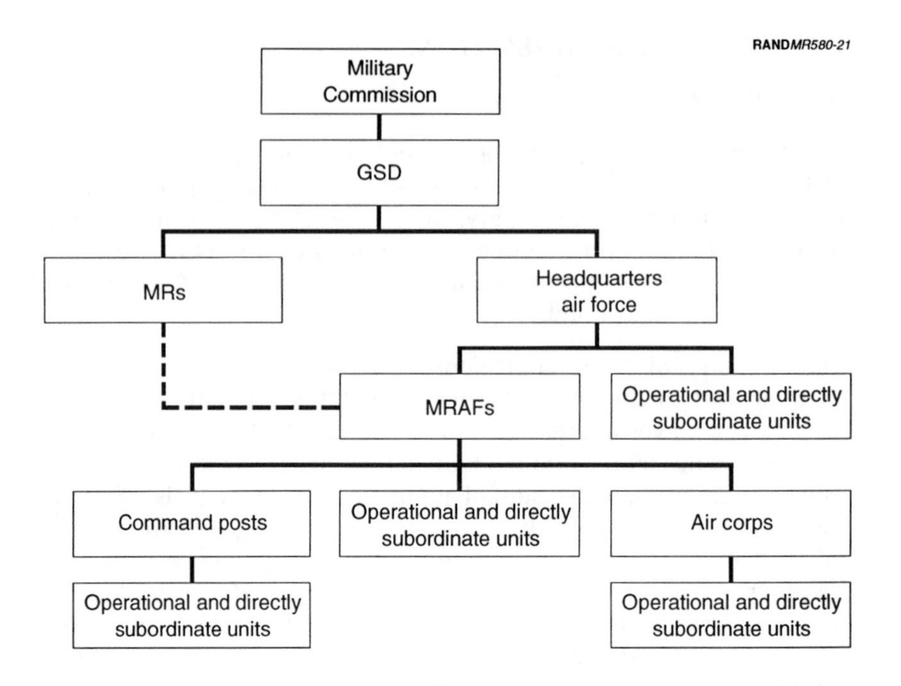

Figure 21—PLAAF Chain of Command

The command center uses a semi-automated system of advanced electronics technology to indicate every movement inside Chinese territorial airspace, keeping in touch with tens of thousands of air force personnel and the nearly 10,000 sorties flown daily. A computer in the aeronautical engineering (maintenance) department is linked with several hundred microcomputers from all air force units and can conduct a comprehensive statistical analysis of the quantity and quality of all equipment three months faster than in the past and 10 times more efficiently than using the previous method.

---

are administratively organized more like a command than a department and have a much larger staff than the other major departments.

Military Region Air Forces

Administratively and operationally, the PLA is organized into seven MRs: Shenyang, Beijing, Lanzhou, Nanjing, Guangzhou, Jinan, and Chengdu. Singly or in combination, these MRs can be considered as theaters of operation, with the primary emphasis being placed on regional defense (see Figure 5). It was not until 1985, when the number of the MRs and MRAFs and their borders coincided for the first time, that the air force finally looked like it was preparing structurally to move away from strictly air defense to supporting the ground forces. Further evidence of this came in 1988, when the seven MRAF commanders also became MR deputy commanders for the first time. While the seven MR commanders are responsible for combined operations, the MRAF commanders, acting as the MR commander's air component commander, are responsible for flight and air defense operations within the MR.[7]

Within each MR, air force units have one of four basic chains of operational command. First, some units, such as various aircraft overhaul facilities and logistics elements, are directly subordinate to HqAF. Second, some units, such as fighter bases, and AAA and SAM units in the immediate vicinity of the city where the MRAF headquarters is located, are directly subordinate to the MRAF headquarters. Third, the majority of the aviation and air defense units located away from the city where the MRAF headquarters is located are subordinate to a command post or air corps. Fourth, some units, such as schools, are jointly subordinate to HqAF and the appropriate MRAF headquarters. For example, HqAF is responsible for the curriculum, while the MRAF headquarters is responsible for the facilities.

In terms of command and control, the 1979 Vietnam border conflict provides a good example of how the air force chain of command works in time of a crisis. At that time, the commander of the

---

[7]An MRAF commander literally "wears two hats" or—in the Chinese case—two uniforms. When General Larry Welch, the former USAF Chief of Staff, visited the Guangzhou MR in April 1989, PLAAF Lieutenant General Liu Heqiao met the Welch delegation wearing a green PLA uniform in his capacity as a Guangzhou MR deputy commander. At the PLAAF-hosted dinner, Liu wore the blue PLAAF uniform of the MRAF commander. In addition, any air force or navy person working in one of the three general departments or other national-level PLA organizations wears an army, not an air force or navy, uniform.

Guangzhou MR, Xu Shiyou, was appointed commander of the southern front; Yang Dezhi, the new commander of the Kunming MR (and future chief of the General Staff) was the deputy commander; and Zhang Tingfa, the PLAAF commander, was the chief of staff and concurrently controlled all the air force operations.

Command Posts and Air Corps

The PLAAF currently has eight command posts and four air corps, which are subordinate to the various MRAF headquarters (Figure 22).[8] Historically, these intermediate-level command elements were established for the air defense of key cities that were not designated as MRAF headquarters. Practically speaking, there are no functional differences between the two organizations, although an air corps is viewed as having slightly less stature than a command post. The number of air corps and command posts has changed frequently over the years, with some command posts replacing air corps in the 1980s. The trend during the 1990s presumably will be for command posts to replace the remaining air corps. PLAAF officers generally state that the air corps and MRAF headquarters are structured almost identically as operational *and* administrative organizations. Command posts are structured primarily as operational organizations, with their administrative functions being performed by an MRAF headquarters.

PERSONNEL

Following the Military Commission's 1985 mandate for the PLA to cut its forces by one million, the PLAAF had reduced its total active-

---

[8]The four active air corps are the First (Changchun), Seventh (Nanning), Eighth (Fuzhou), and Tenth (Datong). The Second (Dandong) and Fifth (Hangzhou) Air Corps were abolished. The eight command posts are Dalian (former 3rd Air Corps), Tangshan (former 6th Air Corps), Xian (former 11th Air Corps), Wulumuqi (former 9th Air Corps), Shanghai (former 4th Air Corps), Wuhan (former Wuhan MRAF Hq), Kunming (former Kunming MRAF Command Post), and Lhasa. Although these organizations are primarily responsible for defending major cities, the 7th Air Corps became the PLAAF's "forward command post" during the 1979 Sino-Vietnamese border conflict. It was responsible for virtually all air force units in the operational area.

Figure 22—PLAAF MRAF, Command Posts, and Air Corps

duty force by one-fourth by 1990, at which time it had 170,000 military and civilian officers and 330,000 conscripts.[9] Although there are

[9]The 25-percent reduction in force figure is routinely cited. There is perhaps an assumption among Chinese and foreign analysts that the reduction was applied across the board in all services. According to China Today (1989a), p. 675, the Military Commission authorized only a 20-percent reduction for the PLAAF on August 5, 1985. The 500,000 figure comes from Dou (1990). The figure of 470,000 PLAAF personnel is given in IISS (1994), p. 173. The average PLA ratio of officers to conscripts and volunteers is 1 to 3.3, compared to 1 to 2.45 before the 1985 reduction in forces (*Wen Wei Po* [Hong Kong], April 29, 1987, p. 3, and May 3, 1987, p. 7). Based on the figures supplied by Senior Colonel Dou Dezhong, the PLAAF air attaché at the Chinese embassy in Washington, D.C., the PLAAF still had not reached the average PLA ratio. Dou's figure includes, however, "civilian officers." If they are excluded, the PLAAF probably comes

comparatively few air force or "joint" (i.e., GSD, GPD, and GLD) billets in Beijing, total PLAAF personnel in the Beijing area in 1990 may have been as high as 50,000—nearly a tenth of the air force. In addition, about one-sixth of all PLAAF personnel are involved in political, not operational, work.

Some of the largest reductions in the PLAAF during that period were realized by a personnel sleight of hand trick. For the first time, the Chinese armed forces created a civilian support bureaucracy. Large numbers of officers from the support units—especially schools, academies, hospitals, research institutes, and service units—were required to become civilian defense employees in August 1988. An implicit objective was to alter the ratio of officers to conscripts from 1:2.4 to 1:3.3. For the PLAAF, the greatest impact was felt in the logistics department, which controlled most support organizations. At HqAF, approximately 20 percent of its personnel became civil servants. Most instructors in the air force schools and academies also became civilians.

Like the rest of the PLA, the air force does not have a professional NCO corps. However, the air force began to establish one in the mid-1980s, including opening an NCO school in Dalian. In many cases, PLAAF officers do the work that NCOs in the USAF are responsible for. For example, PLAAF maintenance officers attend a four-year engineering academy and are capable of completely repairing any aircraft in the inventory. The same is true for each of the other academies, such as the antiaircraft and SAM academies. At the aviation unit level, the officer-to-enlisted ratio in a maintenance element is about 1:1.

The majority of PLAAF personnel—officers, NCOs, and conscripts—serve their entire careers in the same MR and perhaps even in their native province. Pilots, for example, normally spend their entire careers in the division to which they are assigned after transition flight training. This situation strikes U.S. military manpower managers as unusual, because American servicemen are frequently transferred.

---

close to the general PLA officer-conscript ratio. The PLA has published little segmented data regarding military manpower. Although there are specified numerical limitations on the number of general officers each service can have, the PLA has only referred to "ratios" for all other officer ranks. When ranks were assigned in 1988, the PLAAF had 126 general officers. See *Zhongguo Kongjun*, November 1988, p. 1.

In reality, the infrequent transfer of troops is a fairly common practice throughout the world. In the case of the PLAAF, the prevalence of regional service and the normally ample manpower distributions among the MRs has meant that stringent centralized control of all air force personnel is not viewed as especially necessary.

Although PLA and PLAAF personnel do not routinely serve great distances from the area where they joined the military, extended family separations are an ongoing source of dissatisfaction within all the services. Except for pilots, whose dependents can live with them almost immediately, other PLAAF officers must be 35 years old, have 15 years of service, and have battalion commander status before family members can join them. Some cities also require that the spouse have a job, that the officer already have quarters, and that the child already have a guaranteed place at a school.[10]

NAVAL AVIATION

Naval aviation seldom, if ever, works or trains directly with the air force. Naval aviation was established in August 1950 as a separate administrative department within the navy headquarters and as a separate PLA navy operational branch. The first naval flying school was founded in 1956 at Changzhi, Shanxi Province. Naval aviation, with 25,000 personnel and about 1,000 aircraft in its inventory, consists of the headquarters at Liangxiang Airfield near Beijing and units assigned to the three fleets.[11]

Fleet aviation is organized much the same as the air force, including its own aviation troops (divisions, regiments, groups, and squadrons), radar troops, communications troops, logistics troops, antiaircraft artillery troops, and technical reconnaissance units. Naval aviation also has aircraft assigned to independent regiments and groups. The primary aircraft in the inventory include three divi-

---

[10]The separate requirements of local jurisdictions underscore the friction that may exist between military units and neighboring communities. This kind of local discrimination prompts military units to establish enterprises to provide employment for dependents and military-supported schools to educate dependents.

[11]There is very little open-source information available about naval aviation, even from the PLA navy's official history. Information in this section came from a compilation of bits and pieces and conversations with PLA naval aviation officials.

sions of B-5 and B-6 bombers (the B-6D variant is designed to fire the C-601 antiship missile); six ground-attack and fighter divisions, including 100 A-5 ground-attack aircraft and about 600 J-6, J-7, and J-8 fighters; and an assortment of shipborne helicopters (Z-5, SA-321, and Z-9) (IISS, 1994, p. 172). More than likely, naval aviation will eventually receive at least one regiment of Russian-produced Su-27s (24 aircraft), which will probably be stationed on Hainan Island.

Naval aviation's main tasks are to protect China's coastal airspace, support the navy fleets and the army, protect China's ocean resources, escort fishing boats and convoys, and provide search-and-rescue operations. Naval aviation also has the mission of liberating islands. Since the mid-1970s, China has paid particular attention to the Paracel and Spratly Islands in the South China Sea. China, along with Taiwan, the Philippines, Vietnam, Malaysia, and Brunei, claims all or part of the Paracels and Spratlys. In 1974, Chinese naval units evicted Vietnamese forces from the Paracels and occupied some of the islands. In 1988, another military encounter between China and Vietnam occurred, resulting in Beijing's occupation of additional islands in the Spratly chain. Naval aviation became involved when, on November 8, 1980, two B-6s from the 3rd Division's 8th Regiment conducted the first reconnaissance flight over the Spratlys.

It is important to emphasize that any possible Chinese assault on the Spratly Islands will most likely be carried out by naval aviation, not by air force units. The biggest reason for this is the separation of responsibilities between the two. Although the PLAAF states that one of its missions is support of the navy, it does not train over water. In fact, the *PLAAF Officers Handbook* specifically states (IISS, 1994, p. 172):

> [F]lying over water and over land is completely different. When flying over the ocean, there are no ground markers as reference points; it is difficult to estimate altitude and distance; weather changes quickly, visibility is low, and the horizon is difficult to discern; there is no navigation equipment on the ocean, and it is difficult to deal with special situations when they appear. Pilots encounter control problems over water every day, which greatly complicates training. Therefore, the farther one flies from the coastline, the more problems there are and the more difficult it becomes.

LEADERSHIP IN THE 1990s

The PLAAF has had eight commanders and nine political commissars since 1949. General Cao Shuangming and Lieutenant General Ding Wenchang, the political commissar, assumed their positions in November 1992 and served in this capacity until November 1994, when Cao was succeeded by Lieutenant General Yu Zhenwu. Recent commanders and political commissars have continued to promote the regularization process that began in 1977 under Zhang Tingfa and Gao Houliang, and continued in 1985 under Wang Hai and Zhu Guang.[12] Foreign observers who have been close to the PLAAF have given high marks to the cooperative spirit maintained by these pairs of officers. Although there was considerable political soul-searching within China's military after June 1989, the senior leadership of the PLAAF seems to have weathered it well. One reason is that the air force leadership concentrated on the tasks assigned by the Military Commission and found little time to become involved in the controversial aspects of reform. But this also reflects the air force's subordinate political status.

PLAAF leadership changes have become more stable and predictable.[13] There have been virtually no surprises since June 1989. Recent commanders and political commissars have maintained adherence to the long-term plan that Wang Hai and Zhu Guang mapped out for a leadership transition for the next generation of air force leaders. The Military Commission and three PLA general de-

---

[12]Of note, when the PLAAF celebrated its 40th anniversary in November 1989, all senior retired air force leaders, including Gao Houliang, attended the ceremonies, but Zhang Tingfa was conspicuously absent. The authors have not been able to find any authoritative views on why this occurred, especially since Zhang still maintains his official air force residence, his office at HqAF, and his limousine and retainers. There was speculation that Zhang and Deng Xiaoping had a falling out in the early 1980s, thus leading to Zhang being replaced by Wang Hai; however, this should not have been enough to keep Zhang from celebrating his role in guiding the PLAAF as the chief of staff, deputy commander, political commissar, and commander from 1962 to 1985.

[13]According to PLAAF officials, considerations associated with the 1989 Tiananmen situation were not some of the primary reasons it took three years after the PLAAF's 40th anniversary in 1989 to select a new commander and political commissar. Rather, there was no space to build a house for them in the HqAF housing compound. The reason for this is that, unlike the USAF, all senior headquarters staff members (about 5 to 15 positions) at all levels of the air force retain their housing when they retire—in other words, the housing belongs to the person rather than the position. So each time someone retires, the air force has to find a new house for the replacement.

partments approve all senior-level PLAAF personnel changes, but none of the changes that took place in 1992 and 1993 were altered by the Tiananmen crisis in June 1989. In other words, despite the upsurge in political themes and rhetoric by the PLA GPD evident for several years after Tiananmen, the regularization of the PLAAF promotion process has led to stability.

Leadership stability has been easier to predict because career and experience have become clear indicators for upward mobility. First, future PLAAF commanders are henceforth likely to be aviators; nonaviators will be the exception. General Wang Hai was the first commander to have been a pilot and the only one who did not begin his career in the ground forces.

Second, antecedent assignments for the air force commander and most deputy commanders will be jobs as an MRAF deputy commander and commander. While Wang Hai had been the Guangzhou MRAF deputy commander and commander and PLAAF deputy commander, Cao Shuangming had been the Shenyang MRAF deputy commander and commander. Career progression to political commissar position may involve variations. Zhu Guang, whose previous air force command experience was as the Shenyang MRAF deputy political commissar, came directly to HqAF from jobs in the GPD and Military Commission. Ding Wenchang was previously the Director of the Political Department at HqAF.

Third, although Cao Shuangming was a Korean War veteran, almost all of the senior leaders at HqAF and in the MRAFs with Korean War experience had been replaced by younger leaders by early 1994. Prior to Cao Shuangming's accession to leadership, three of the HqAF deputy commanders; four of the seven MRAF commanders, including Cao; and at least two MRAF deputy commanders in 1989 had flown with Wang Hai during the Korean War.[14] By early 1994,

---

[14]Cao Shuangming was born in 1929 and joined the PLA in 1946. Having served in the 2nd Field Army, he was later sent to pilot training, which he completed in 1952. In 1953, he joined the "People's Volunteer Air Force" and participated in the Korean War as a deputy squadron commander (each squadron only has two to three aircraft). During the 1958 Taiwan Strait crisis, Cao was deputy commander of the 16th Air Division's MiG-17–equipped 48th Regiment. While Wang Hai was commander, the HqAF deputy commanders who are Korean War veterans were Lin Hu, Li Yongtai, and Liu Zhitian. The other three MRAF commanders were Liu Yudi (Beijing), Sun Jinghua

HqAF had reduced the number of deputy commanders from four to three, and only two of Wang's deputy commanders remain. Yu Zhenwu, the new PLAAF commander, joined the service at the conclusion of the Korean War but followed Wang Hai as the deputy commander and commander of the Guangzhou MRAF, and Lin Hu was Wang Hai's commander in the Korean War. The third deputy commander, Yang Zhenyu, a Korean War veteran without any MRAF command experience, came from being the commandant of the PLAAF Command College in Beijing. As with Yu Zhenwu, who had previously been the director of the training department at HqAF, and Lin Hu, who had been a deputy commandant at the PLAAF Command College, Yang Zhenyu's appointment emphasizes the importance the PLAAF places on training.

Fourth, the commander and political commissar have continued the process initiated by Wang Hai and Zhu Guang of moving younger officers into key HqAF and MRAF command positions. The reinstitution of ranks and mandatory retirement ages in October 1988 made this task easier. It became possible, for example, to put talented younger officers in command positions with lower ranks than an older deputy.[15] Overall, the new officers are better educated than their predecessors. In addition, many of them have had the opportunity to travel abroad with Wang Hai or other PLAAF and PLA delegations.

The PLAAF has received over 100 visiting foreign air force delegations from over 40 countries and regions, which include 38 foreign air force commanders (BBC, 1993a). For example, former PLAAF Commander Wang Hai visited the United States in 1986 and hosted USAF Chiefs of Staff Charles Gabriel in 1985 and Larry Welch in 1989. He also visited Chile, Peru, and Colombia (with a stopover in London) in March and April 1991, and he hosted his Egyptian, Zimbabwean, and Tanzanian counterparts in November and December 1991 and October 1992, respectively. The PLAAF Chief of

---

(Lanzhou), and Hou Shujun (Chengdu). The MRAF deputy commanders were Yao Xian (Beijing) and Han Decai (Nanjing). Almost all of these leaders were replaced by mid-1994 under the new commander, Cao Shuangming.

[15]There are still several cases in which deputy unit commanders outrank their commanders because they have more time in service. It will therefore take several years before the oldest officers reach retirement age and the rank structure becomes fully rational.

Staff, Lieutenant General Yu Zemin, accompanied President Yang Shangkun to Pakistan in October 1991.

Fifth, Cao Shuangming maintained Wang Hai's practice of traveling abroad and taking his MRAF commanders with him to gain firsthand knowledge of foreign air forces. Cao led a six-member delegation on a visit with his counterparts in Pakistan, Thailand, and Bangladesh in May 1993.[16] In June 1994 he led a delegation to Russia to confer with senior Russian air force and civilian officials and to visit the Sukhoi Design Bureau and other aerospace technical facilities.[17] He also continued Wang's practice of hosting high-level visitors, including the visit of USAF Chief of Staff Merrill McPeak in Octorber 1994. In May 1995, Yu Zhenwu became the second PLAAF commander to visit the United States.

All of these leadership trends indicate that there is a long-term leadership plan for the air force and that certain officers are being groomed for specific senior leadership positions. Furthermore, there is a concerted effort to see foreign air forces first-hand and have face-to-face discussions with other air force leaders.[18]

---

[16]Multiple Chinese publications.

[17]"Chinese Air Force General Begins 10 Day Visit" (1994).

[18]It is the authors' opinion that a review of Chinese military literature and analyses of the PLAAF's structure reveals that the air force is the most open of the three services and has made a concerted effort to move away from the shroud of secrecy surrounding the other services. For example, many air force units are referred to in open-source publications by their true names rather than by a five-digit cover designator.

Appendix B

THE PLAAF BUDGET

Although there is some fragmentary information available about the administrative organizations responsible for the PLAAF's budget, no reliable data are available about the air force's actual budget. Even though there is a central air force budget, PLAAF officers often imply that the budget process is not rigidly fixed. The PLAAF relied on three-year budget plans from 1978 to 1986, but then changed its system to match the State Council's seventh five-year plan cycle in 1986 (China Today, 1989a, pp. 489 and 491). In 1987, it had already completed its report on the plans for weapon development in the year 2000. Furthermore, the PLAAF did not have a financial accounting system of its own until mid-1989.[1]

Once the GSD establishes its total budget requirements, centralized funding for the PLAAF comes from the State Council through the GLD finance department. Moneys are normally dispersed between March and June. Within the air force, the finance department (a second-level department subordinated to the HqAF logistics department) is responsible for the PLAAF's overall budget and finance matters.

In general, the PLAAF receives three kinds of central budgetary allocations. The first is "fenced" or specifically earmarked money (i.e., to buy a specific number of aircraft). The PLAAF can only spend this money as specified by the GLD. The second allocation is "constrained funds." These funds are also earmarked by categories, but the PLAAF has some latitude in how it expends this money. The third

[1] *China Daily*, August 16, 1989, in FBIS-CHI-89-160, August 21, 1989, p. 39.

category is discretionary funds, which have no strings attached. According to the allocation constraints, these funds trickle down to the basic level units of the PLAAF based on budgets and plans.[2]

A second source of funds, which is not centrally controlled, represents an off-budget source of income for all four PLAAF administrative levels. This source consists of commercial enterprises, hotels, hospitals, factories, farms, mines, and even airline services. Profits from these activities are substantially discretionary in nature. Unlike centrally apportioned funds that trickle down, the profits of military enterprises are carefully husbanded. In theory, there is supposed to be a "trickle up" flow to the next highest administrative level where portions of the profits are redistributed down to poorer units.[3]

The net effect is that HqAF has budgetary control of big-ticket items, major capital construction, and expenditure categories that central government planners endeavor to control through the state budget allocation process. It has much less control over the daily operating expenses of the units; housing; care of dependents; and morale, welfare, and recreation activities.

---

[2]"The Military Budget System in the PRC" (1985), pp. 1–2. Another Hong Kong publication identifies the following PLA budgetary divisions: development (30 percent), maintenance (33 percent), and living expenses (36 percent). Additionally, the same source claims the military budget comprises two broad parts: "the overall national defense budget and the combat readiness budget." In peacetime the latter is only about 10 percent of the total military budget. See Wan (1990), pp. 17–18.

[3]The PLAAF has not stated how many enterprises are run by units (*budui*). In 1989, however, it reported that more than 100 PLAAF enterprises earned profits in excess of renminbi $50,000 while several earned more than renminbi $1 million (*Jiefangjun Bao*, 1989, p. 1). Like other military services, the PLAAF has held conferences to enforce strict management of military enterprises. Presumably, the managers of these activities are no less creative than their civilian counterparts in devising accounting methods to retain more money for the use of the enterprise or parent unit.

Appendix C

THE POLITICAL COMMISSAR SYSTEM

The PLA's political commissar system has always been a puzzling institution to foreigners. During the earliest professional exchanges between USAF and PLAAF delegations, both sides grappled awkwardly with the existence or absence of this "system" in the other's service. Western analysts tend to regard it as a Leninist artifact that is intrusive and obstructs the pursuit of military efficiency. The attitudes of PLA officers are opaque, but they all tend to agree that the political commissars' only real power comes from their control of personnel assignments. In addition, one military official metaphorically described the system as follows: "Every child needs a mother and a father to grow up correctly. Within the Chinese military, the commander is like the father, the political commissar is like the mother, and the soldiers are like the children."[1]

Apart from the strictly political dimension of the commissar system, it nonetheless is responsible for a variety of services that are almost nonpolitical. These services include routine personnel administration, education, security, information dissemination and propaganda, welfare and recreation activities, sponsoring cultural events, counseling soldiers and dependents with problems, and maintaining the general morale of soldiers. In foreign militaries, many of these missions fall within the purview of personnel affairs or a chaplain's office.

---

[1]Interview with a Chinese officer, February 1988. The maternal part of the metaphor has been used to describe the GSD's Foreign Affairs Bureau, which Chinese officers describe as "our mother-in-law. It is a little different."

Organizationally, the party component consists primarily of party committees and branches that are led by party secretaries. Party committees and their standing committees, which handle day-to-day affairs, exist at the regiment level and above. The "grassroots level," as it is called, is found in organizations below the regiment level. On the military side, the party operates through the political departments, which are administrative organizations. At the regiment level and above, there is a political commissar who is a counterpart to the commander. There are "political instructors" at the grassroots level who interact with servicemen—Party and non-Party members. Virtually every new air force political officer receives training at the PLAAF Political Academy in Shanghai. Political commissars receive mid-level training at the Air Force Command College in Beijing.

In 1989, 6 percent of the PLAAF—about 30,000 people—worked within the commissar system. Given the relatively small number of PLAAF personnel working at the MRAF level or above, it is clear that most of the air force's full-time political workers are in operational units and support organizations.[2]

At each level of the air force, major issues are decided by the Party committee, although there is a division of responsibilities. If an issue concerns military affairs, the commander or line military officer carries out the decision. If the issue concerns political matters, political officers are responsible. For example, a commander decides how many sorties will be flown on a given day, but the political commissar participates in deciding who flies those sorties, because that decision involves both military and political matters (i.e., reliability, attitude).[3] In a commander's absence, the political commissar is re-

---

[2]Interview with the PLAAF's former Political Commissar, Lieutenant General Zhu Guang.

[3]When this practice was explained to Western air force officers, PLAAF officials were routinely vague about how command jurisdictions are resolved when the distinction between a military and political issue is unclear. A synthesis of various explanations is that through years of experience, line and political officers have acquired an unwritten understanding or tolerance of the recurrent differences. Understanding the distinctions has become part of the air force's culture and a necessary staff skill. Additionally, commissars and commanders frequently work together at different organizational levels, where they may develop personalized working relationships. (Five of the seven MRAF political commissars in 1990 had previous HqAF or MRAF command staff posi-

sponsible for carrying out the unit's mission in conjunction with the deputy commanders. In theory, a commander and a political commissar are coequal, but in practice the relationship may be quite variable. Personality and leadership style play an important role that is largely invisible to foreigners who try to understand the meld of commander and commissar.

Finally, an important consequence of the PLA's policy of "opening up to the outside" is that even the political commissars have been directly exposed to foreign cultures and military systems. In October 1988, for example, the then-director of HqAF's political department and the then-political commissar, Lieutenant General Ding Wenchang, accompanied the director of the PLA GPD, General Yang Baibing, on a visit to Eastern Europe. This was the first time a PLA political commissar had visited a foreign country. Soon thereafter the PLAAF Political Commissar, Lieutenant General Zhu Guang, visited the United States as a guest of the Secretary of the Air Force.

---

tions. The Shenyang and Beijing MRAF commanders and political commissars had worked together for several years.) Disagreements or conflicts are normally viewed as depending more on personality than on jurisdiction. The rationality of the explanation collapses when political struggles within the Party lead to a politicalization of even the most routine operational matters—as frequently happened during the Cultural Revolution.

Appendix D

THE PLAAF RANK SYSTEM

On 1 October 1988, the PLA instituted a new rank system for the first time since ranks were originally established in 1955 and then abolished at the beginning of the Cultural Revolution in 1965. Not only were insignia indicating rank and the branch of service abolished, but all PLA personnel, regardless of service or branch, wore the same standard uniform. During this period, the only way to tell the difference between an officer and an enlisted member was the number of pockets on the jacket: Officers (known as commanders or cadres) had four, and enlisted soldiers (known as fighters) had two. In addition, the material used in the officers' uniforms was of better quality (Defense Intelligence Agency, 1976, pp. 5-21 and 10-1). This caused major problems during the 1979 border conflict with Vietnam, when several units converged and no one could tell who was in charge. Even in everyday conversations, the only way to know where one fit in the pecking order was to ask what position the person held. For example, officers introduced themselves as "division deputy commander Zhang" or "bureau director Wang."

When the ranks were reinstituted, the PLA as a whole had 17 three-star; 146 two-star; and 1,251 one-star generals and admirals. Of the 128 PLAAF general officers, only one was a full general (three star)—the commander. The exact numbers of lieutenant generals (two stars) and major generals (one star) were not specified. Besides the three general officer ranks, the officer corps also has the rank of senior colonel, colonel, lieutenant colonel, major, captain, first lieutenant, and second lieutenant. The enlisted ranks include master sergeant, technical sergeant, sergeant first class, sergeant, corporal, private first class, and private.

The new rank system was both welcomed and feared. After more than 20 years without ranks, it was difficult to establish criteria that took into account seniority, different job responsibilities, and rational organizational structures. Within the air force, rank determinations were easiest to make in operational units. Problems arose, however, when assigning appropriate ranks to people working in technical, administrative, and political fields. Consistency among the military services was an additional concern. The solution, in part, was to create a dual-track officer corps: command (i.e., line officers or "operators") and technical personnel in support positions. Technical officers and nontechnical officers wear the same ranks, but they wear different collar insignia.

In the U.S. military, the terms "rank" and "grade" are effectively synonymous. In the PLA, however, they are quite distinct. Even with the reinstitution of ranks, the PLA still considers grade, or what it calls AEP, is still a more accurate reflection of authority and responsibility across service, branch, and organizational lines. For example, regulations regarding retirement ages refer to AEP, not rank. In addition, military pay is calculated on the basis of rank, AEP (grade), and time in service.

Thus, while rank is a key indicator for foreigners, AEP is still the key indicator within the PLA. Even today, officers still refer to each other in terms of their position, not their rank. For example, the PLAAF commander and political commissar have different ranks but they have the same grade—each has the AEP of an MR commander. A more striking case is found in the PLA navy: The commander in 1988 had a lower rank than the political commissar, but each had the same grade or AEP. In addition, when Cao Shuangming became the PLAAF commander in November 1992, he was not promoted to general from lieutenant general until sometime in late 1993.

All personnel within the PLAAF, regardless of whether they are in a nonoperational administrative element or an operational unit, have an AEP at the MR, army, division, regiment, battalion, company, or squad level. The relative importance of departments cannot necessarily be determined by first- or second-level status, or by the military rank of the department directors. For example, the HqAF political and logistics department directors and the chief of staff (director of the headquarters department) all have the AEP of an MR deputy commander; however, the aeronautical engineering department director only has the AEP of an army commander—the same as the deputy chiefs of staff and deputy directors in the other first-level departments.

Appendix E

AIRCRAFT PROCUREMENT PROGRAMS

This appendix discusses the circumstances surrounding the procurement of each type of combat aircraft in the PLAAF. The dates, numbers and particular problems associated with each type contribute to a complete picture of PLAAF inventory development and future alternatives. The spreadsheet model presented in Appendix F attempts to match production with reported inventory levels, from 1954 to the present. It should be used to see the evolution of the combat inventory over time, to place projected force evolution arguments in context.

FIGHTERS

MiG-15

MiG-15s were introduced into China following the start of the Korean War, in 1950. The Chinese probably lost more than 1,000 aircraft during the war, but survived to be reequipped and strengthened by the Soviets (Bueschel, 1968, p. 24). In December 1951, the Chinese government asked the aviation industry to implement a plan of production for the YAK-18 primary trainer and the MiG-15Bis. In October 1954, before achieving production capability, a decision was made to switch the jet production effort to the MiG-17F (Duan, 1989, p. 28). The MiG-15 never reached full production in China, so all the Chinese MiG-15 inventory is of Russian origin. The Chinese did produce a large number of MiG-15UTI trainers for domestic use and export. It is estimated that 1,300 MiG-15s were in service in 1954, and these are assumed to have been maintained by attrition-replacement stocks from Russia until the 1961 Sino-Soviet split. Almost all of these aircraft were the improved MiG-15Bis variant.

F-5 (MiG-17)

MiG-17s were first confirmed in PLAAF service by pictures taken during a Chinese attack on a reconnaissance plane from Taiwan in early 1956 (Bueschel, 1968, p. 31). The first Chinese-produced MiG-17, referred to as the F-5, was delivered from Shenyang in the fall of 1956 (Bueschel, 1968, p. 40). Initial production aircraft had a substantial number of Russian components. Chinese-production F-5s corresponded to later model MiG-17s, incorporating the VK-1A (Chinese designation WP-5) afterburning engine. Some models were manufactured with limited all-weather radar capability. The F-5 was the primary interceptor for the PLAAF from the late 1950s until the late 1960s, when it was replaced by the F-6. In later years it served as a fighter-bomber, along with the MiG-15. From 1956 to 1959, 767 F-5s were produced, before production shifted from Shenyang to Chengdu to allow F-6 production at Shenyang (Duan, 1989, p. 119).

F-6 (MiG-19)

The MiG-19 first flew in 1952 or 1953. It was provided to the PLAAF in 1958, along with air-to-air and surface-to-air missiles, to counter Nationalist high-altitude and high-performance jet reconnaissance of the Chinese mainland (Bueschel, 1968, p. 57). Production of the F-6 was immediately initiated at Shenyang, with a Chinese-assembled MiG-19 flying in 1958, and the first F-6 flying in September, 1959. The early 1958 to 1960 "Great Leap Forward," the complex design of the MiG-19, and the Sino-Soviet split of 1961 caused successful series production to be delayed until 1963 (Duan, 1989, p. 115). A slowdown in production accompanied the 1966 through 1970 period of the Cultural Revolution. Further complicating the problem, almost all F-6s manufactured during that time had to be recalled to the factory to be rebuilt and modified to make them safe for flight. More than 3,000 F-6s were built before production ceased in early 1980s at Shenyang, with production of all-weather and reconnaissance variants (Pocock, 1991, p. 138). The estimated peak of F-6 service was 1984, when more than 3,300 aircraft flew with the PLAAF and naval aviation. The F-6 is still the most numerous fighter in service with the Chinese today, making up more than 65 percent of the force.

F-7 (MiG-21)

The MiG-21 first flew in 1955 and entered service in the Soviet Union in 1958. China received a license to produce the MiG-21F-13 in 1961. A few aircraft were delivered to serve as pattern and early production models before the Sino-Soviet split caused the Soviets to abandon the program. The Chinese decided to reverse-engineer the MiG-21 at Shenyang. Production occurred at Chengdu and Guizhou to allow Shenyang to concentrate on development of the F-8. The first F-7 prototype flew in January 1966, with production commencing in 1967. Initial production was hindered by the Cultural Revolution and later by poor acceptance of the aircraft by the PLAAF. Production totaled less than 100 aircraft between 1967 and 1979. The Chinese almost abandoned the program in the late 1970s. These F-7s were limited to day operations of short range and endurance. Early Chinese variants are comparable to the early Soviet MiG-21s, NATO code-named Fishbed-B. China was able to steal several later-model day and all-weather MiG-21s from shipments to North Vietnam during the mid-1960s (Bueschel, 1968, p. 91). Lessons learned from these aircraft, combined with force structure deficiencies uncovered during the 1979 border war with Vietnam, caused the Chinese to reevaluate the F-7 program. The F-7 reevaluation received high-level support, enabling provision of requisite funding and satisfactory resolution of the principal problems. If this is emulated in other comparable challenges in military aviation, the Chinese could be expected to meet with greater success than has generally been the case in their aviation programs.

F-7-2 development began in 1975 at Chengdu. The aircraft was approved for production in 1979. The F-7-2 improvements included a more powerful engine, a new ejection seat, external fuel tank capability, and a better drag chute. It is roughly comparable to the Soviet MiG-21F, or NATO Fishbed-C. The incorporation of the F-7-2 into the PLAAF and its export sales, as the F-7A, F-7B, and F-7M, attest to its success.

The F-7-3 is a further development, based on the all-weather MiG-21pf models stolen from Soviet shipments to Vietnam. While it is not a direct copy, it shares many of the general capabilities associated with the NATO Fishbed-D. The F-7-3 design began in 1981, with the first flight in April 1984. Series production began in 1989. The F-7-3 includes a major fuselage redesign with an all-weather radar and fire-control system, a more powerful engine, more internal fuel capacity, and other improvements.

Further plans to improve the F-7 resulted in the proposed Super-7 version, to be developed jointly with Grumman and Pakistan, under a U.S. assistance contract. The Super-7 would have been another major redesign and included an APG-66 radar in a redesigned nose and a General Electric F404 engine with side-mounted intakes. Its development was canceled when U.S. assistance was suspended following the Tiananmen incident. Efforts continue to develop a similar upgrade from other sources. GEC-Ferranti is discussed as the source for its Blue Hawk pulse Doppler radar, with power provided by an RD-33 engine, used in the MiG-29, from Russia. If developed, it could be used primarily for export, and there is no certainty that it would see wide service in the PLAAF, because of aviation ministry hard-currency payment requirements and budget requirements.[1]

Production for domestic use and export continues today for the F-7-2, F-7-3 and FT-7 trainer. Future fighter force level requirements will govern F-7 production requirements. The F-7 is the most successful fighter now available to the PLAAF, and can be expected to take on more missions as F-6 aircraft are phased out of the inventory.

A-5

Design of the A-5 began in 1958. After a long development cycle, the airplane was approved for production in 1969. The A-5 is manufac-

---

[1]One of the reasons the PLAAF and naval aviation might not purchase any of the aircraft with Western systems is the cost. For example, the air force only has a few F-7Ms, which have Western subsystems incorporated in them, in its inventory because they are simply too expensive. While the air force insists that it pay only renminbi for the aircraft, the aviation ministry insists that the air force pay hard currency for any portions of the aircraft that include Western systems that were originally purchased with hard currency. Therefore, the more foreign components future aircraft have, the more expensive the aircraft will be to the air force. If the air force must pay hard currency for the foreign components, it is highly unlikely that the air force will buy too many, if any, of the Super-7.

tured at Nanchang and is identical to the F-6/MiG-19 from the center section back. The nose is pointed, but no radar was included in its weapon system. The aircraft's nuclear capability was demonstrated on January 7, 1972 with a live drop. Early versions had a bomb bay, for internal weapon carriage, but the plane's short range caused versions built after 1981 to be redesigned with fuel tanks in this area. The later version, known as the A-5-1, also has more powerful engines and other refinements. Recent efforts to upgrade the plane have added a ranging radar to naval variants and a laser rangefinder to export and experimental versions. No comprehensive upgrade of PLAAF assets has materialized. If inventory maintenance is essential to the PLAAF, the A-5 could be continued in production, but its utility in combat is limited by its crude weapon system and MiG-19 ancestry. Orders for export sales to Pakistan will keep the A-5 in production through 1998 (Cohen, 1994, Table 4.12). Pressures to maintain an adequate inventory of attack aircraft could force the Chinese to procure more of this aged design.

F-8

The F-8 is visually and dimensionally similar to the Mikoyan Ye-152A Flipper. The Flipper was an unsuccessful MiG-21 based twin-engined fighter which was displayed during the 1961 Tushino air show.[2] Design of the F-8 began at Shenyang in 1964. Two prototypes were constructed, with the maiden flight in June 1969. The design was not validated for production until December 1979. This long development can be attributed to the effects of the Cultural Revolution, inadequate prototypes for testing, and the teething pains of China's first indigenous fighter development effort. About 150 F-8s have been built. They are considered to be underpowered, have inadequate weapon systems, and be ineffective as interceptors.

The specifications for the F-8-2 were formulated in 1980, with the first flight in June 1984. The aircraft had a solid nose, which provided room for a more capable fire-control radar, more powerful engines, side-mounted intakes, and other improvements, based on MiG-23

---

[2]"J-8 and J-8 II Finback" (1990), p. 18.

aircraft acquired from Egypt.[3] Five prototype aircraft were manufactured to speed testing and evaluation of the aircraft. From 1985 to May 1990, the F-8-2 development program actually consisted of two development efforts. Shenyang continued the Chinese effort, while the U.S.-funded "Peace Pearl" program attempted to improve the fighter by developing a western avionics suite. Grumman used the APG-66 radar with a new HUD, Litton inertial navigation system, and other supporting equipment to give the F-8-2 a modern intercept capability. There were also preliminary discussions on equipping the aircraft with the General Electric F-404 engine. The $502 million program was structured to provide two aircraft with five sets of spares and equipment for 50 aircraft by January 1995, but no technology transfer.[4] The program was suspended by the United States following the June 1989 Tiananmen incident and was canceled by the Chinese in May 1990. The Chinese development program continued, with F-8-2 production commencing in the late 1980s, resulting in the first aircraft entering service with naval aviation in the early 1990s. It is equipped with a domestically designed and built SR-4 pulse Doppler radar (Zhang, 1993, p. 880). It is capable of using IR and semiactive air-to-air missiles, along with various air-to-ground ordnance, and is reportedly capable of in-flight refueling. The F-8-2 is in batch production of 20 to 24 aircraft per year. Production expansion is possible, but could be limited by the tactical utility of the aircraft's high-altitude interceptor design.

FB-7

The FB-7 is a twin-engined fighter-bomber under development at Xian for the Chinese navy. It has a two-man crew in tandem seating. Its primary mission is interdiction, with a secondary fighter mission. The aircraft has a fixed compound sweep wing with lateral intakes and a low-mounted horizontal tail. The first two prototypes were rolled out in August 1988. They are powered by Chinese WS9 afterburning turbofans (Chinese-assembled Rolls-Royce Spey Mk 202).[5] The aircraft is reported to have Chinese-designed terrain-following

[3]"Air Force of the People's Liberation Army," (1991), p. 76.

[4]"J-8 and J-8 II Finback" (1990), p. 18.

[5]"XAC JH-7 (FB-7)" (1993), p. 58.

radar and other advanced avionics. In its naval attack configuration, it is expected to carry two C-801 ship-attack cruise missiles and two drop tanks.

The negative aspects of this program are a lack of high-level support, air force participation, and an active engine-manufacturing capability. The Chinese had assembled 50 WS8s when the program was terminated in late 1980.[6] Several plans are being discussed for using other engines for production versions, but this greatly increases program risk. The LMC WS6 turbofan was developed between 1966 and 1980 and has a suitable thrust rating, but was never produced in quantity. It is highly unlikely that the FB-7 will play a major role in the future.

Su-27

China purchased 26 Su-27s from Russia in 1991, which were delivered in mid-1992. The Su-27 is among the most modern and capable fighter aircraft in the world. It has a state-of-the-art weapon system and is capable of using a wide variety of air-to-air and air-to-ground ordnance. The PLAAF is operating the aircraft from Wuhu, 250 km east of Shanghai. The integration of the Su-27s has proven to be difficult, and full operational capability is not expected until the end of 1995 at the earliest. The Su-27 has long-range and high-speed multi-role capabilities but does not fill all roles required for a modern fighter force. It has no air-to-ground guided weapon capability and is a large and lightly armored close air support aircraft. Later versions have been adapted by Sukhoi as ground-attack aircraft, but these are substantially different from the baseline fighter. If the Su-27 is chosen to be the next standard fighter, a lengthy development cycle could again result in China building its air force around an aircraft that is old by the time it sees service in large numbers.

---

[6]"Air Force of the People's Liberation Army" (1991), p. 76.

BOMBERS

Tu-4

The Tu-4 is a Soviet copy of the American B-29. A small number of Tu-4s were provided to the Chinese beginning in 1951. There were reportedly two regiments, consisting of nearly 100 Tu-4s, in service in 1955 (Bueschel, 1968, p. 34). The program to equip the PRC with a strategic bombing capability gave them the ability to threaten the Nationalists on Taiwan, along with the U.S. fleet and bases in Japan. The effort apparently suffered from high attrition in attempting to train the PLAAF to fly and maintain such a sophisticated aircraft (Bueschel, 1968, p. 201). Tu-4s remained in Chinese service until the mid-1980s as test, development, and reconnaissance platforms.

B-5/Il-28

The Il-28 first flew in 1948 and entered service in the Soviet Union in 1950. It is a twin-engined, turbojet-powered, light bomber with straight wings and a tail turret. It was provided to the Chinese in 1952. The aircraft underwent a 40-percent redesign for Chinese manufacture as the B-5. The aircraft was reverse-engineered from drawings provided for the repair of Il-28s and from examples in Chinese possession, beginning in 1963. The first B-5 flight was in September 1966, and full production began at Harbin in 1967. The aircraft was produced in light bomber, torpedo bomber, nuclear weapon carrier, and trainer versions until 1988.[7] The B-5 has since been retired from air force service but continues to serve in small numbers in naval aviation.

B-6/Tu-16

The Tu-16 first flew in 1952 and entered service in the Soviet Union in 1955. It is a high-subsonic, twin-engined, turbojet-powered, medium bomber. In 1956, the USSR agreed to build a factory for

---

[7]In 1988, the Harbin Aircraft Factory responded to the in-flight failure of a B-5's entire electrical power system by examining all of the remaining 424 aircraft that had been produced to date (this probably did not include those sold abroad). The results of the examination showed that 65 of the 425 aircraft had the same problem that led to the power failure. (PLAAF Aeronautical Engineering Department, 1988, p. 31.)

medium bomber manufacturing in China and granted a production license for the Tu-16 in 1957. Prototype production began at Harbin and Xian in 1959. Prototype assembly, using Soviet components, was completed quickly, and the first aircraft flew in September 1959. A small number of aircraft were completed in the following years. Following the Sino-Soviet split, all production was transferred to Xian. In 1964, work was completed on modifications to allow the B-6 to drop nuclear weapons. A successful delivery was completed on May 14, 1965. The first Xian-manufactured aircraft flew in December 1968, and series production began the following year. A second-generation navigation system was installed in the B-6A beginning in 1982. The B-6D is a naval variant equipped with a large chin-mounted radar and is capable of carrying C-601 cruise missiles. It began development in 1975 and was approved for production in 1985. The Tu-16 was used as a tanker aircraft and an electronic warfare platform in Soviet service and has been proposed for future use in the same roles by the Chinese.

Appendix F

FIGHTER AIRCRAFT PROJECTION

METHODOLOGY

In this research, we have sought to construct a model that matches past Chinese inventory estimates, enabling us to project future force levels and examine likely options to the year 2005. Air force and naval aviation totals are aggregated for these estimates.

China does not publish official figures on inventory and airframe life, making it necessary to estimate these numbers to project future inventories. Constructing a spreadsheet with data from 1954 to 2005 allowed us to compare inventory levels for all aircraft to ensure consistent trends in production, service life, and retirement. Cross-checking totals with numerous open sources provided some degree of confidence in the individual types and overall totals. When inconsistencies between sources were encountered, they were resolved by smoothing the results over a number of years.

The most often used source in this methodology is issues of the IISS's *The Military Balance* from 1960 to 1993–1994. Volumes of Aviation Advisory Services Limited's *International Air Forces & Military Aircraft Directory* dating from 1972 to 1991 were also frequently referenced. The major source for cross-checking was Jonathan A. Cohen and Randall Forsberg's *Sources and Methods for the IDDS Master Table of World Bomber, Attack, and Fighter Aircraft 1972, 1982, 1992 and Derivative Tables,* the issues of 9 June 1993 and April 1994. Other sources are noted as appropriate.

Attrition rates are assessed against inventory in each year. The Chinese do publish some attrition data, but they are not complete enough to support this model. To reflect the learning curve associated with jet aviation, we used a rate of 1 percent for the 1950s, 0.5 percent for 1960 to 1975, 0.3 percent for 1975 to 1985, and 0.2 percent for 1985 to 2005. These rates are somewhat below those for other countries, reflecting conservative Chinese training and flight scheduling. A rate of 0.5 percent corresponds to an accident rate of 5 per 100,000 hours if all airplanes average 100 hours per year with sorties of one hour duration.

MiG-15

The Su-15 never reached full production in China, so all the Chinese MiG-15 inventory is of Russian origin. It is estimated that 1,300 MiG-15s were in service in 1954 and are assumed to have been maintained by attrition replacement stocks from Russia until the 1961 Chinese-Russian split. Almost all of these aircraft are the improved MiG-15bis variant. A 15-year airframe life is assumed for the MiG-15. Some aircraft are kept in service slightly longer, reflecting low aircraft flight hours per year and pressure to maintain a large inventory.

F-5 (MiG-17)

Chinese production F-5s corresponded to later-model MiG-17s, incorporating the VK-1A (Chinese designation WP-5) afterburning engine, and some models have a limited all-weather radar capability. The Shenyang Aircraft Factory had produced 767 F-5s from 1956 to 1959, when production shifted to Chengdu to allow F-6 production at Shenyang (Duan 1989, p. 119). Production was lower following the factory change, because of the emphasis on the F-6 and production of the FT-5 trainer. Chengdu produced 1,061 FT-5s between 1966 and 1986. These are not included in the inventory model but were considered in setting production rates. A maximum service life of 23 years for combat F-5s is assumed.

F-6 (MiG-19)

The MiG-19 was provided to the PLAAF in 1958. Production of the F-6 was initiated at Shenyang, with a Chinese-assembled MiG-19 flying in 1958 and the first F-6 flying in September 1959. The early 1960s "Great Leap Forward," the complex design of the MiG-19, and the Sino-Soviet split of 1961 caused successful series production to be delayed until 1963 (Duan, 1989, p. 115). Between 1973 and 1986, 634 FT-6s were built, but these are not included in the inventory projection (Duan, 1989, p. 120). Production slowed down during the 1966 to 1970 period of the Cultural Revolution. A 28-year life span is assumed for the F-6. With so many of this type in service, changes to this assumption will have large effects on the future size of the PLAAF. The air force and aviation ministry undertook a major study in 1989 to determine ways to increase the service life of the existing F-6s, but the results of the study are not known. However, the most likely recommendation was to fly the aircraft less, which would impact pilot proficiency.

F-7 (MiG-21)

China received a license to produce the MiG-21F-13 in 1961. A few aircraft were delivered to serve as pattern and early production models before the Sino-Soviet split caused the Soviets to abandon the program. The first reverse-engineered prototype flew in January 1966, and production commenced in 1967. Production totaled less than 100 aircraft between 1967 and 1979. F-7-2 development began in 1975 at Chengdu. It was approved for production in 1979. The F-7-3 design began in 1981, with the first flight in April 1984. Series production began in 1989. Production for domestic use and export continues today for the F-7-2 and F-7-3. A 25-year service life is used for F-7 combat aircraft.

A-5

Design of the A-5 began in 1958. Production began in 1969 and is programmed to continue through 1998, to maintain the active inventory at more than 600 aircraft. Aircraft are assumed to be retired at 20 years of service. This is a shorter service life than the F-6 because of a higher projected utilization. F-6 pilots are reported to fly 100 hours per year, while A-5 pilots reportedly fly 150 hours per year.

F-8

Design of the F-8 began in 1964. The design was not validated for production until December 1979. About 150 F-8s were built. The specifications for the F-8-2 were formulated in 1980, and the first flight was in June 1984. F-8-2 production commenced in the late 1980s, resulting in the aircraft entering service with naval aviation in the early 1990s. The F-8-2 is in batch production. The F-8-2 is assumed to have a 25-year service life.

FB-7

The FB-7 is a twin-engined fighter-bomber under development at Xian for the Chinese navy. The first two prototypes were rolled out in August 1988. The negative aspects of this program are a lack of air force participation and no active engine manufacturing capability. It is unlikely that the FB-7 will play a major role in the future of naval aviation or any role at all in the PLAAF. In 1989, one military attaché in Beijing described the FB-7 as "a program that began with an engine looking for an airframe, and is now an airframe looking for an engine."

Su-27

China received 26 Su-27s from Russia in 1992. Reports indicate that China will purchase at least one more batch of 24 Su-27s. Issues of payment method, technology transfer, and future weapon system buys have complicated agreement on licensed production of the aircraft.

Appendix G

INDIGENOUS SAM SYSTEMS

The HQ-1 SAM system began as a licensed production version of the Soviet SA-2a/b Guideline. The first Chinese SAM unit was formed by January 1959, equipped with the five SA-2 launchers and 62 missiles. System technical information was transferred in 1959; prototype production began in 1961; and the first missile was test-fired in July 1963. The system was manufactured and deployed between 1965 and 1970. The air force used its HQ-1 and SA-2 systems to shoot down five Nationalist U-2s between 1962 and 1965. The HQ-2 is a redesign of the HQ-1, which began in 1965 to add longer range and electronic countermeasures resistance to the missile. The improved missile entered the inventory in March 1966. The HQ-2 has been produced in three variants: the HQ-2B, HQ-2F, and HQ-2P.

Assistance in the evolution of the missiles and radars was obtained by stealing Soviet equipment shipped to Vietnam on Chinese railways in 1966 and 1967 (Bueschel, 1968, p. 90). A significant advance over the original SA-2 system has been the SJ-202 guidance radar, which provides a two-target attack capability with up to four missiles at one time. This is an improvement over the single-target capability found in Soviet SA-2 systems. The Chinese have approximately 120 SAM battalions, each battalion containing an HQ-2 battery of six launchers, providing protection to population and strategic centers within China.

The HQ-7 is a Chinese adaptation of the Thomson-CSF Crotale SAM system. The Crotale was purchased for use aboard Chinese destroyers and was reverse-engineered between 1978 and 1988. The system has a maximum range of 6.6 n mi (12 km). It uses a command-guided missile with radar, TV, and IR tracking capabilities. Other nonstrategic SAMs manufactured by the Chinese include the HN-5, a reverse-engineered version of the SA-7 Grail, and the PL-9 vehicle-mounted IR SAM, which is roughly comparable to the U.S. Chaparral system.

The HQ-61 SAM began development in the 1960s as a response to the Soviet's refusal to provide the SA-6 system to the Chinese. It was first seen in public in 1986 and was operational in the late 1980s. It is similar in appearance to the U.S. Sparrow but is larger, weighing approximately 200 lb more. The HQ-61 was developed as a truck-mounted mobile SAM for army use. Each battery contains a reverse-engineered Soviet-designed Flat Face radar for target acquisition, a truck-mounted illuminating radar, and four trucks equipped with twin rail launchers. The missile has a maximum range of 6.8 n mi (12.5 km) with a single-stage solid-fuel motor and uses continuous wave illumination with semiactive homing and anti-jam features. It has been adapted to naval use from a twin rail launcher and is marketed as the PL-10 in an air-to-air adaptation.

The KS-1 SAM was first revealed in 1991. It is a large, 900 kg, single-stage, solid-fuel command-guided missile with a maximum range of 23 n mi (42 km). It can be used in conjunction with the SJ-202 phased-array guidance radar used with later HQ-2 systems. The KS-1 is believed to be on order for the Chinese armed forces. It may prove to be an improvement over the 2,300-kg liquid-fueled HQ-2 but will not compare well with the recently purchased SA-10.

China acquired four batteries of Russian SA-10 (S-300) SAM systems in 1993 and expected to receive 12 more in 1994. The S-300 is a state-of-the-art air defense system available in transportable and self-propelled versions with three different missiles. The exact version that China purchased cannot be determined at this time. The S-300 has a jam-resistant three-dimensional pulse radar for target detection and a phased-array multipurpose missile-guidance radar that can simultaneously engage up to six targets, with two missiles each.

The SA-10a has a maximum range of 26 n mi (47 km), the SA-10b has a maximum range of 50 n mi (90 km). Recent intelligence updates have incorporated the SA-12 system into the S-300 family of weapons. The missiles formerly associated with the SA-12, now the

SA-10c, have a maximum range of 82 n mi (150 km). The S-300 has the capability to engage aircraft, cruise missiles, and tactical ballistic missiles. In Russian use, a regiment is composed of three batteries. The 1993 Chinese purchase would allow one battery to be used for training with one operational regiment, followed by four operational regiments in the 1994 purchase. The combination of sophisticated radars, highly automated target processing, and highly capable missiles makes the S-300 a major technical improvement in Chinese air defense. (Cullen and Foss, undated, pp. 27–28, 103–104, 116–118, 234–239.)

BIBLIOGRAPHY

"1993 Forecasts—Part 7 of 7—Asia Pacific," *Flight International*, December 23, 1992, p. 30.

Acharya, Amitav, and Paul M. Evans, *China's Defence Expenditure: Trends and Implications*, Toronto: Joint Centre for Asia Pacific Studies, Eastern Asia Policy Papers, 1994.

Ackerman, Julia A., and Michael Collins Dunn, "Chinese Airpower Revs Up," *Air Force Magazine*, July 1993.

Agence France Presse, "China, Russia Jointly Developing Fighter," November 9, 1993.

"Air Force of the People's Liberation Army," *International Air Forces & Military Aircraft Directory*, AL-361, November 1991.

Allen, Kenneth W., *People's Republic of China, People's Liberation Army Air Force*, Washington, D.C.: Defense Intelligence Agency, May 1991.

Aviation Advisory Services Limited, *International Air Forces & Military Aircraft Directory*, issues from 1972 to 1991.

Baum, Julian, "Winged," *Far Eastern Economic Review*, January 12, 1995.

BBC—See British Broadcasting Corporation.

Bodansky, Yossef, "The PRC's Force Modernisation Efforts Finally Begin to Show Results," *Strategic Policy*, March 31, 1993.

Bowie, Christopher J., et al., *Trends in the Global Balance of Airpower*, MR-478/1-AF, 1995.

British Broadcasting Corporation, "Hong Kong Paper on Sino-Soviet Relations: USSR to Train Chinese Pilots," *British Broadcasting Corporation, Summary of World Broadcasts*, May 3, 1991a.

_____, "More Air Force Pilots Trained for All-Weather Flying," *British Broadcasting Corporation, Summary of World Broadcasts*, December 24, 1991b.

_____, "Part 3 (The Far East)," *British Broadcasting Corporation, Summary of World Broadcasts*, FE/1263/B2, 1991c.

_____, "Awesome Eagles Soar in the Vast Skies," *British Broadcasting Corporation, Summary of World Broadcasts*, September 7, 1992.

_____, "Chinese Air Force Modernization Drive," *British Broadcasting Corporation, Summary of World Broadcasts*, August 7, 1993a.

_____, "*Lien Ho Pao* Claims Chinese Air Force has AWACS Aircraft," *British Broadcasting Corporation, Summary of World Broadcasts*, December 10, 1993b.

Bueschel, Richard M., *Communist Chinese Air Power*, New York: Frederick A. Praeger, 1968.

Chen Jian, *China's Road to the Korean War—The Making of the Sino-American Confrontation*, New York, Columbia University Press, 1994.

Chen, King C., *China's War With Vietnam, 1979: Issues, Decisions, and Implications*, Stanford, Calif.: Hoover Institute Press, 1987.

Cheng, Nien, *Life and Death in Shanghai*, London: Grafton Books, 1986.

Chengdu Military Region Campaign Training Office, *Jituanjun Yezhan Zhendi Fangyu Zhanyi Kongjun de Yunyong* [*Air Force Utilization During the Campaign to Defend Group Army Field Positions*], February 1982.

Cheung, Tai Ming, "Comrades in Arms: China Signals Willingness to Resume Soviet Ties," *Far Eastern Economic Review*, July 19, 1990.

China Daily (Beijing), August 16, 1989, in FBIS-CHI-89-160, August 21, 1989.

"China Favors Russia over Rolls Royce," *Flight International*, July 7, 1993.

China Today Series Editorial Committee, *Dangdai Zhongguode Hangkong Gongye* [*China Today: Aviation Industry*], Beijing: China Social Sciences Press, 1988.

_____, *Dangdai Zhongguo Kongjun* [*China Today: Air Force*], Beijing: China Social Sciences Press, 1989a.

_____, *Dangdai Zhongguo Haijun* [*China Today: Navy*], Beijing: China Social Sciences Press, 1989b.

"China's Military Aircraft Inventory," *Flight International*, November 25, 1992.

"China Orders Il-76 Transports," *Interavia Air Letter (IALEA)*, May 25, 1993.

"China Sets Up Army Air Arm to Increase Modernized Combat Effectiveness," *Hsin Wan Pao* (Hong Kong), April 18, 1989, p. 4, in FBIS-CHI-89-079, April 26, 1989.

"China Switches IRBMs to Conventional Role," *Jane's Defence Weekly*, February 4, 1994.

"Chinese Air Force General Begins 10 Day Visit," Xinhua, June 2, 1994.

"Chinese Combat Refuelling Needs Tanker," *Flight International*, April 3, 1991.

Cohen, Jonathan A., "China's Combat Aircraft Domestic and Export Production Schedules for Firm Orders 1992–2000," Memorandum to Glenn Krumel, May 17, 1994.

Cohen, Jonathan A., and Randall Forsberg, *Sources and Methods for the IDDS Master Table of World Bomber, Attack, and Fighter Aircraft 1972, 1982, 1992 and Derivative Tables*, June 9, 1993.

"Command of the Skies," *Far Eastern Economic Review*, February 14, 1991, pp. 8–9.

"CPC Views Various Aspects of Gulf War," in FBIS-CHI-91-050, March 14, 1991.

Cullen, Tony, and Christopher F. Foss, ed., *Jane's Land-Based Air Defense 1993–94*, undated.

Defense Intelligence Agency, *Handbook on the Chinese Armed Forces*. Washington, D.C.: Defense Intelligence Agency, July 1976.

Dou Dezhong, "The Chinese Air Force," Tallahassee Air Force Association, Tallahassee, FL, May 31, 1990.

Duan Zijun, ed., *China Today: Aviation Industry*, Beijing: The China Aviation Industry Press, 1989.

Editorial Group of the Changsha Military Engineering Academy, Hunan Military District, *Jun Xun Shouce* [*Military Training Handbook*]. Changsha: Hunan Education Press, May 1988.

Fairbank, John K., Edwin O. Reischauer, and Albert M. Craig, *East Asia: Tradition and Transformation*, Cambridge, Mass.: Harvard University Press, 1973.

FBIS, *Daily Report*, October 26, 1984 and March 3, 1986.

Fink, Donald E., and Paul Proctor, "China Aviation: Chengdu Aircraft Corporation Builds Export F-7M, Upgraded F-7-3," *Aviation Week and Space Technology*, December 11, 1989a, pp. 82–83.

_____, "Shenyang Focuses on Commercial Projects as Military Aircraft Requirements Shrink," *Aviation Week and Space Technology*, December 11, 1989b, p. 70.

Fulghum, David A., "New Chinese Fighter Nears Prototyping," *Aviation Week and Space Technology*, March 13, 1995, pp. 26–27.

Futrell, Robert F., *The United States Air Force in Korea 1950–1953*, Rev. Ed., Washington, D.C.: U.S. Air Force, Office of Air Force History, 1983.

Godwin, Paul H.B., "Chinese Military Strategy Revised: Local and Limited War," in Allen S. Whiting, ed., *China's Foreign Relations, The Annals of the American Academy of Political and Social Science,* Vol. 519, January 1992, pp. 191–201.

_____, *The Chinese Communist Armed Forces,* Maxwell Air Force Base, Ala.: Air University Press, June 1988.

_____, ed., *The Chinese Defense Establishment: Continuity and Change in the 1980s,* Boulder, Colo.: Westview Press, 1983.

Goncharov, Sergei N., John W. Lewis, and Xue Litai, *Uncertain Partners: Stalin, Mao, and the Korean War,* Stanford: Stanford University Press, 1993.

Gordon, Yefim, and Vladimir Rigmant, *MiG-15,* Osceola, Wisc.: Motorbooks International, 1993.

Gregor, James A., "Modernization of the Air Force of the PRC and the Military Balance in the Taiwan Strait," *Issues & Studies,* Vol. 21, No. 10, October 1985, pp. 58–74.

Hamamoto, Ryoichi, in *Yomiuri Shimbun,* January 8, 1995, p. 4, in FBIS-CHI-95-006, January 10, 1995, p. 34.

Hangkong Shibao, November 24, 1988, p. 1.

He Chong, "China's Military Budget this Year and the Ridiculousness of the 'China Threat' Theory," *Zhongguo Tongxun She,* in FBIS-CH1, March 23, 1995, pp. 34–35.

He Di, "The Last Campaign to Unify China: The CCP's Unmaterialized Plan to Liberate Taiwan," *Chinese Historians,* Vol. 5, No. 1, Spring 1992, pp. 1–16.

Henley, Lonnie D., "China's Military Modernization: A Ten Year Assessment," in Larry M. Wortzel, ed., *China's Military Modernization,* New York: Greenwood Press, 1988.

Hinton, Harold C., ed., *The People's Republic of China: A Handbook.* Boulder, Colo.: Westview Press, 1979.

Hong Baocai, "The Development of China's Military Air Transport," *Liaowang Overseas* (Hong Kong), Vol. 30, July 24, 1989, in FBIS-CHI-89-151, August 8, 1989, pp. 6–7.

Hu, Timothy, "Chinese Army: Fewer Men, More Arms," *The Nikkei Weekly*, February 1, 1992.

Huus, Karl, "Learn from Li Peng: To Understand China's Economy Listen to its Buzzwords," *Far Eastern Economic Review*, August 25, 1994, p. 44.

Indian Express, December 29, 1992.

"Inflation, Budget Constraints Force Deep Reductions in Spending Power, Modernization for China's Military," *Aviation Week and Space Technology*, March 18, 1991.

International Institute for Strategic Studies, *The Military Balance*, various annual issues.

IISS—See International Institute for Strategic Studies.

"J-8 and J-8 II 'Finback,'" *World Air Power Journal*, Autumn/Fall 1990.

Jiefangjun Bao, October 1, 1989, p. 1.

Joffe, Ellis, *The Chinese Army After Mao*, Cambridge, Mass.: Harvard University Press, 1987.

"K-8 Makes International Debut," *Flight International*, March 4, 1992.

Karnow, Stanley, *Mao and China: A Legacy of Turmoil*, London: Penguin Books, 1990.

Kaye, Lincoln, "Deafened by Decree, China's Currency and Tax Reforms Spread Confusion," *Far Eastern Economic Review*, January 13, 1994.

_____, "Reduce Speed Ahead," *Far Eastern Economic Review*, March 16, 1995, pp. 14–15.

Kristoff, Nicholas D., "Experts Fret Over Reach of China's Air Force," *The New York Times*, August 23, 1992.

Latham, Richard J., *Selected Bibliography of PRC National Defense Literature, 1980–1991,* unpublished manuscript, 1991.

Latham, Richard J., and Kenneth W. Allen, "Reform of China's Air Force," *Problems of Communism,* May–June 1991, pp. 30–50.

Lee, Ngok, *China's Defence Modernisation and Military Leadership,* Sydney: Australian National University Press, 1989.

Lenox, Duncan, ed., "YJ-1/2", *Jane's Air-launched Weapons,* Issue 11, undated.

Li, Man Kin, *Sino-Vietnamese War.* Hong Kong: Kingsway International Publications, Ltd., 1981.

Li Yuanchao, "The Politics of Artillery Shelling: A Study of the Taiwan Strait Crises," *Beijing Review,* September 7–13, 1992, pp. 32–38.

Liang, Heng, and Judith Shapiro, *Son of the Revolution,* New York: Vintage Books, 1983.

Liu Dajun, and Wang Zemin, eds., *Zhongguo Shehuizhuyi Guofang Jingjixue* [*Chinese Socialist Defense Economics*], Beijing: PLA Press, 1987.

Lo Ping, "Defense Minister Has Courageously Defeated Generals of the Yang Family," FBIS-CHI-90-164, August 23, 1990, p. 35.

"'Made in China' Deal Is Forged for Su-27s," *Jane's Defence Weekly,* May 6, 1995, p. 3.

"Mainland Researches and Develops Jian-10 Fighters Modeled on Israel's Lavi," *Lian Ho Pao* (Taipei), December 27, 1994, in FBIS-CH-I-94-249, December 28, 1994, p. 25.

Mann, Jim, "China Cancels U.S. Deal for Modernizing F-8 Jet," *Los Angeles Times,* May 15, 1990.

_____, "China Seeks Russian Weapons," *Los Angeles Times,* July 12, 1992.

_____, "U.S. Says Israel Gave Combat Jet Plans to China," *Los Angeles Times,* December 28, 1994.

Mecham, Michael, "China Updates Its Military, But Business Comes First," *Aviation Week and Space Technology*, March 15, 1993, p. 58.

Military History Department, Academy of Military Science, *Kangmei Yuanchao Zhanshi* [*History of the War to Resist America and Aid Korea*], Beijing: Chinese Academy of Military Science, 1988.

Milton, David, and Nancy Dall Milton, *The Wind Will Not Subside Years in Revolutionary China—1964–1969*, New York: Pantheon Books, 1976.

Oksenberg, Michel, and Robert B. Oxnam, eds., *Dragon and Eagle: United States–China Relations Past and Present*, New York: Basic Books, 1978.

O'Lone, Richard G., "Chinese Air Force Developing Few New Aircraft Designs," *Aviation Week and Space Technology*, December 7, 1987, pp. 55–56.

_____, "China Modernizes Military Aircraft in Atmosphere of Fiscal Austerity," *Aviation Week and Space Technology*, December 11, 1989, pp. 55–59.

Ostankino TV (Moscow), "PRC Seeks License to Build Su-27 Aircraft," March 12, 1995.

"Pakistan Is Expected to Confirm the First K-8 Order," *Flight International*, November 17, 1992.

PLAAF Aeronautical Engineering Department, *Hangkong Weixiu* [*Aviation Maintenance*], No. 10, 1988.

PLAAF Headquarters Education and Research Office, *Kongjun Shi* [*History of the Air Force*], Beijing: PLA Press, November 1989.

PLAAF Second Aviation School, *Zhongguo Renmin Jiefangjun Kongjun Dier Hangkong Xuexiao Jianshi* [*Brief History of the PLAAF Second Aviation School*], Chengdu: Air Force Second Aviation School, August 1982.

"Playing Catch-up," *Airline Business*, September 1993, p. 65.

Pocock, Chris, "Far East Air Arms: Northern Region," *World Air Power Journal*, Autumn/Winter 1991, pp. 138–142.

Pollack, Jonathan D. *Perception and Action in Chinese Foreign Policy: The Quemoy Decision,* Ph.D. Dissertation, University of Michigan, 1976.

_____, "Structure and Process in the Chinese Military System," in Kenneth G. Lieberthal and David M. Lampton, eds., *Bureaucracy, Politics, and Decision Making in Post-Mao China,* Berkeley and Los Angeles: University of California Press, 1992.

"PRC Plans to Purchase Soviet Su-25 Fighters," *Nihon Keizai Shimbun* (Tokyo), December 29, 1990, p. 6.

Reuters News Service, "Taiwan Ends Campaign to Lure Chinese Military Defectors," May 1, 1991.

_____, "China to Build Advanced Fighter by 2000," *China News,* January 20, 1994a, p. 1.

_____, "China Unveils Plan to Hike Defense Budget," *China News,* March 12, 1994b.

Schwartz, Harry, *Tsars, Mandarins, and Commissars: A History of Chinese-Russian Relations,* New York: Anchor Books, 1973.

Segal, Gerald, *Defending China,* London: Oxford University Press, 1985.

Sheng Lijun, "China's View of the War Threat and Its Foreign Policy," *Journal of Northeast Asian Studies,* Vol. XI, No. 3, Fall 1992, pp. 47–69.

Shijie Junshi Nianjian [*World Military Yearbook*], Beijing: PLA Press, annual issues 1985, 1987, 1989, 1990, 1991, 1992.

Sun Maoqing, "Fly Toward the 21st Century—An On-the-Spot Report on the Modernization Drive of the People's Air Force." Xinhua, November 10, 1994, in FBIS-CHI-94-228, November 28, 1994.

Swaine, Michael D., *The Modernization of the Chinese People's Liberation Army: Prospects and Implications for Northeast Asia,* The National Bureau of Asian Research, Vol. 5, No. 3, October 1994.

Tanham, George, and Marcy Agmon, *The Indian Air Force: Trends and Prospects,* RAND, MR-424-AF, 1995.

Teng Lianfu and Jiang Fusheng, eds., *Kongjun Zuozhan Yanjiu* [*Air Force Operations Research*], Beijing: National Defense University Publishers, May 1990.

"The Military Budget System in the PRC," *China Tech* (Hong Kong), Vol. 1, No. 2, June 10, 1985.

"U.S., French Fighter Sales to Taiwan Nudge Mainland China Closer to Russia," *Armed Forces Journal International,* January 16, 1993.

"US Defence Envoy's Trip Set to Boost Military Ties," *South China Morning Post,* November 1, 1993.

"USA Cancels Defunct Chinese Contracts," *Flight International,* January 6, 1993.

USAF Historical Division, *Air Operations in the Taiwan Crises of 1958,* Washington, D.C.: United States Air Force, November 1962.

Wan Li-hsing, "China's Military Expenditure to Increase Drastically in 1990," *Dang Dai* (Hong Kong) Vol. 18, March 31, 1990, pp. 17–18, in FBIS-CHI-90-078, April 23, 1990, pp. 46–49.

Wang Baocun and Dong Haiyan, "Maikenamala Junshi Gaigede Gongguo Deshi [The Successes and Failures of the McNamara Military Reforms]," in Yang Dezhi and Huan Xiang, eds., *Guofang Fazhan Zhanlue Sikao* [*Thought on Strategies of Defense Development*], Beijing: PLA Press, 1987, pp. 239–251.

Wang Chenggang, ed., *Shijie Junshi Nianjian* [*World Military Handbook*], PLA Press, Beijing, 1991.

Wang Shouyun, "Xinshiqide Guofang Keji he Wuqi Zhuangbei Fazhan Zhanlue Yanjiu [A Strategic Study of the Development of Defense S&T, Weapons and Equipment in the New Period]," in *Zong Canmoubu Junxunbu,* ed., *Guofang Xiandaihua Fazhan Zhanlue Yanjiu* [*A Study of Development Strategy for Defense Modernization*], Beijing: Military Translation Press, 1987.

Woon, Eden Y., "Chinese Arms Sales and U.S.-China Military Relations," *Asian Survey,* Vol. XXIX, No. 6, June 1989, pp. 601–618.

Worden, Robert L., Andrea Matles Savada, and Ronald E. Dolan, eds., *China, a Country Study,* Washington, D.C.: Federal Research Division, Library of Congress, July 1987.

"XAC JH-7 (FB-7)," *Jane's All the World's Aircraft 1993–94,* 1993, p. 58.

Xinhua [New China News Agency], November 17, 1992.

Xu Yan, "Chinese Forces and Their Casualties in the Korean War," *Chinese Historians,* Vol. VI, No. 2, Fall 1993, pp. 45–58.

Yang Dezhi and Huan Xiang, eds., *Guofang Fazhan Zhanlue Sikao* [*Thought on Strategies of Defense Development*], Beijing: PLA Press, 1987.

Young, Kenneth T., *Negotiating with the Chinese Communists: The United States Experience, 1953–1967,* New York: McGraw-Hill, 1968.

Zalonga, Steven, "Russian Air-to-Air Missiles: Part 2—Tactical AAMs," *Jane's Intelligence Review,* May 1993, p. 195.

Zhang Yihong, in *International Defense Review,* November 1993.

Zhongguo Kongjun [*China's Air Force*], various issues.

Zhongguo Renmin Jiefangjun Junguan Shouce—Kongjun Fence [*Chinese People's Liberation Army Officers Handbook—Air Force*], Beijing: Qingdao Publishers, May 10, 1990.

Zhu Daqiang, "China Has Manufactured Over 10,000 Fighter Planes of Over 60 Models," *Zhongguo Xinwen She,* April 26, 1991.

Zhu Yaping, photo caption, *Zhongguo Hangkong Hangtian Bao,* June 7, 1990.

Zielenziger, Michael, "Without You I'm Nothing: New Report Says China Fuels Pacific Rim Growth," *Far Eastern Economic Review,* June 23, 1994, p. 59.